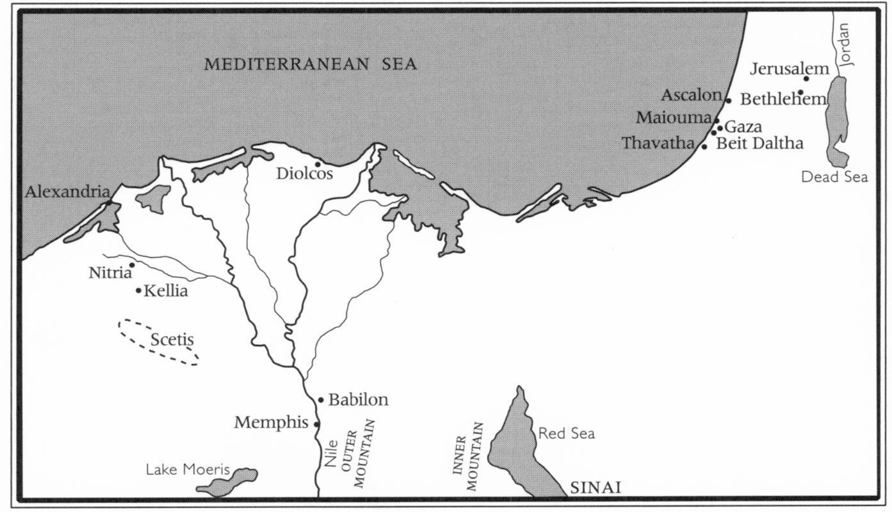

Egypt, Sinai and Southern Palestine.

Cistercian Studies Series: Number One Hundred Fifty

Abba Isaiah of Scetis
Ascetic Discourses

Cistercian Studies Series: Number One Hundred Fifty

Abba Isaiah of Scetis
Ascetic Discourses

Translated, with an Introduction and Notes,

by

John Chryssavgis

and

Pachomios (Robert) Penkett

CISTERCIAN PUBLICATIONS
Kalamazoo, Michigan
2002

Available from

Cistercian Publications
Editorial Offices and Customer Service
Institute of Cistercian Studies
Western Michigan University
Kalamazoo, MI 49008

British and European Customer Service
97 Loughborough Road
Thringstone, Coalville, Leic. LE67 8LZQ

http://www.spencerabbey.org/cistpub/

The work of Cistercian Publications
is made possible in part by support from Western Michigan University
to The Institute of Cistercian Studies

Library of Congress Cataloguing available upon request.
ISBN 0-87907-5503 (hc)
0-87907-7506 (pb)

Dedicated to

SISTER BENEDICTA WARD SLG

and

BISHOP KALLISTOS WARE

Table of Contents

Table of Abbreviations

AB	*Analecta Bollandiana*
CSCO	*Corpus Scriptorum Christianorum Orientalis*
DS	*Dictionnaire de Spiritualité*
HE	*Historia Ecclesiastica*
JTS	*Journal of Theological Studies*
OCA	*Orientalia Christiana Analecta*
OgtI	Abba Isaiah, *On Guarding the Intellect*
P	*Plerophoriae*
PL	*Patrologia Latina*
PG	*Patrologia Graeca*
PO	*Patrologia Orientalis*
RAM	*Revue d'Ascétique et de mystique*
Sayings	*The Sayings of the Desert Fathers*
Sch	*Sources Chrétiennes*
VI	*Vitae Isaiae*
VP	*Petrus der Iberer*

Preface

BY THE END OF THE FOURTH and the early part of the fifth centuries, the monks of Egypt were characterized by a sense of movement; not only were they increasingly being 'discovered', but they also began to be 'dispersed', gradually becoming attracted to other places. After the passing of the founding generation of monasticism—Antony, Pachomius, Amoun of Nitria, and Macarius of Scetis—the second generation—among them Silvanus—left their homes and places of training, and journeyed abroad, often in search of isolation. During the 430s, Abba Isaiah settled in Gaza and it is from here that we have a series of ascetic *Discourses* attributed to him. Now, for the first time in English translation, we, too, discover the wealth of spiritual and theological insight that Isaiah shares with his audience, as pertinent today as it was fifteen centuries ago.

John Chryssavgis
Pachomios (Robert) Penkett
Boston and Oxford
Easter, 1998

Introduction

Historical and geographical setting

IN THE FIFTH AND SIXTH CENTURIES, the Gaza region proved to be historically, geographically, theologically, and spiritually a bridge between the Egypt of the fourth century (or earlier) and the Byzantium of the seventh century (or later). Located at 31° 31' (N. Lat.) and 34° 28' (E. Long.), the southwest palestinian city of Gaza was uniquely situated to provide communication between East and West, as well as between North and South. It was surrounded by numerous small streams, rather than by one main channel. It was accessible to the Mediterranean, and yet also sheltered from the sea by sand dunes. It was established on very fertile soil and stood at the hub of an extensive road network and thereby proved an important trading center. The most important of these roads was the caravan route that linked Syria with Egypt, dating from as early as the first century CE.[1] Another road connected Gaza with Jerusalem from the second century CE. In the twentieth century, a road was discovered leading from Gaza to the eastern desert, dating back to the early second century. Maiouma was its port, which enabled sea-trade throughout the Mediterranean. The region was on one of the main spice and perfume routes as early as the third century BCE.

1. Ac 8:26.

Apart from its spice trade, Gaza was also famous for its prosperous grape produce and wine trade. The region boasted a sophisticated system of irrigation and elaborate wine presses. Jerome's *Life of Hilarion*[2] even attests to the fact that monks were occupied in cultivating vines in the fields. Abba Isaiah adopts the imagery of winemaking in *Discourse* 12.

Constantine the Great (d. 337) separated pagan Gaza from christian Maiouma (or Constantia), and the two cities were not reunified until the time of Julian the Apostate (323–63). Gaza, with its temple, the Marneion, was to become a center of Hellenistic paganism. During the rule of Arcadius (395–408) an edict was passed, forbidding pagan worship, and Gaza was christianized, largely through the zeal of Porphyrius. Arcadius' wife, the Empress Eudoxia (d. 404), built a basilica, the Eudoxiana, on the ruins of the Marneion. The christian community of Gaza, however, remained a small minority until the fifth century. The city recalled the ethiopian eunuch's conversion by Philip on the road to Gaza.[3] It took pride in some prominent martyrs. Its bishop attended the First Ecumenical Council in Nicaea (325). During the fourth century, Gaza was embroiled in the arian controversy, and the reinstatement of the local athanasian bishop required the intervention of the pope and the emperor. The monk Hilarion (291–371) was also born around this time in Thavatha, a town about five miles south of Gaza which later acquired the significant reputation as the location of the famous monastery of Seridos directed by Abba Barsanuphius at the turn of the sixth century. Hilarion is said to have traveled to Egypt and met Antony, the father of monasticism. Afterwards, he returned to Palestine and introduced monasticism to that region, which was also known for its own flat desert and fine yellow sand, which must have resembled the desert of Egypt to the dwellers and travelers there.

Porphyry of Gaza (347–420) was appointed bishop of Gaza in 394 and, according to Mark the Deacon's *Life*, felt the need to build a pilgrim hostel to cater to the increasing number of

2. Jerome, *Life of Hilarion*, cc. 25–27. For complete bibliographical information for texts noted, see 'Bibliography'.

3. Ac 8:26–40.

christian travelers. Shortly after the Fourth Ecumenical Council of Chalcedon (451), the controversial theologian, Peter the Iberian (d. 491), was elected Bishop of Maiouma. Peter was the disciple of Abba Isaiah and he publicized his master's teaching widely. We know that he traveled to Alexandria and to the Egyptian desert, as well as to Arabia and Phoenicia.

It is only toward the end of the fifth century, however, that Gaza suddenly flourished as a center for literary studies and spiritual pilgrimage, attracting numerous students and pilgrims alike, and becoming renowned for its teachers of rhetoric. In addition to a number of orators and poets, the Gaza community produced Aeneas (d. 538), who combined neoplatonist philosophy with his christian beliefs and whom Abba Isaiah possibly influenced through conversation, and Procopius (465–c. 530), a rhetorician and eminent theologian of the early sixth century. Other renowned examples of the Gaza School include Zosimas, Choricius, Isidore, Timothy, and John. In 637, Gaza was conquered by the Arabs and withdrew into obscurity, at least from the christian perspective.

The transmigration of monks in the early- to the mid-fifth century was common. The *Spiritual Meadow* of John Moschos (550–619/34) and the *Lives* of Euthymius (d. 473) and Sabas (d. 532) by Cyril of Scythopolis (c. 525–557) attest to the movement of ascetics from Egypt (especially Scetis) to Palestine (especially Gaza). Abba Isaiah himself was a later emigrant from Egypt. He moved to Beit Daltha, midway between Gaza and Thavatha, sometime after the Second Ecumenical Council of Constantinople (431), taking with him the monastic way and the spiritual wealth of the semi-eremitic milieu of Scetis. Perhaps he left Egypt after the second devastation of Scetis in c. 434.[4]

The period covering the years of turmoil from 431 to 451 and after was a critical time for imperial authority, for ecclesiastical jurisdiction, and for doctrinal formulation. We know from the *Life of Peter the Iberian*, written by Zacchariah the Scholar of Gaza (early sixth century), that both Abba Isaiah and Bishop Peter avoided obeying the Roman emperor Zeno's summons to the capital (c. 485) in

4. See, however, Chitty, *The Desert a City*, 73.

order to sign the *Henotikon* (482). Abba Isaiah enjoyed great esteem among the monks in Egypt, as attested by the inclusion of some sayings in the *Apophthegmata*, the three last of which correspond with passages in the *Discourses*. He must already have acquired a wide reputation as an ascetic also of Gaza in his venerable age. This is evinced by Zeno's summons, and it would seem to imply that he arrived in Gaza several decades earlier, possibly in the late 430s. We know that Peter feigned illness in order not to sign, but there is no evidence that Abba Isaiah did not accept to sign this imperial endeavor to reconcile the Chalcedonian and Monophysite groups.

As a monk in fifth-century Gaza, Isaiah could not but be a part of the spirit of reconciliation and communication that was characteristic of both his place and period.

Abba Isaiah

The name 'Isaiah' seems to have been a common one at the time and in the region of the desert fathers—that is to say fourth- and fifth-century Egypt, Syria, Palestine, and Asia Minor. It appears, for example, in at least five sources of great importance for the history of early christian monasticism. The first of these, *The History of Monks in Egypt* 11, a collection of descriptions of Egyptian monks made in 394 by a deacon and a group of laymen traveling through Egypt, mentions a devout man and ascetic, Isaiah, who, in the company of Abba Sourous, visited the great confessor, Abba Anouph.[5] There is another reference to an Isaiah in the company of Paesios, a fourth-century Egyptian anchorite, in Bishop Ammon's letter on Pachomius and Theodore, recorded in the *Pachomian Koinonia*.[6] A third source, *The Histories of the Monks of Upper Egypt* 42 of Paphnutius, describes several incidents in the life of a late fourth-century bishop of Alexandria named Isaiah.[7] *The Lausiac History* 14, another collection of descriptions, this time of both

5. *Historia monachorum in Aegypto*, in *The Lives of the Desert Fathers,* c. 11.
6. *Pachomian Koinonia*, 1:120.
7. Paphnutius, *History of the Monks of Upper Egypt,* c. 42.

male and female ascetics (mainly Egyptian but also, to a lesser extent, Palestinian), made around 419–420 by Palladius (c. 363-before 431), the galatian monk and bishop, for Lausus, chamberlain to the eastern roman emperor, Theodosius II (401–50), refers to an Isaiah, again in the company of Paesios, at Nitria.[8] The name Isaiah also occurs several times in the *Alphabetikon*, the Alphabetical Series of Apophthegmata, linked with Achilles (3), Ammoes (2), Macarius (27), and Poemen (20). Any study of the writer of the *Discourses* must, therefore, proceed with caution. It is generally agreed that toward the end of the fifth century, or during the first half of the sixth, the Palestinian lawyer and ascetic, Zacchariah the Scholar, also known as Zacchariah the Rhetor, wrote a syriac *Life of Isaiah*. In it, Zacchariah refers to certain writings in syriac of one, Isaiah.[9] Within a couple of centuries a second syriac *Life of Isaiah* was written, this time by the nestorian, Dadišo of Beth Qatraya. In this second *Life,* which serves as a preface to Dadišo's *Commentary on the Discourses*, the name of the writer of the *Discourses*, Isaiah, is linked with Scetis for the first time.[10] According to the *Discourses* themselves, Abba Isaiah had a disciple called Peter. The three names Isaiah, Peter, and Scetis are all combined in a story recorded in a ninth-century manuscript, in which Peter, a follower of Abba Isaiah, relates that he once ate with his *abba* and other old men in the company of Abba Isaac of Scetis.[11] Care is to be taken with these references, however. For instance, another tale that brings together Isaiah, Peter, and Elisha of Scetis proves, in fact, to have been set in the time of Eulogius, a sixth-century bishop of Alexandria and correspondent of Gregory the Great.

There are, in addition, certain fifth- or sixth-century *Lives* of another Peter, the monophysite Peter the Iberian (d. 491), bishop of Maiouma, near Gaza, which can add to our knowledge of Abba Isaiah. The anonymous *Life of Peter the Iberian* records that Isaiah was brought up and educated in Egypt, trained as a monk at an

8. Palladius, *Historia Lausiaca*, c. 14.
9. Zacchariah the Scholar, *Vitae Isaiae*, hereinafter referred to as VI, 12.
10. Dadišo Qatraya, *Commentaire du livre d'abba Isaie*.
11. Karakallou 251. On this manuscript, see Draguet, 'Une section "isaienne" d'apophtegmes dans le Karakallou 251' *Byzantion* 35 (1965) 44–61.

egyptian *coenobium* and withdrew into the isolation of the interior desert, which might imply Scetis, although the place is not named.[12] It is possible, too, that this might refer to the spiritual desert. The egyptian connection is confirmed in Zacchariah the Scholar's syriac *Life of Severus of Antioch* in which Isaiah is described as 'this grand ascetic of Egypt'.[13] Isaiah soon discovered, however, that his reputation hindered the search for solitude. Finding that he had many followers, Isaiah moved up to Palestine. Having visited the holy places, Isaiah settled at first in the desert near Eleutheropolis but judean monks and visitors still sought him there.[14]

After the Council of Chalcedon (451), several collections of stories, or *plerophoriae*, were made with the intention of confirming the anti-Chalcedonian position. Perhaps the most famous of these, the *Plerophoriae* assembled around 515, during the pontificate of Severus of Antioch, by John, a monk at the monastery of Beth Rufina and, later, bishop of Maiouma, refers to Isaiah visiting the aged monk, Paul, in the Thebaid about the year 431 before settling in Palestine in 452/53.[15] Isaiah is reported talking with Peter the Iberian, bishop of Maiouma, during the palestinian rebellion at the Council of Chalcedon.[16] Isaiah is known to have received two scholars, Nestorius the Bouletes and Dionysius.[17] Several documents, the *Ecclesiastical History*[18] and syriac *Chronicle* of Zacchariah the Scholar[19] and a letter written by Severus of Antioch,[20] mention extreme anti-Chalcedonians looking to Isaiah for guidance.

The anonymous *Life of Peter the Iberian* refers to Abba Isaiah being installed at Beit Daltha, near Gaza, by the autumn of 485, that is, after Peter the Iberian had been living at Thavatha for three

12. *Petrus der Iberer*, hereinafter referred to as VP, 101–23.
13. Zacchariah the Scholar, *Vita Severi*, 283.
14. VI, 6.
15. John Rufus, *Plerophoriae*, hereinafter referred to as P, 27–28.
16. VP, 81–82.
17. VP, 100–101.
18. Zacchariah the Scholar, *Historia Ecclesiastica*, 5/9 and 6/1.
19. Zacchariah the Rhetor, *Historia Ecclesiastica*, hereinafter referred to as HE, 2.3–6.
20. Severus of Antioch, *Ep*. 38 also refers to Abba Isaiah as 'the very famous, the statue of philosophy and of life in God'.

years.[21] Zacchariah the Scholar's *Life of Isaiah* confirms this point,[22] and, together with John of Maiouma's *Plerophoriae*, adds that Isaiah lived here as a recluse, controlling a *coenobium* through his disciple Peter.[23] John of Maiouma also records that Abba Isaiah and Peter the Iberian, not to be confused with Isaiah's disciple of the same name, were in close contact for three years.[24] The anonymous *Life of Peter*,[25] syriac *Chronicle*,[26] and *Plerophoriae*[27] all record Cosmas the Spartharius coming with orders to bring both Isaiah and Peter to Constantinople. Isaiah excused himself on grounds of ill health and Peter, forewarned, escaped to Phoenicia. The *Chronicle* mentions that sometime later Peter did in fact go to Constantinople[28] and the anonymous *Life* refers to him excusing himself from attendance at court after Pentecost, 489, and returning to Palestine where he settled near Jamnia in the autumn of 490.[29] It was at Jamnia that Peter heard of Isaiah's death on 11 August 491. The anonymous *Life* records Peter's own death during eve of 4 December in the same year.[30]

During the last hundred years scholars have been in dispute over the identity of Isaiah. In 1900 Kugener argued that the *Discourses* were written by the Isaiah known to have been at Gaza but were later circulated under the name of Isaiah of Scetis. A few years later, Augoustinos, the editor of the Greek text of the *Discourses* claimed that there were two distinct Isaiahs. In his publication of the syriac versions of the *Discourses*, René Draguet postulated a number of Isaiahs.

Was there more than one Isaiah involved with the writing of the *Discourses*? Certainly, as we have seen, Isaiah was a common name. We have also seen that the name Isaiah was associated with certain

21. VP, 101–104.
22. VI, 9.
23. VI, 9–10; VP, 100–104; and P, 101.
24. VP, 100–104.
25. VP, 103.
26. HE, 2.6.3.
27. P, 68.
28. HE 2.6.4.
29. VP, 124–26.
30. VP, 145.

fifth-century writings by Zacchariah the Scholar. The name was also linked with Scetis by the commentator Dadišo of Beth Qatraya. The *Discourses* themselves mention Peter as a disciple of the writer, and the three names Isaiah, Peter, and Scetis are combined in a ninth-century manuscript. The early writers of the *Life of Peter the Iberian* and the *Life of Severus of Antioch* and John of Maiouma have no difficulty in associating Isaiah with Egypt. The writer of the *Life of Peter the Iberian*, Zacchariah the Scholar, and John of Maiouma also have no problem over linking Isaiah with Palestine.

Why, then, were Kugener, Augustinos, and Draguet uncertain as to the identity of Isaiah? One of the *Sayings of the Desert Fathers* combines Isaiah with Macarius.[31] If we are to assume that this was the egyptian anchorite and monk, Macarius the Great, who died in 390 may we not also assume that Isaiah was, like Paul the Theban, at least one hundred twenty years old when he died? This does not seem impossible.

However, in the same way that there was more than one Isaiah, it may perhaps be argued that there was more than one Macarius. One of the chapters in the syriac version of the *Discourses* refers to certain other fourth-century Desert Fathers whom Isaiah knew. These, however, are not referred to in the Greek text and the reader is directed to Draguet's edition of the syriac *Discourses* to pursue this argument further. It might be added, in conclusion, that Draguet's arguments are comprehensively disproved by Derwas Chitty in his extended article on Abba Isaiah and the reader is encouraged to read this for a balanced view of the argument.

Monastic and scriptural sources

The *Discourses* were written during one of the most formative periods of christian monasticism in Egypt and Palestine. In the second half of the third century, Antony the Great (251–c. 355), the father of monasticism, had gone alone into the desert in order to live in isolation but his asceticism immediately attracted followers

31. *Sayings*, Macarius 27.

who came to live in community near him and in the opening years of the fourth century he came out of solitude to be their spiritual father. Soon after Antony's death, Athanasius (c. 295–373) wrote his biography of the monk, a work that was to have a profound influence on monasticism throughout Christendom.[32] Toward the end of the fourth century, the desert had become the home of innumerable hermits leading similar lives to Antony's, ascetics living as disciples of an *abba,* or spiritual father, and communities of monks, united in prayer and work.

In addition to those living in Egypt and Palestine, theologians in Cappadocia wrote on the monasticism of the desert. Basil the Great (c. 330–379), who had come to the desert to live as both monk and hermit, for example, later organized monastic life in and around Caesarea during his episcopacy there. Two of his works, *The Longer Rules* and *The Shorter Rules*,[33] became models of eastern monasticism and were widely quoted in the *Rule of Saint Benedict.*

The desert also attracted many travelers, some of whom recorded stories about monks they had encountered there. The best-known collection of these stories, *The History of the Monks in Egypt*,[34] recorded in Greek by a group journeying through Egypt in 394, was translated into Latin by Rufinus of Aquileia, who had lived as a disciple of Didymus the Blind and later founded a community for men on the Mount of Olives. The popular character of these histories gave them great interest.

Other visitors to the desert included Evagrius Ponticus (*c.* 345–99), who became a monk and lived at Nitria and the Cells, and in his *Practical Treatise* and *Chapters on Prayer* wrote on the spiritual life he experienced there.[35] John Cassian (360–435), who came from his monastery at Bethlehem to study egyptian and syrian monasticism collected his accounts of monastic life in his *Institutes* and *Conferences* for a monastery in Marseilles.[36] The works became classics in the

32. Athanasius, *Vita Antonii*, PG 26:838–976. New translations by T. Vivian from the Greek and Coptic are forthcoming in the Cistercian Studies series.
33. W. K. L. Clarke, *The Ascetical Works of St Basil* (London. 1925).
34. *The Lives of the Desert Fathers* (Oxford and Kalamazoo, 1981).
35. Evagrius Ponticus, *The Praktikos and Chapters on Prayer* (1978).
36. John Cassian, *Conferences* (New York, 1985).

medieval west, with quotations from them abounding in the *Rule of Saint Benedict*. Palladius (c. 363/4-before 431), who became a disciple first of Dorotheus and later of Evagrius, recorded stories of monks he had met in his *Histories*, a work of unashamed edification, emphasizing the spiritual value of the desert life.[37]

Collections of sayings, or *apophthegmata,* were also made during the fourth and fifth centuries. They were circulated and added to, orally at first, amongst the monks themselves and, later, were preserved in two series, the *Alphabetical Collection,*[38] in which sayings were grouped according to the desert father, from Antony to Or; and the *Anonymous Collection,*[39] in which sayings were grouped according to subject. It was, then, a very rich literary field which included biography, hagiography, rules, spirituality, and history that Abba Isaiah inherited.

The hermits', ascetics', and monks' liturgy, spiritual reading, and prayerful meditation were imbued, of course, with Scripture. There is also throughout the sources mentioned above much evidence of studying the Scripture. Those, on the other hand, who were illiterate would most probably have known the liturgy and psalms by heart. Both Testaments would have been known in Greek, the Old in its Septuagint version, or possibly even in Sahidic Coptic. By the time of Abba Isaiah, the Bible had been opened up to a variety of interpretations and hermeneutical methods and we read of it being spoken between abba and disciple, saint and demon, holy man and prostitute.[40]

In the *Discourses*, Abba Isaiah shows that he is indebted first all, to the Scriptures, both Old and New, and also the Apocrypha. From the Old Testament, Genesis and the Psalms predominate, but quotations are taken from most of the books. Of the gospels, Matthew appears most frequently. Scripture is cited copiously throughout, from

37. Palladius, *The Lausiac History* (London and Maryland, 1965).

38. *The Sayings of the Desert Fathers: Alphabetical Collection* (Oxford and Kalamazoo, 1983r).

39. *The Wisdom of the Desert Fathers: anonymous series* (Oxford, 1986r); and *The World of the Desert Fathers: anonymous series* (Oxford, 1986).

40. On the place of scripture in eastern christian monasticism, see D. Burton-Christie, *The Word in the Desert: Scripture and the Quest for Holiness in Early Christian Monasticism* (Oxford and New York, 1993).

a few words to extended passages. Sometimes Isaiah acknowledges the writer before quoting him, on other occasions the writing is so integrated into the text that it can easily be missed. Moreover, Abba Isaiah expects his reader to know his source, simply reminding him on occasion how such and such a theme is dealt with in the Bible.

The *Discourses* also show a strong influence of some of the early monastic writers. These, however, are almost never acknowledged and it is possible to argue that while a particular phrase, for instance, appears in an earlier text there is not always sufficient evidence to suggest that Abba Isaiah knew this specific work. There are echoes to be found of Antony the Great, Athanasius, Evagrius Ponticus, John Cassian, and Macarius the Great. On the other hand, Isaiah seems to be almost silent on Basil the Great. As soon as the original Greek text is translated into Syriac, during the course of the sixth century, quotations from many other desert fathers, especially of the fourth century, are added.

Spirituality and theology in the Discourses

The *Discourses* are full of interest in terms of information about the monastic life and rules of the time. They are also full of insight in terms of theological and spiritual doctrine. They are marked by a faithfulness to tradition, drawing as they do on the former and formative generations of egyptian asceticism; yet they are equally marked by a note of originality, founding as it were a current of thought that becomes distinctive of the Gaza region.

It has already been observed that the *Discourses* is not a systematic exposition of monastic thought. It should be added here that they are also not a scholastic treatment of ascetic theology. The work is intellectual, even at times creative, and it does have a sense of unity in its basic structure and theme. Nevertheless, it does not contain any explicitly philosophical speculation or exclusively doctrinal elaboration. Indeed, at times, Abba Isaiah's writing is expressly hostile toward any intellectualism.[41] Abba Isaiah is described by

41. See *Discourse* 6.

his biographer, Zacchariah the Rhetorician as a *praktikos*, and this term appropriately and succinctly summarizes the character of the *Discourses*. They constitute a practical guide for the monk on the life of *ascesis*, the way of prayer, the discipline of work, the fulfillment of the commandments, and the attainment of accordance with the nature of Jesus.[42]

There is very little that could be regarded as strictly theological, and not a word that may be construed as controversial.[43] Abba Isaiah's emphasis is on the practical life. Even when he adopts, once, the term *ousia* and, on numerous occasions, the term *physis*, the reference is to the human nature that requires both reformation and transformation, renaissance and resurrection alike. Never are these terms used to refer to the divine nature. He is not, however, simple. He is, rather, humble. In Isaiah we see the positive spirituality of the monophysite tradition, stripped of all negations and anathemas.[44] This cannot be said of every friend or disciple of Isaiah. For example, his disciple Peter deplores the decisions of Chalcedon, but, of course, he is a bishop and not just a monk. Nevertheless, although non-Chalcedonian by confession, Abba Isaiah is ecumenical by conviction. It is no wonder that, in the centuries that followed, Chalcedonians, Monophysites, and Nestorians alike preserved and profited from his works.

One aspect of Abba Isaiah's thought that is indicative of his monophysite inheritance is his emphasis on the imitation of Jesus Christ and on the intimacy of the monk's relationship with Jesus. Although not entirely absent from eastern byzantine thought, such an emphasis is certainly afforded a centrality by Isaiah not frequently found in spiritual and mystical writers of the East. Perhaps it is further evidence of the open-mindedness of Abba Isaiah's work that in reading, for example, *Discourse* 16 one can almost imagine that one is reading the *Imitation of Christ* by Thomas à Kempis. (However,

42. We are indebted to the work Derwas J. Chitty and, in particular, to his article on Abba Isaiah in the *Journal of Theological Studies*. Chitty, 'Abba Isaiah', JTS, 22.1 (April 1971) 69.

43. See Augustinos, 66.

44. Chitty, 'Abba Isaiah', 70.

this is more likely to be a reflection of the practical nature of the *corpus*.) The references to the 'sweetness' and 'tenderness' of Jesus[45] are typical of a simple piety and practical spirituality. Yet, much more than this, they are also signs of Isaiah's own very delicate nature and of his sensitivity to details in the interpersonal relations of the members of his monastic community.[46] In fact, nothing is more detestable and dangerous in the spiritual life, for Isaiah, than insensitivity toward others and toward God.[47] Isaiah believes that we ought to 'follow in the steps' of Jesus,[48] and plainly, in Pauline terms,[49] to be 'dressed with Jesus'.[50]

Abba Isaiah's indebtedness to Saint Paul is particularly evident in *Discourse* 13, where the monk develops his most favorite expression of 'ascending the cross of Jesus'. It is a passionate devotion to and contemplation of the Cross.[51] It also includes a perceptive distinction between *bearing* the Cross, which signifies the preparatory stage of ascetic discipline, and *mounting* it, which implies the higher stage of silence.[52] Finally, it proposes an appealing Christological corrective to other more intellectual representatives of the contemplative tradition, such as Clement of Alexandria and Evagrius of Pontus (although Evagrian language is accepted unreservedly). Again, however, there is no systematic development of the Christological doctrine.[53] It should be noted briefly here that Abba Isaiah is also one of the few early ascetic authors to stress the importance of the Holy Spirit.[54]

Another fascinating and consequential aspect of the *Discourses* is the development of a theology of nature. Abba Isaiah adheres to the classical distinction between that which is 'according to nature'

45. See *Discourse* 13 and 25.
46. See *Discourse* 4.
47. See *Discourse* 5, 16, 18 and 26.
48. See *Discourse* 22 and 25.
49. Cf. Ga 3:27.
50. See *Discourse* 2 and 21.
51. See *Discourse* 21, 25 and 27.
52. See *Discourse* 8.
53. See *Discourse* 2 and 21.
54. See *Discourse* 19.

(*kata physin*) and that which is 'contrary to nature' (*para physin*), but he even coins two terms hitherto unknown in the Greek language: *é kataphysis* and *é paráphysis*.[55]

It is in *Discourse* 2 that Abba Isaiah develops his optimistic understanding of human nature and the passions. The ascetic tradition is often perceived as treating nature in an unduly harsh, if not out rightly negative way, and there is certainly much evidence to support this perception, even in the *Apophthegmata*. Abba Dorotheus said of the body, 'It kills me, I kill it',[56] although Abba Poemen provides a milder statement, 'We were taught not to kill the body, but to kill the passions'.[57] Nevertheless, such rigoris attitudes are not determinative in the ascetic tradition, where other writers also played a decisive and different role. For example, Pachomius and Ammonas differ in this regard, and Isaiah too clearly constitutes an exception. Isaiah describes the human nature, which God created, as having 'a healthy sense' which, however, was 'altered'. Formerly, similar to 'the nature of Jesus', human nature has been perverted by the fall. Abba Isaiah is not the first ascetic writer to adopt this line, but his *Discourses* offer an explicit and consistent teaching in this regard. 'Desire is the natural state of the intellect', he writes, 'for without desire . . . there is no love.'[58] He continues his discussion by presenting the positive content of other passions such as zeal, anger, hatred, and pride. These, he suggests, have been distorted from natural to shameful passions.

In spite of this refreshing peculiarity in Abba Isaiah's writings, much of his spiritual teaching echoes the traditional teaching of the egyptian desert, with its emphasis in the *Apophthegmata* on obedience, silence, struggle against the thoughts, reading of the Scriptures, and manual labor. Yet Isaiah presents these monastic virtues in an original way, proving not only a faithful disciple but himself a spiritual master.[59] Concepts of central significance include 'neglect' (*améleia*, which appears in almost half of the discourses) and

55. See *Discourse* 8, 16, 18 and 25.
56. Cf. *Lausiac History* 2:17.
57. Cf. *Sayings* 184.
58. See *Discourse* 2.
59. See Regnault, DS col. 2090; and Draguet, CSCO 293, 127.

its corrective virtue 'attention' (*prosoché*, which is mentioned twenty times in *Discourse* 27 alone); 'repentance' (*metanoia*, which is also found in five) and the corresponding 'virtues of sorrow' (*penthos*) and pain (*ponos*); as well as 'humility' (*tapeinosis*) and, especially, his favorite phrase 'do not measure yourself' *(me metrein seauton,* which occurs in *Discourses* 1, 3, 5, 6, 7, 9, 15, and 16).

Doctrine, then, is always closely related to asceticism,[60] but, always, the most striking feature and spiritual foundation of Abba Isaiah's writing is *balance*.[61] Any excessive measure—even in the treatment of his favorite topics like the gift of tears—is attributed to the demonic, though he is also mild in his concept of demons. Isaiah clearly enjoyed a wide reputation for discernment. He was moderate and modest, while at the same time not mediocre in his discipline and doctrine.

In the fourth century, Egypt was the forging-ground and the testing-place of all kinds of monastic life and all extremes of monastic tolerance. Yet in the fifth century, the middle or *royal* way was transmitted to the Middle East (Palestine and Gaza) and the West (Rome and Gaul). Much as Cassian did in translating egyptian thought to the West, Abba Isaiah not only introduced the same spiritual legacy to the palestinian region, but also introduces contemporary readers to the heart of daily life in palestinian monasticism.[62]

Throughout the *Discourses* Abba Isaiah emphasizes the need for the monk to control his passions and enable his virtues to develop through the imitation of Christ. The ideal was to become apathetic, dispassionate, that is, to lose the passions that hindered the spiritual ascent of the soul and prevented the intellect from becoming united with God. Because the monk was human, however, he was subject to the assaults of the devil and had sinned against God since infancy. Such sins were manifold: avarice, love of worldly things, the desire to dominate, greed, impurity, jealousy, lethargy, negligence, vainglory, and the wish to hold on to one's own will. Indeed, all that was contrary to nature, that is, the nature of Christ, was considered to

60. See *Discourse* 7, 13 and 21.
61. See *Discourse* 4.
62. See *Discourse* 1, 3–5, and 9.

be evil. In renewing his imitation of Christ, which Isaiah describes as ascending the cross, or stripping away the old flesh in order to put on the new, the monk could repent of his sins. The image of Christ on the cross symbolized for Isaiah the bronze serpent of the Old Testament. In the same way that the bronze serpent had worked miracles of healing, so Christ, too, cured the soul. Looking at Christ crucified, Isaiah saw God taking upon himself all the infirmities of humanity. Looking at Christ crucified, the monk was inspired to repent, to look for the healing of his soul, and the theme of repentance was of such importance to Abba Isaiah that one of the chapters from the first part of the *Discourses* and the whole of the second deal with the subject. It was so integral to the monk's spiritual journey, however, that all of the *Discourses* are imbued with it.

Of central importance to repentance was the feeling of *penthos* or compunction. The monk was to hold his sins, as well as death and the fear of judgment, before his eyes at all times and not to become preoccupied with the sins of others. Fear of God, which has its source in humility, the first and fundamental virtue, and is engendered through tears of compunction, was considered by Abba Isaiah to be a positive feeling. It was the mother of all virtues. It guarded a monk against his passions. It chased away every evil. On the other hand, a heart that held no fear of God was insensible to the prick of conscience. It was therefore held to be pleasing to God. Those who knew that they feared God were blessed. If a monk ignored his own sins, destructive passions would grow in him, replacing the virtues. If he committed the same sins a second time, he would not be forgiven. If he did not regain the innocence of his infancy, he would not enter into the kingdom of God. If the passions won the battle against the virtues, he would enter Gehenna.

Repentance, bringing pardon of sins, was an essential virtue for the monk who wished to serve God and any study of Scripture would reveal how essential this was. Having its source in God, it was seen as a gift from God to the monk. It turned the monk away from his sin and towards God. It restored his original nature; it purified him. It was like a mother who cared for her infant. Without repentance, the monk could not breathe or have any being. It could not be found in any material thing, however, but belonged to the cross.

Abba Isaiah's audience

In the chapter headings of the *Discourses* the author himself describes the text as a collection of 'rules', 'commands', 'precepts', or 'discourses'. They are a series of formative regulations, a list of didactic propositions, even a form of spiritual 'constitution' for men choosing, perhaps, to follow the lifestyle of Abba Isaiah,[63] or else to enter the nearby monastery directed by Isaiah' s closest disciple, Abba Peter.[64]

These men were literate, possessing books in their cells, and in some instances wealthy, having slaves. Some of them were even married and had children. The disciples who read, or heard, these discourses included young, baptized beginners, and brothers who were living both in community and in isolation, with their elders or else under an abba. Their way of life included prayer in the cell, psalmody, the study of Scripture, communal liturgical worship, the sacraments of Communion and Confession, spiritual direction and manual work. Some of them also went on journeys to towns and cities for work or visitations.[65]

The *corpus* appears to have been assembled by Abba Isaiah's disciple Abba Peter, himself also an Egyptian, who quotes his master's words of advice in many of the *Discourses*, or else his own questions to his elder. In either case, the advice reflects the needs and interests of Abba Isaiah's audience. At least one discourse is a letter addressed to Peter on entering the monastic life;[66] others may be addressed to him,[67] or to others.[68] Others still are general homilies.[69] In some discourses it is not clear whether it is Isaiah or Peter who is speaking;[70] others are memorable words of Isaiah simply reported by Peter.[71] In fact, most of the discourses in the Greek manuscript

63. See *Discourse* 3.
64. See *Discourse* 1.
65. See, for example, *Discourse* 3.
66. See *Discourse* 25 and 26.
67. See *Discourse* 15 and 16.
68. See *Discourse* 21.
69. For instance, *Discourse* 11, 'On the grain of mustard seed'; cf. *Discourse* 19 and 22.
70. See *Discourse* 5 and 9.
71. See *Discourse* 8 'Apophthegmata', and 26.

tradition include the phrase, 'Again [the Father] said . . .', and the distinctive, homiletical endings to many of these discourses may be clues to their author, or else to their literary genre. Perhaps Isaiah is, through Peter, addressing other disciples from whom he is separated either by choice and seclusion, or by circumstance and sickness.[72] In both cases, he was one of the first monks to introduce a lifestyle that acquires prominence in the next generation with the peculiar practice of the great 'Old Men', Barsanuphius and John. From the seclusion of his cell, Barsanuphius directed a nearby monastery (formally, or nominally, supervised by Seridos). He may well have learned or liked this manner of spiritual direction from Isaiah and his similar relationship to Peter (who may have acted as administrative superior in the nearby community).

It is possible that Abba Isaiah and Abba Peter are jointly responsible for the authorship of the first draft or layer of the treatises, while Peter and/or a disciple of his is the compiler of the entire *corpus*. The fifth discourse makes reference to earlier, or 'first writings'. Chitty suggests that, supposing Peter had considered or even possibly commenced the writing of the treatises during Abba Isaiah's lifetime, then the latter would have insisted on his own contribution remaining anonymous, and on other material from earlier ascetics in Egypt being included.[73] Furthermore, the purpose of the publication by Peter of any 'lives' or 'sayings' of Egyptian Fathers, would surely have been the transmission of events and words recalled by Isaiah from his time in Scetis, or, more probably, the events and words relayed to Isaiah by the disciples of those who survived the first devastation of Scetis (c. 407). The expectation of Abba Isaiah's audience was precisely to hear from him, as their bridge to an earlier generation of elders, about the teaching and conduct of monks in former times. This would mean that Isaiah was remembering conversations held between his own elders, or simply informants, and leading personalities from the egyptian generation of monastics in the 430s: Arsenius, Agathon, and Sisoes, all of whom did not die

72. See *Discourse* 26.

73. See Chitty, JTS, 52–53. The question of the plurality of authors is further complicated by the more recent appearance of the syriac *Asceticon*.

before 434. Isaiah's information was probably gathered sometime during the 450s.

One of the highlights of this corpus is precisely the way in which contemporary readers are able to connect the early monastic generations of the third and fourth centuries to the later developments found in the teachings of, for example, Barsanuphius and John (mid-sixth century). Abba Isaiah describes in almost pedantic detail the life of the monk in the fifth century, from the least significant aspects to the most spiritual dimensions of life in community.[74] In so doing, he reveals certain personal characteristics, such as his acute sensitivity in issues of social relations, his profound insight in matters of spiritual life, as well as his balanced understanding in questions of orthodox doctrine. These are all characteristics also of the Desert Fathers.

Abba Isaiah's generation is, and clearly feels, responsible for recollecting and perhaps even for collating the primary corpus of the *Apophthegmata* in order to preserve the authenticity of earlier generations and to perpetuate their authority among later generations. If there is a lack of systematic plan in Isaiah's words and in Peter's product, their purpose is certainly defined by clarity of mind; 'elder' and 'disciple', both migrants from Egypt to Gaza, are reminiscing about the 'golden age' of egyptian monasticism. This, in part, is why it is difficult to say whether the *corpus* is the personal exposition of a single author. It is more likely to embrace a variety of authors, including even pre-isaian material. Nevertheless, the personality of Abba Isaiah pervades every page of the *Discourses*—whether as inspiration, as witness, as writer, as speaker, or as compiler.

Manuscripts, versions and commentaries

Until now, the only writings of Abba Isaiah known to the reader of English have been the twenty-seven extracts *On Guarding the Intellect* included in the first volume of the *Philokalia*[75] and certain

74. See *Discourse* 5.

75. Saint Nikodemus of the Holy Mountain and Saint Macarius of Corinth, *The Philokalia*, 4 vols. (London, 1979–95) vol. 1, c. 1.

of his sayings from the Alphabetical Collection included in *The Sayings of the Desert Fathers.*[76] The present volume, then, is the first complete translation into English of Abba Isaiah's *Discourses* and is based on several manuscripts of the Greek text, ranging over many centuries. The earliest known fragment of the Greek text, existing in a late fifth-/early sixth-century papyrus, is now at Columbia University (Inv. N. 553). The next oldest manuscripts of the Greek text, from the eleventh century, are at Athens (Atheniensis 549), the British Library (Add. 39609), and the Bibliothèque Nationale, Paris (Coislin 123). Five manuscripts dating from the following century are at Athens (499 and 500), in the Bibliothèque Nationale (Coislin 281 and 283), and in the Museum of History, Moscow (320 = Vladimir B Synodale 177). Two thirteenth-century manuscripts are in the Bodleian Library (Cromwell 14) and Library in Venice (B. Marcianus 132). Two manuscripts going back to the fourteenth century are now in the Bibliothèque Nationale (Coislin 284) and at Moscow (gr. 926). An incomplete manuscript of the Greek text dating from the seventeenth century, is at Jerusalem (Patr. 109). The most recent manuscript, from the nineteenth century, of the Greek text is Panteleimon 273. Doubtless in addition to these fifteen manuscripts there are further copies of the Greek text, as yet not identified.

The seventeenth-century manuscript, with its lacunae tilled in by Metropolitan Cleopas of Nazareth, with translations back into Greek from a Latin version, was edited and published by Augoustinos, a monk from the Saint Gerasimos Lavra in the valley of the Jordan, at Jerusalem in 1911, and was reprinted, without any additions, by S. N. Schoinas at Volos in 1962. The late fifth-/early sixth-century papyrus fragment is described by E. R. Hardy, Jr. in a paper 'A fragment of the works of the abbot Isaiah'.[77] The British Library and Bodleian manuscripts were collated by Derwas Chitty

76. *The Sayings of the Desert Fathers: the alphabetical collection* (Kalamazoo, 1984r) 69–70 and passim.

77. E. R. Hardy Jr., 'A fragment of the works of the abbot Isaias', *Annuaire de l'Institut de Philologie et d'histoire orientales et slaves de I'Universite Libre de Bruxelles,* 7 (1944) 127–40. See also Chitty, JTS, 47.

in a typescript by Derwas Chitty, now in Saint Gregory's House Library, Oxford.[78]

Extracts from the Greek text of the *Discourses* are also known, existing under different titles and authors, for example, in a sermon by Athanasius,[79] and in the *Sacris Parallelis* of John Damascene.[80] In addition, there are extensive references to the Greek text of the Discourses throughout the vast ascetic collection, *Synagogē,* of Paul of Evergetinos (d. 1054), first published at Venice in 1783.

Almost fifty manuscripts of various syriac versions also exist, five of which go back as far as the sixth century.[81] These are of exceptional importance, reflecting early additions to the original Greek text. A further syriac work, *Concerning the Steps of the Monastic Life*, has also come to light in recent decades.[82] Two syriac *Commentaries* on the *Discourses* are also of interest, one by the seventh-century nestorian Dadišo Qatraya,[83] the other by an anonymous writer, whose manuscripts date from the twelfth century.[84]

In addition, there are versions of the *Discourses* in no less than six other languages. The arabic translations of Abba Isaiah's writings exist in no less than four categories. There are shorter and longer recessions of *Precepts to novices,* writings taken from the *Discourses.*[85]

78. Copies of this typescript are also in a handful of private libraries.

79. Athanasius, *Sermo pro iis qui saeculo renuntia sunt,* PG 28:1409–20. See also, J. Kirchmeyer, 'A propos d'un texte du pseudo-Athanase', *RAM* 40 (1964) 311–313.

80. John Damascene, *Sacris Parallelis*, PG 96:325, 420 sq.

81. R. Draguet, *Les cinq recessions de l'Ascéticon syriaque d'abba Isaïe,* CSCO 289/Syr 120 and CSCO 290/Syr 121 (Louvain, 1968). See also, R. Draguet, *Les cinq recessions de 1'Ascéticon syriaque d'abba Isaïe: les témoins et leurs parèlleles non-syriaques*, CSCO 289/Syr 120, CSCO 290/Syr 121 (Louvain, 1968); and 'Notre édition des recessions syriaque de "1'Ascéticon" d'Abba Isaïe', *Revue d'Histoire Ecclésiastique* 63/3–4 (1968) 843–57.

82. F. Graffin, 'Un inédit de 1'abbé Isaïe sur les étapes de la vie monastique', *OCA* 29 (1963) 449–54.

83. Dadišo Qatraya, *Commentaire du livre d'abba Isaïe*, CSCO 326/Syr 144 and French translation CSCO 327/Syr 145 (Louvain, 1972).

84. *Commentaire anonyme du Livre d'abba Isaïe (fragments)*, CSCO 336/Syr 150 and CSCO 337/Syr 151 (Louvain, 1973).

85. The shorter recession, included in Vat. arabe 398, the longer in four manuscripts, all translated from Latin into Arabic, and ranging from the early tenth to the seventeenth centuries, are discussed by J. -M. Sauget, 'La double recession arabe des Préceptes aux novices de 1'abbé Isaïe de Scété', *Melanges E. Tisserant*, 3 vols., Studi e Testi 231, 232 and 233 (Vatican City, 1964) in vol. 3, 299–336. The

There are also fragments from the *Discourses* in a ninth-century manuscript, Vatican arabe 71, which, at certain points, are so freely translated from the Greek that their identification as the work of Isaiah is difficult.[86] There is a further fragment from the *Discourses* wrongly attributed to Ammonas.[87] A series of sayings in a tenth-century manuscript, Sinai arabe 547, completes the Isaian corpus in Arabic.[88]

An armenian translation of some of the *Discourses* was published at Venice in 1855.[89] A leading Isaian scholar, A. Guillaumont, edited nineteen fragments of a Sahidic Coptic version, existing in two manuscripts, one dating from the tenth century and the other from the eleventh, of the Greek text of twelve of the *Discourses*.[90] In addition, there is an Ethiopian version of nine of the *Discourses*,[91] and fragments and citations of a Georgian version of five of the *Discourses*.[92] There is a Latin version of the *Discourses* in a twelfth-century manuscript, Darmstadt 1943, which was published by Petrus-Franciscus Zino of Verona at Venice in 1558 and again in 1574, which was then printed by Migne in the *Patrologia Graeca* series.[93]

---

longer recession, in Latin, is given in PL 103:427–34. See also G. Graf, *Geschichte der christlichen arabischen literature*, vol. 1, Studi e Testi 118 (Vatican City, 1944) 402–403.

86. J. -M. Sauget, 'Les fragments de I'Ascéticon de 1'abbé Isaïe du Vatican arabe 71', *Oriens Christianus* 48 (1964) 235–59.

87. J. -M. Sauget, 'Un fragment ascétique d'abba Isaïe en traduction arabe sous le nom d'abba Moise', *Proche Orient Chrétien* 27 (1977) 43–70. See also PO 11:458–71.

88. J. -M. Sauget, 'Un nouveau témoin de collection "d'Apophthegmatum Patrum". Le "Paterikon" du Sinai arabe 547', *Le Muséon* 86 (1973) 14–16.

89. *Vitae Patrum*, vol. 2, pp. 505–635. Venice, 1855. See also B. Outtier 'Un patéricon arménien', *Le Muséon* 84 (1971) 299–351.

90. A. Guillaumont, *L'Ascéticon copte de 1'abbé Isaïe*, I'Institut français d'archeologie orientale, Bibliothèque d'Etudes coptes 5, Cairo, 1956. See also, A. Guillaumont, 'La recession copte de I'Ascéticon de 1'abbé Isaïe' in *Coptic Studies in honor of W E. Crum*, The Byzantine Institute (Boston, 1950) 49–60. Other previously unidentified Coptic fragments had been edited by L. Th. Lefort. 'Fragments coptes', *Le Muséon* 58 (1945) 97–120, esp. 108–14 and 118–20.

91. V. Arras, *Ascéticon*, CSCO 458, SA 77; French trans. 459, SA 78 (Louvain, 1963).

92. G. Garitte, *Catalogue des mss georgiens litteraires du Mont Sinai*, CSCO 165, SA 9 (Louvain, 1956).

93. *Beati Esaie abbatis opera e graeco in latinum conversa*, Petrus Franciscus Zino, Venice, 1558. See also PG 40:1105–1206.

There is a French translation of the Greek text of the *Discourses* made by the monks at Solesmes under the direction of Herve de Broc, with an introduction by Lucien Regnault.[94]

The later tradition

The *Discourses* provide ample advice on work and prayer, on how to behave in one's cell, on monastic renunciation and sexual abstinence, on spiritual direction and discernment, on sleep and study, and on the importance of silence.[95] Thus, the teachings and the text itself of the *Discourses* were deeply respected and highly recommended by a wide variety of writers in the East and the West from at least the eighth century onwards. For instance, Theodore the Studite (d. 826) included them among the 'accepted' books after Scripture.[96]

However, textual reference to Abba Isaiah is much earlier than this. The *Discourses* were regarded, from a very early period, as foundational and formative reading for monastics at all stages of maturity, from the young novice to the advanced solitary. Already a generation later, his successors, Barsanuphius the Great and John the Prophet (both d.c. 542–5) refer to Isaiah at least four times by name, but clearly either imply or else echo Isaian doctrine on numerous other occasions. Curiously, Dorotheus (mid-sixth century) does not refer directly to Isaiah, although he is clearly aware of and quotes the corpus, and Isaiah may even be described as his 'spiritual ancestor'.[97]

The palestinian tradition assimilated the thought of Abba Isaiah in terms of general themes as well as of fundamental principles which later writers either assumed as ideas or adopted as terminology. With Barsanuphius and John, and before them Isaiah and Peter, we have three generations of an ascetic pedigree, a monastic succession or evolution that begins in the egyptian desert. Indeed, in spite of the contrast drawn between Isaiah and Evagrius, there is also a sense in

94. Abbé Isaïe, *Receuil ascétique*, Spiritualité Orientale 7, Abbaye de Bellefontaine 49 (Bégrolles, 1970).
95. See, for example, *Discourse* 1, 3–6, and 9.
96. *Testament* PG 99:1816.
97. Cf. *Dorotheos of Gaza: Discourses and Sayings* (Kalamazoo, 1977) 30.

which the two authors are comparable with respect to their lasting influence through the centuries and across the literary traditions.[98]

The precise evaluation and determination of Abba Isaiah's later influence is a complicated matter, partly as a result of the anonymity of many references to him, also perhaps due to the fact that some Isaian writings exist under other people's names. Another reason for this is the general and considerable influence of the *Apophthegmata*, a tradition with which Abba Isaiah is confused and to which he also contributed. In the sixth century the *Discourses* are cited by Zosimas (Dorotheus' contemporary), in the *Long Letter* by the nestorian bishop and ascetic writer Philoxenus of Mabboug (d. 523), as well as by Abraham the Great (d. 588). In the seventh century, he is quoted by Isaac the Syrian, of Nineveh (d.c. 680), by Symeon of Taybuthe and by Dadišo Qatraya. Abba Isaiah also considerably influenced Gregory of Cyprus (a nestorian monk of the seventh century) and John Climacus (570–c. 649).[99] In the following century, John of Daljatha informs us that young monks were encouraged to read Abba Isaiah. The nestorian ascetic Rabban Bar'Idtâ could repeat the entire discourses 'from end to end'; this was true not only of the Syriac, but also of the Arabic and Armenian traditions. All of these examples of Isaian influence imply continual and increasing respect of our author, to which later centuries also bear witness.

Numerous writers refer to Abba Isaiah in general terms: John of Damascus (c. 550–749), Anthony of Melissa (eleventh century), and John of Antioch (twelfth century) rank Isaiah among the inspired authors of the patristic tradition. Sophronius of Jerusalem (c. 550–638) is an exception in this regard, ranking him among the heretical authors of the heresy known as the *Akephaloi*, together with Isaiah's disciple Peter, in his long *Synodical Letter to Patriarch Sergius of Constantinople*.[100]

However, more specifically, it is Abba Isaiah's teaching on prayer, silence, and attentiveness that proved most influential. The tenth

98. F. Neyt, 'Citations «isaïennes» chez Barsanuphe et Jean de Gaza', *Le Muséon*, 65–66.

99. Cf. K. Ware, in *John Climacus: The Ladder of Divine Ascent* (New York, 1982) 30.

100. PG 87(3):3192.

century anthology of Paul Evergetinos (d. 1054) incorporated a great part of Isaiah's work, referring to Isaiah by name no less than seventy-six times.[101] This widespread influence is also observed in another anthology of writings on prayer, namely the *Philokalia*, the late eighteenth-century collection of texts by Nikodemus of the Holy Mountain of Athos (1749–1809) and Macarius of Corinth (1731–1805). The first volume of the *Philokalia* opens with a brief selection, in twenty-seven paragraphs, of Isaiah's *Discourses* under the title 'On Guarding the Intellect'. In the *Philokalia*, it is especially Nicephorus the Hesychast (thirteenth century)[102] and Gregory of Sinai (d. 1346) who draw from Isaiah's method of prayer. Nicephorus numbers Isaiah among the fourteen patristic authorities who preserve the 'guarding of the heart',[103] while Gregory appeals to him as a 'witness' for *the* technique of breathing in prayer.[104]

Abba Isaiah's influence is not entirely restricted to the East. He was also considered as an author of significance for his monastic teaching in the West, where his sayings were preserved in a fragmentary or partial way. Passages from the corpus are found in the work of Peter Poussines (1609–1686), and the abbot Benedict of Aniane (c. 750-d. 821). Nevertheless, in the Latin tradition, Isaiah was better known through the *Apophthegmata*. Following the sixteenth-century translation of the *Discourses* by Francesco Zino, Isaiah was recommended to novice masters of the Jesuit Order.[105] However, this lack of familiarity is also shared by the christian East, where in the slavic world for example, Isaiah was little known until the late eighteenth century when the *Philokalia* was translated by Paissy Velichkovsky (1722–1794) and, later, by Theophan the Recluse (1815–1894).

101. Cf. R. Draguet, *Les Cinq Recensions*, CSCO 289, 51–56.

102. Nicephorus, for example, describes Abba Isaiah as 'this great Father', cf. *Philokalia*, vol. 4, 201.

103. *On Sobriety and the Guarding of the Heart* PG 147:956–57.

104. *On Silence* 3 PG 150:1316.

105. Cf. PL 40:1072–74 and PL 103:427–34.

1

Rules for the Brothers who Live with Him

THOSE WHO WISH TO STAY WITH ME should listen for the sake of God.

Each of you should stay in his cell with fear of God.[1] In accordance with God's command,[2] do not despise your manual work, nor neglect your study or continual prayer,[3] and preserve your heart from foreign thoughts,[4] lest you think anything <evil> against any person or anything in this world. Always examine where you falter, and try to correct yourselves, asking God with pain of heart, tears,[5] and much toil, to forgive you and keep you henceforth from

1. Fear of God is a fundamental and positive virtue in the monastic tradition. Cf. *Sayings*, Anthony 32 and 33. See note 6 below.

2. Abba Isaiah is a deeply evangelical monastic and writer, constantly emphasizing the need to obey the divine commandments.

3. The palestinian tradition of prayer constitutes a significant milestone in the development of the Jesus Prayer and is a precursor to the Hesychast tradition. See Serapion, *Letter to Monks* 3 PG 40:928; Athanasius, *Life of Antony* 3; and Barsanuphius, *Letter* 441.

4. As in most ascetic writers, the heart is the source of all thoughts and the center of spiritual struggle. Cf. *Sayings*, Pambo 10, Poemen 34, and John the Dwarf 10. See also Gregory of Nyssa, *On the Creation of Man* 8 and 15 PG 44:145 and 177; and Mark the Monk, *To Nicholas* 6 PG 65:1037.

5. The role of tears is central in the monastic life and thought of Abba Isaiah. Cf. also Barsanuphius, *Letters* 37, 77, 257, 461 and 570; Mark the Monk, *Chapters on Sobriety* 28 PG 65:1069; and Abba Dorotheus, *Instruction* 21. See also *Sayings* Dioscorus 6, Poemen 119, and Arsenius 41; and Antony, *Letter* 20 PG 40:1055–1066.

falling again in the same way. Keep death before your eyes daily,[6] and be concerned about how you will leave this body, pass the powers of darkness that will meet you in the air, and encounter God without hindrance, foreseeing the awesome day of his judgement and reward for all our deeds, words, and thoughts. *Everything lies naked and exposed to the eyes of the one with whom we have to reckon.*[7]

Do not speak at all in the refectory[8] or church,[9] unless there is great urgency, nor correct anyone who is chanting, unless he asks you something.

Carry out the kitchen duties[10] on a weekly rota with godly fear, and without forsaking your study.

Let no one at all enter another brother's cell,[11] do not try to see one another before the <ninth> hour,[12] and do not be concerned with each other's manual work, whether your brother has achieved more than you, or you more than he. When you leave <your cell> for a duty, do not speak in any idle or bold way whatsoever, but let each one with godly fear observe himself, his work, study, and soul in secret.[13]

When the office concludes, or when you rise from the meal table, do not delay one another by speaking[14] either about God or about the world, but let each one of you enter his own cell and weep for his sins. If it is necessary to speak to each other, converse only a very little with humility and respect, as if God was listening to you.

6. Continual remembrance of death is another form of formative fear. The monastic is at all times and in all things accountable before others and before God.

7. Heb 4:13.

8. Pachomius, *Canon* 9 PG 40:948.

9. Pachomius, *Canon* 8 PG 40:948.

10. Abba Isaiah has in mind a specific monastic community that leads a common life of prayer and service. Cf. John Cassian in PG 28:860.

11. The monastic cell is a sacred space of solitary silence. See *Sayings* Daniel 5, Moses 6, and Paphnutius 5.

12. Palladius, *Lausiac History* 7. Another indication of a detail that reveals the community experience in a monastery. The ninth hour was the time when monastics would come together to pray in common prior to sharing a common meal.

13. The communal experience neither precludes nor excludes the solitary experience. Society and silence are not contradictory concepts. See note 14 below.

14. Pachomius, *Canon* 12 PG 40:948.

Do not argue with each other about anything, and do not criticize anyone. Do not judge or crush anyone either by <word of> mouth, or even in your heart. Do not complain at all about anyone, and let no lie leave our mouth, do not desire to speak or hear anything that does not benefit you. Do not allow evil, or hatred, or envy against your neighbor in your heart,[15] and do not let one thing be in your mouth and another in your heart, for God is not ridiculed, but sees everything, both secret and manifest.[16]

Do not conceal any of your thoughts, sorrows, or desires, but confess them openly and freely to your elder,[17] and try faithfully to carry out whatever you hear from him.

Take care not to forget to follow my rules; otherwise, you will understand, I will not let you stay with me.[18] However, if you follow them, both secretly and openly, I will give account for you before God. If you do not follow them, he will demand account from you both for your neglect and also for my rejection. Whoever keeps my rules secretly and openly will be guarded by our Lord God from all evil and protected by him in every temptation that comes, secretly or openly.

I entreat you, brothers, learn the reason why you left the world and show concern for your salvation, so that your renunciation will not have been to no avail, and so that you will not be shamed before God or the saints who renounced everything and struggled for his sake.

So let these become your virtues:[19] lack of strife, toil and humility,

15. Silence in solitude does not violate sensitivity in relations. Abba Isaiah's rules of conduct are an application of Evagrius' definition of a monk who is 'apart from all, and yet a part of all' (Cf. *Chapters On Prayer*, 124).

16. Abba Dorotheus, *Epistle* 1:182 PG 88:1797.

17. The role of the spiritual director is very important in Abba Isaiah's life and writing. The elder not only directs his disciples in this life, but gives account for them before God in the next (see the next few lines). See *Discourse* 9. Cf. also Athanasius, *Life of Antony* 3–4; *Sayings*, Rufus 2; and Barsanuphius, *Letters* 554, 694, and 703.

18. The setting is clearly that of a middle-sized community directed by Abba Isaiah who lives within the community.

19. The practical life of the monk includes a struggle against the passions in order to acquire the virtues. Cf. *Sayings*, Poemen 207; and Barsanuphius, *Letter* 258.

consciously cutting off your will in all things,[20] not trusting in your own righteousness but always having your sins before your eyes. Know this, relaxation, boasting, and vainglory dispel all the monk's toil.

20. *Sayings*, Anthony 37, 38 and 44; Barsanuphius, *Letter* 40.

2

On the Natural State of the Intellect

I DO NOT WANT YOU TO FORGET, brothers, that in the beginning, when Adam was created, God placed him in Paradise with healthy senses that were established according to nature. When Adam listened to the one who deceived him, all of his senses were twisted toward that which is contrary to nature, and it was then that he fell from his glory.[1] Our Lord, however, on account of his great love, took compassion on the human race. *The Word became flesh*,[2] that is to say completely human,[3] and became in every way like us except without sin,[4] in order that he might, through his holy body, transform that which is contrary to nature to the state that is according to nature. Having taken compassion on Adam, God returned him to Paradise, resurrecting those who followed his steps and the commandments which he gave us so that we might be able to conquer those who removed us from our glory, indicating to us holy worship and pure law, that we may stay in the natural state in which God created us.

The person, then, who wishes to attain this natural state removes all his carnal desires, in order that God may establish him in the

1. Gregory of Nyssa, *On Virginity* 7 PG 46:352; and Thalassius, *Century* 4:10 PG 90:1460. See also Barsanuphius, *Letters* 192 and 246; and Abba Dorotheus, *Instruction* 10:106. There is also an implicit reference to Abba Isaiah's notion of 'nature' from this *Discourse* in John Climacus, *Ladder*, Step 26.

2. Jn 1:14.

3. Abba Isaiah is aware of the christological debates, and conscious of the importance of doctrinal precision.

4. Cf. Heb 4:14.

state according to nature. Desire is the natural state of the intellect because without desire for God there is no love. This is why Daniel was called *a man of desires*,[5] but the enemy twisted this into a shameful desire, a desire for every impurity.

Ambition, also, is the natural state of the intellect for without ambition there is no progress toward God, as it is written in the epistle, *be ambitious for the higher gifts*.[6] However, our godly ambition has been turned into an ambition that is contrary to nature, so we are jealous, envious, and deceitful toward each other.

Anger, too, is the natural state of the intellect for without anger we cannot even attain purity unless we are angry toward all that which is sown in us by the enemy.[7] Just as Finees, the son of Eleazar, became angry and slaughtered the man and woman, the Lord's temper against his people was shattered.[8] Yet this anger within us was turned against our neighbor in regard to such senseless and useless matters.

Likewise, hatred is the natural state of the intellect. When Elijah discovered this, he killed the prophets of shame,[9] and Samuel acted similarly against Agag, the king of the Amalechites,[10] for without hatred against the enemy, no honor is bestowed on the soul. This hatred of ours has been twisted, however, into a state that is contrary to nature, so that we hate and loathe our neighbor, and this hatred chases away all the virtues.

Similarly, a sense of pride over the enemy is the natural state of the intellect. When Job found this sense, he reproached his enemies,

5. Dn 9:23. Abba Isaiah's concept of passions is both innovative and illuminating. The passions in their natural state are positive forces that lead to communion with God. In their perverted state, they require redirection and purification, ultimately transformation, but not destruction. Cf. Athanasius, *Against the Heathen* 1:3–5; Gregory of Nyssa, *On the Creation of Man* 18; Theodoret, *The Healing of Hellenic Maladies* 5:76–79; Mark the Monk, *On Those who Think . . .* 89 PG 65:944; Abba Dorotheus, *Instruction* 11:113–23; John Climacus, *Ladder* Step 27; and Maximus Confessor, *Chapters on Love* 3, 67 PG 90:1037. See *Discourse* 28. See also K. Ware, 'The Meaning of Pathos in Abba Isaias and Theodoret of Cyrus', in *Studia Patristica* 20 (1989) 315–322.

6. 1 Co 12:31.

7. Cf. Mt 13:25.

8. Cf. Nm 25:7.

9. Cf. 1 K 18:40.

10. Cf. 1 S 15:33.

saying to them, '*Unworthy, mean, and good-for-nothing people, whom I would not consider as worthy as the dogs in my pastures*'.[11] Yet even this interior sense of pride over our enemies was twisted, and, instead, we were humiliated by them, taking pride against and goading each other, proving ourselves righteous over our neighbor. Consequently, on account of this pride, it is God who becomes our enemy.

Now these things are innate to humanity. But when Adam tasted disobedience, these were changed within him into shameful passions.

Therefore, dear friends, let us endeavor and be careful to leave these things behind, achieving what our Lord Jesus Christ has shown us in his holy body; for he is holy and dwells among the holy. Let us, then, take care of ourselves, in order to please God by leading our practical] life in the best way we can, and by taking control of all our <bodily> members until they are established in the state that is according to nature, so that we may find mercy in the hour of temptation which will come over the whole universe. Let us pray, at all times, to his goodness, that his help may come, together with our humility, in order to save us from our enemies, for his is the power and the help and the might to the ages of ages. Amen.

11. Jb 30:4.

3

On the Condition of Beginners and Anchorites[1]

ABOVE EVERYTHING WE REQUIRE HUMILITY, always being prepared to say, 'Forgive me' for anything we say or do. Through humility the enemy is entirely destroyed.[2]

In order that you may be calm in your thoughts, do not measure yourself[3] in anything you do. Keep a solemn and meek face when you are with strangers, so that the fear of God may dwell in you. If you are traveling with brothers, keep a short distance[4] so that you may be silent and, as you journey, do not look here and there but examine your thoughts, or pray to God in your heart. Wherever you arrive, do not be impudent <in your conversation> but remain modest in all matters. When food is laid out before you, eat your

1. Abba Isaiah is perhaps also spiritually responsible for a number of monastics attached to but not living within the community. Therefore he addresses his advice to beginners within his monastery as well as hermits who live nearby. In fact, the advice that follows provides detailed regulations for a healthy and caring community. Much of the counsel also relates to rules when one is travelling. Isaiah has in mind a group of monastics who journey a great deal for the affairs of the community or for personal business. These itinerant monks are, nevertheless, members of a community whether inside or outside the monastery.

2. Cf. Abba Dorotheus, *On Humility* PG 88:1640.

3. 'Μὴ μέτρει σεαυτόν' is a key phrase in Abba Isaiah's spiritual teaching that is influential on later palestinian and sinaite monasticism. The emphasis is on not comparing oneself with others, good or evil, in order to retain a personal and peaceful connection with God. The spiritual life should not resemble a thermometer that rises or falls according to outside forces.

4. Pachomius, *Canon* 38 PG 40:952.

meal as if in a hurry, and, since you are younger, do not dare to reach out your hand to feed another person. At the place where you must sleep, do not share the bedcover with anyone else, but recite a number of prayers in your heart before you sleep. If you grow weary along the way and wish to rub some oil on your feet because of the tiring journey, anoint only your own feet, revealing them modestly, but do not allow anyone to anoint your body with oil, except in the case of an emergency or illness. When you are sitting in your cell and an unknown brother visits you, do the same to him. Anoint his feet and say to him, 'Be so kind as to take some oil and anoint your own body' but if he does not readily wish to do so, do not trouble him. If, however, he is an elderly ascetic, then oblige him until he anoints himself entirely.

When you sit at the table with brothers, if you are younger than the others, do not say to anyone, 'Eat this', but remember your sins, lest you eat with sensual pleasure. Stretch out your hand only [to the area immediately] before you, but if something lies in front of another person, do not reach out to it.[5] Let your clothes cover your legs, while your knees should be held firmly together. If those at the table happen to be guests, gladly offer them whatever they need. When they finish eating, say to them once or twice,[6] 'Please, eat a little more'. When you are eating, do not raise your head toward your neighbor, nor look here or there, and do not speak unnecessarily. Do not reach out to anything you may want without first excusing yourself, and when you are drinking water, do not make a noise as secular people do.

When you are sitting with brothers and wish to spit, do not do so in their presence but stand up and move outside. Do not stretch your body when others are looking. If you must yawn, do not open your mouth and this will be avoided.[7] Do not open your mouth widely when you laugh; it is rude to do so.

Do not covet anything you see that belongs to your neighbor, whether it is a garment, or a belt, or a hat, and do not satisfy your

5. Barsanuphius, *Letter* 87.
6. Isaac of Nineveh, *Homily* 7 (Wiesbaden, 1969) 67f.
7. Evagrius, *To Anatolius* 66 PG 40:1240.

desire by acquiring a similar one for yourself. If you buy a book for yourself, do not exaggerate its decoration. It is a passion for you to do so.

If you do something wrong, do not lie, being shy about it, but show repentance saying, 'Forgive me',[8] and the error will pass unnoticed. If someone says something harsh to you, do not raise your heart against him, but try to be reconciled with him before any blame arises in your heart, for anger arises very swiftly. If someone falsely accuses you of something, do not be frightened, but excuse yourself saying, 'Forgive me, I am no longer doing this', whether you are aware of it or not. All of this leads to progress in beginners.

When you are carrying out your manual labor, do not despise it but perform it carefully and in godly fear, lest you fall into the sin of ignorance. Irrespective of the manual labor that you are being taught and without ever being shy, ask your teacher, 'Please tell me if this is satisfactory, or not'. If your brother calls you while you are working, try to find out what he wants and help him out, leaving your own work behind.

When you finish eating, enter your cell and carry out your duties. Do not stay for conversation with those who will not benefit you. On the other hand, if those who are speaking the word of God are elders, then ask your Abba, 'Shall I stay and listen, or should I withdraw to my cell?', and do whatever he tells you.[9] If he sends you away for anything, ask him, 'Where do you want me to stay?', and do whatever he tells you. *Neither add to, or subtract from* what he says.[10] If you hear something while outside, do not retain it with a view to telling the others when you return. If you protect your ears, your tongue will not sin.

If you want to do something and the person you are staying with does not, surrender your will to him, so that there is no argument to upset him. When you are staying with a brother as his guest, do

8. Abba Dorotheus, *Instruction* 16.

9. Barsanuphius, *Letter* 305.

10. Strict and precise obedience is attested to in both the earlier and the later monastic tradition of the desert. The aim is not blind adherence to certain rules, but the discernment of the word and will of God among the many words of people. Cf. *Sayings* Antony 37–38; and Barsanuphius, *Letter* 40. See also, Dt 13:1.

not give him orders in anything, nor seek to control him. If you are staying with other brothers, do not attempt to compare yourself with them, or their conversation, lest you upset them, or lose your freedom and peaceful dwelling with them. If you are to stay with a brother and he says, 'Cook something for me', ask him, 'What do you want me to make?' If he gives you the choice[11] saying, 'Whatever you wish', then cook whatever is available, with godly fear. If you are living in a community and there is a job to be done, then share the task with all the others. Do not take care of your body for the sake of everyone else.

When you wake up each morning, first study the word of God before resuming your manual labor. If there is anything to be set in order, whether a mat, or a jug, or anything else, attend to it quickly and without hesitation. If it is a job for which you require assistance, your brother should help you but do not hold any grudge against him. If it is a small task and one person says to the other, 'Go off and do your own work, brother, I can do this alone', then be obedient. The one who obeys is the greater.

If a brother comes over to stay with you as a guest, be cheerful toward him as you greet him, and if he is carrying a vessel, hold it gladly for him, and when he is leaving, do the same. Let your greeting of him be kind and God-fearing, in order that no harm is caused to him. However, refrain from asking him about matters that are of no benefit to you but say a prayer with him and, when he sits down, ask him, 'How are you?', and then stop talking.[12] Give him a book to read. If he has a long way to go, let him rest and wash his feet. If he converses inappropriately, say to him in a loving manner, 'Forgive me, but I am weak and unable to hear such things'. If he is weary and his clothes are unclean, wash them. If he is simple and his dirty clothes are torn, sew them. If he is an itinerant monk, and there are some of the faithful staying with you, do not show him up before them, but show him mercy in the love of God. If your visitor is a brother for the sake of God and he approaches you asking for rest, do not turn your face away from him, but accept him gladly to

11. Literally, 'authority'.
12. Barsanuphius, *Letter* 308.

stay with your other faithful guests. If he is poor, do not send him away empty-handed, but show him the blessings you have received from God, since you know that whatever you have is not yours, but a gift from God.

If a brother offers you something, do not go away and open it to find out what is inside. Moreover, if the gift is very expensive, say to him, 'Please place it in my hands'. If you visit someone's home and he leaves you alone for a moment, do not raise your head to examine the vessels in his house, or open anything, whether a small door, or a pot, or a book. As he is leaving, say to him, 'Give me something small to do until you return', and do whatever he suggests without hesitation.

Do not be complimentary to anyone except in regard to what you have seen. And do not say that you have seen what, in fact, you have only heard. Do not reproach anyone for his clothing.

If you stop to urinate, or for your urgent necessities, do not act in a disdainful manner, but remember that God is watching you. If you rise in your cell to attend to your duties, do not look down upon them with neglect; otherwise, instead of honoring God, you may find yourself angering him. Stand in fear of God. Do not lean against the wall, nor relax by standing on one leg while resting the other, like foolish people do.[13]

Train your heart not to come around to your desires, in order that God may receive your sacrifice. When you are chanting in community, let each one of you say his own prayers. But if a guest is staying with you, invite him politely to say the office. Repeat your request only two or three times, without arguing with him.[14] When it is time for Communion, resist your thoughts and let your senses be attentive with godly fear, so that you may be worthy of the sacrament, and that the Lord may bring you healing.

Be careful not to allow your body to look ugly in squalor, lest vainglory has the better of you. Beginners, however, should allow their body to look entirely unsightly. This is to their benefit. Let the beginner never wear a beautiful garment until he reaches a mature

13. Cf. Evagrius, *Chapters on Prayer* 110; Barsanuphius, *Letter* 509.
14. Barsanuphius, *Letter* 319.

age. This is to his healing. A beginner should put a stop to the drinking of wine after three glasses at the most.[15] He should not entirely bare his teeth when laughing, but keep his face modestly lowered. When he is about to sleep, he should fasten his belt. Also, he should struggle not to place his hands inside his clothes, for the body has many passions that the heart fulfils.[16] If there is any need to go outside, he should put on his sandals, but while he is in his cell, he should try not to wear sandals. When walking, his hands should be held firmly against his side, so that they do not move to and fro as in the case of secular people.

If walking with your seniors, on no occasion should you move in front of them.[17] If your elder stops to talk to someone, do not despise him by sitting down, but stand there until he gives you a sign to sit. If you travel to a city or town, let your eyes look downward so that no inner warfare is aroused once you return to your cell. Do not sleep over at anyone's house where your heart is afraid of sinning. If you are going to have a meal at a particular place and you learn that a woman will also be eating there, then, under no circumstance, should you stay.[18] It is better for you to offend the person who has invited you than for your heart to commit adultery in secret. If you can, do not even look at the clothes of a woman. If you are journeying on the road, and a woman says, 'Peace be with you', respond to her within your heart, keeping your eyes lowered.

If you are traveling with an elderly person, do not allow him to carry the luggage. If, however, both of you happen to be young, take turns carrying the luggage for a while, and let the one who is carrying walk ahead.

15. *Sayings* Sisoes 2 and Xoios 1.

16. The palestinian school of thought retains a more unified, semitic anthropology and worldview. Cf. also Mark the Monk, *On Those who Think* . . . 15 PG 65:932; and Gregory of Nyssa, *On the Creation of Man* 8 and 15 PG 44: 145 and 177. See also *Discourses* 6 and 16.

17. Isaac of Nineveh, *Homily* 7, 67f.

18. Barsanuphius, *Letter* 351.

4

On the Conscience[1] of Those who Stay in Their Cells

IF YOU ARE ON A JOURNEY and there is a sick person traveling with you, allow him to walk in front of you, so that he may sit down, if he needs to do so.

If you are all beginners and you are away from home, arrange to take turns to be first to use the basin, or to begin to eat at the table, so that there may be no trouble when the time comes to use the basin; thus, if one of you enters first on one occasion, someone else should be first on another.

If you wish to ask an elder about some thought, bare your thought to him voluntarily, if you know that he is trustworthy and will keep your words.

If you hear about a weakness of your brother, do not tell it to anyone, for this will lead to your <spiritual> death.

If some brothers are talking about thoughts that trouble you, do not try to hear them, lest they cause you inner warfare.

Force yourself to repeat many prayers, for prayer is the light of your soul.

Every day ponder your mistakes. And, if you pray about them, God will forgive you.

1. On the link between conscience and heart, see *Sayings* Poemen 201; Mark the Monk, *To Nicholas* 6 PG 65:1037; Barsanuphius, *Letters* 13 and 40; and Dorotheus, *Instruction* 3 and *Discourses and Sayings* 105–7.

If a brother obliges you to slander someone, do not pretend to be modest or convinced by him, otherwise you sin against God. Instead, say to him in humility, 'Forgive me, brother, but I am wretched and all that you say, in fact, describes me, and so I cannot bear to hear it'.

If a brother harms you and someone else slanders him in front of you, guard your heart[2] so that evil is not revived within you. Instead, remember your own sins before God and that you want him to forgive you these, and *do not return evil*[3] against your neighbor.

If you are out with brothers who are unknown to you and these happen to be younger than you, give them the honor of priority. If you visit the house of a friend, allow the others precedence over you in everything, whether at the washing basin or at the dinner table. And do not give yourself priority because you are supposedly their guest, but allow them the honor, saying, 'God has been merciful to me on account of you'.

If you are traveling with a brother and you need to break the journey in order to say something to a friend, ask your brother to wait for you, but should your friends wish to keep you for a meal, let nothing enter your mouth until you invite your companion to sit with you too. If you are traveling with more brothers and you are embarrassed to take them with you to your friend because there are too many of them, do not slight them, or leave them behind in order to go secretly and eat, but discuss with them what should be done, and humbly listen to whatever they say to you.

While you are walking with them, do not wander about, considering only yourself, and avoiding menial chores.[4] If you are away from home and wish to visit a brother but he does not wish to receive you, then if you should see him on the way, or if he should come to you unexpectedly, try even harder to be good to him. If you hear that someone spoke something against you and you happen to meet this person somewhere, or if he should visit you, maintain a cheerful face and be as kind as you can to him. Do not tell him

2. Athanasius, *Life of Antony* 6; and *Sayings* Poemen 20.
3. Rm 12:17.
4. Isaac of Nineveh, *Homily* 7 [p. 67f].

anything that you have heard, or say, 'Why did you speak in this way?', for it is written in Proverbs, '*Whoever bears a grudge breaks the law*'.[5]

If some of the brothers are together and you all <decide> to visit a poor brother, do not cause him any distress in his poverty, but buy what you will need for yourselves to eat there so that some will be left over for him, and be satisfied with the shelter that you have found.

If you visit some of the elders whom you know and are accompanied by others who are not acquainted with them, do not be bold in your conversation with the elders in their presence, but allow room for those who have come with you to express their thoughts.

If there are brothers who live with you[6] and they are under your authority, take care of them in strict discipline, knowing that you will give account to God for them.

If you live in isolation from the world for the sake of God, do not desire to mingle with those around you, nor converse too much with others, for it would almost be better for you to live instead with your natural relatives. If you depart to a mountain in order to visit certain brothers living in monasteries, stay wherever you go and do not leave for another place unless you ask whether or not you should do so. And if the elder is not happy for you to leave, then do not upset him until you leave from that place.

If you are given a cell at a place that you know, do not receive many friends; one is sufficient, in case of illness. Do not lose the intensity of your isolation.[7] If you do good to a poor person, do not invite him to your cell without good reason, lest you lose the benefit that you rendered him.

If you enter a monastery that you do not know, stay wherever you are asked, and do not enter another cell unless the brother there actually invites you. If you are silent in your cell, do not keep any vessel that might abolish the command to love your brother, should he ask to use it. Use it only for as long as you so need, and no

5. Pr 12:24.
6. Abba Dorotheus, *Instruction* 17.
7. Barsanuphius, *Letter* 348.

longer. Do not try to dissolve the commandment and be upset, *for it is better for you to lose one of your members than for your whole body to be thrown into Hell.*[8] If you have left your natural relatives in order to be in isolation for the sake of God, do not allow the pleasure of their remembrance to come to you while you are sitting in your cell, feeling pity for your father or mother, or remembering your brother or sister, or perhaps feeling compassion for your child or wife in your heart, for you have left all these behind. Instead, remember your departure in relation to the urgency of your death when none of these people will help you. Why should you not leave them behind for the sake of virtue?

If you are silent in your cell and recall someone who has harmed you, then rise up and pray to God with all your heart to forgive that person, and the thought of retribution will leave you.

If you are about to participate in the sacrament of Communion, guard your every thought in order that you may not communicate unto condemnation.[9]

If you are tempted by sexual fantasies during the night,[10] guard your heart so that during the day you do not wonder which particular persons caused the fantasy, lest you are defiled in their [sensual] pleasure and bring upon yourself a wicked wrath. Rather, abandon yourself before God with all your heart, and he will help you, for he has compassion on human weakness.

If you lead an ascetic life, do not let your heart take confidence that it is protecting you, but think to yourself, 'It is because of the mortification of my body that God hears my misery'.

If someone should insult you, do not respond at all until he stops. If you examine yourself and find that what you have heard from him is true, then repent as if you were, indeed, the sinner, and God's goodness will once again receive you.

If you are journeying with brothers[11] and one of them especially happens to be loved by you for the sake of God, do not be bold with

8. Mt 5:29.
9. Cf. 1 Co 11:29.
10. Barsanuphius, *Letter* 258.
11. John Climacus, *Ladder* Step 26.

him while the others are watching, lest one of the weaker brothers should die from envy. Otherwise, you will bear his sin, because you gave him reason to sin. If you visit certain friends, do not expect them to be extremely happy to see you in order that, if they do not receive you, you may give thanks to God.

Should you be taken ill while silent in your cell, do not be discouraged but give thanks to the Lord. If you see your soul disturbed, say to it, 'Is not this illness better for you than the Hell that you will go to?', and you will again find inner peace.

If you are visiting some brothers and one of them says to you, 'I am not happy here; I want to come and live with you', do not give him false hope, lest you scandalize any of the others. If he says to you, 'I am dying to tell you something in secret', find a way for him to leave you, and do not allow him to live with you.

While living silently in your cell, place a limit for yourself so far as eating goes, allowing your body what it needs in order to support you in your duties, and that you do not feel the need to leave your cell.[12] Eat nothing with sensual pleasure, with a desire to taste things, whether they are good or bad for you. Should the need arise for you to visit either another brother, or a monastery, do not overconsume whatever good food you may find there, lest you betray yourself and become reluctant to return to your cell.

If the demons convince your heart to undertake some ascetic discipline that is beyond your capacity,[13] do not listen to them,[14] for they always arouse us in whatever matter we cannot achieve, until we fall into their hands at their pleasure.

Eat only once a day, and give your body what it needs so that you will continue to want to arise from sleep.[15] Keep your vigil modestly, and do not deprive your body of its needs, but perform your duties leniently and sensibly, lest your soul is darkened by the degree of sleeplessness and gives up the struggle. Half the night

12. *Sayings* Poemen 31.

13. Athanasius, *On virginity* 8 PG 28:261; Evagrius, *Praktikos* 40; *Sayings* Syncletica 13 and Poemen 129.

14. Barsanuphius, *Letters* 524 and 518.

15. Pseudo-Athanasius, *To Castor* PG 28:873.

is sufficient for your duties,[16] and the other half for your physical rest.[17] Practice your prayers and psalmody[18] for two hours before sleep, and then rest. When the Lord awakens you, do your duties without hesitation. Should you notice your body growing reluctant, say to it, 'Do you want to rest in this brief life and then be cast to the outer darkness?' Then, if you can bring yourself to rise a little, your strength will return.

Do not be friendly toward people about whom your conscience is afraid to move beyond to other friends,[19] lest you consciously become the cause of a scandal. If you are in a monastery and keep a servant, then you are insulting your <monastic> vocation. If you give him to a brother, you are sinning against God. Either release him and let him go, or grant him his freedom. Should he wish to become a monk, it is his choice, but you should not let him stay with you, because this is not beneficial for your soul.

If you are leading a life of ascetic discipline for the sake of God and people become envious of you, or honor you in regard to this, then leave this discipline and embark upon another, so that your toil may not be in vain.

If you have escaped vainglory, do not pay any attention to people, knowing that whatever you do will win over God's favor. If you have renounced the world, do not allow yourself to keep anything. And if you see that you desire to move from place to place because your senses are still weak, this movement to and fro is destructive for your soul. Try, instead, to apply yourself to your manual labor, in order that you may remain silent in your cell, carefully eating the bread you have earned.

If you go away to the city in order to sell your manual labor, do not argue over the price as secular people do, but give it away for any price, so that you do not lose the intensity of your cell. When purchasing something that you may need, do not argue, saying, 'I

16. Barsanuphius, *Letter* 83.

17. Abba Isaiah is less austere than the desert tradition: cf. *Sayings* Arsenius 15. However, see *Discourse* 16, below.

18. Cf. Evagrius, *Praktikos* 15 and *Chapters on Prayer* 83 and 85.

19. John Climacus, *Ladder* Step 26.

am not giving that much for this'. If you want it, restrain yourself a little, and if you do not have the amount to pay, then leave it quietly, put it down and leave. If your thoughts bother you saying, 'Where will you find it?' then reply, 'I have now become exactly like all the saints who have been tested by God through poverty, until he saw that their disposition was faithful and led them to plentitude'. If a brother sets down a vessel beside you and you happen to need to use it, do not touch it unless you first ask him. If a brother asks you to buy for him a vessel when you go out, if you could buy it for yourself, then buy it also for him. If you are staying with others, do not do so against the wish of those who live with you, in order not to upset them. If you need to visit your hometown for some reason, guard yourself in the presence of your natural relatives, and do not be too bold with them, nor converse too much with them. If you take something from your brothers in order to use it, do not forget about it, but make certain that you return it promptly. And if the vessel is a tool, then return it as soon as you have finished your work. If you break it, do not neglect to make him a better one. If you give something to a poor brother who needs it and you see that he cannot return it, do not upset or compel him in any way, whether it is a matter of money, or clothing, or anything else that you gave him according to your capacity.

If you go and live in a place where you are given a cell and you spend money to construct something in this cell, then, if you leave it and another brother takes it over, do not remove him should you later wish to return there. Ask for another cell, in order not to sin against God. Of course, if he should wish to surrender it to you of his own accord, then you are not to blame. If you left behind some vessels in the cell and he has used them, do not ask him for them. Further, when you leave a particular cell, do not take with you something that may be useful for the next person, but leave it there for a poor brother, and God will provide for you, wherever you go.

Do not be ashamed to confess to your elder every thought that troubles you and you will be alleviated of it, for nothing gives greater joy to the evil spirits than a person who keeps silent about his thoughts, whether these are good or evil.[20] Guard yourself at the time of receiving Communion, that you hold no evil against your brother, otherwise you are deceiving yourself. If the meaning of Scripture is revealed to you through allegory,[21] then go ahead and allegorize; but guard yourself in order not to abolish the literal <interpretation>, so that you may not believe that your knowledge is above holy Scripture, for this is a sign of pride. If your brother is deceived by the words of heretics[22] and in his ignorance strays away from the faith, do not overlook him, should he return again, for this happened as a result of ignorance. Be careful not to enter into dialogue with heretics in your desire to prove your faith right, in case the germ of their shameful words harms you. If you come across a book written by heretics, have no wish to read it, lest it fills your heart with the germ of death, but hold onto the faith into which you were baptized, neither adding to, nor subtracting from it. *Guard yourself*, also, *against that which is falsely called knowledge, which is opposed to healthy doctrine*, as the apostle says.[23]

If you are a beginner and have not yet lived a life of strict discipline, then, when you hear of the sublime virtues of the Fathers, do not pursue them, hoping to acquire these with ease, for they will not come to you unless you first cultivate the soil. If you cultivate the soil, they will come to you by themselves. Guard yourself against boredom, for this obliterates the fruit of monastic life. If you are struggling against a passion, do not lose heart, but surrender yourself to God, saying, 'I cannot do this; help me, the wretched one'. Say this with all your heart and you will find rest. If shameful thoughts are sown in your heart while sitting in your cell,[24] make sure you struggle with your soul, so that you are not overtaken. Try to remember that God is watching over you and that everything you ponder in your heart is revealed before him.

20. Spiritual confession or consultation includes the revelation both of one's evil as well as of one's good thoughts.

21. See *Introduction*, 22 above, and *Discourse* 11, below.

22. Orthodoxy of faith is critical for orthopraxis of ascetic discipline. The precise adherence to doctrinal truth was always treasured in the life of the monastics who struggled for its accurate formulation and austere preservation.

23. 1 Tm 1:10; 6:20.

24. *OGtI* c. 27.

Therefore, say to your soul, 'If you are afraid of other sinners like yourself seeing your sins, how much more should you fear God who watches over all?' This advice will reveal the fear of God to your soul, and if you persevere with it, you will become unmoved by the passions, for it is written, 'Those who trust in the Lord are like Mount Zion, which cannot be moved but abides forever <as the Lord dwells> in Jerusalem'.[25]

If you are leading an ascetic life and struggling against the enemy,[26] should you notice the demons weakening their warfare or even retreating, do not rejoice in your heart that the evil spirits are now behind you, for they are preparing a battle that is worse than the first. They are moving behind the city and ordering their troops to lie still. If you oppose them by attacking them, they run away from you, feigning weakness. Then, if your soul feels proud that it has chased them away and you abandon the city, some of them appear from behind while others attack from the front, thereby leaving the poor soul surrounded and with nowhere to escape.[27] Now the city in this case is the act of surrendering oneself before God with one's whole heart, for he will save you from all the attacks of the enemy. If you pray to God about a particular struggle, in order for him to remove it from you, and he does not hear you, do not lose heart, for he knows better than you what is of benefit to you. If you pray to God generally in the time of spiritual warfare, do not say, 'Take this from me', or, 'Give me this',[28] but pray as follows: 'Lord Jesus Christ, help me and do not allow me to sin before you, for I am deceived. Do not let me follow my own will. Do not let me become lost in my sins. Have compassion on your creature. Do not overlook me, for I am weak. Do not abandon me, for I have sought refuge with you.[29] Heal my soul, for I have sinned against you.[30] All those who trouble me are before you,[31] and I have no other refuge

25. Cf. Ps 125:1–2.
26. *OGtI* c. 2.
27. Cf. Jos 8.
28. Evagrius, *Praktikos* 42; and Barsanuphius, *Letter* 142.
29. Cf. Ps 143:9.
30. Cf. Ps 41:4.
31. Cf. Ps 49:20.

but you, Lord. Save me, Lord, on account of your mercy.[32] Let all those who have risen against me be put to shame, for they seek to destroy my soul.[33] For you, Lord, are mighty in all things, and through you is glory given to God the Father and the Holy Spirit. Amen.' Then your conscience[34] will speak in secret with your heart as to the reason why God is not listening to you. Your duty is not to feel contempt, but simply to do what he commands, for it is impossible for God not to hear you unless you, first, disobey him. He is not far from us, but our desires prevent him from listening to us. Therefore, let no one deceive you. Just as the earth cannot be fruitful without seed and irrigation, so, also, it is impossible for us to be spiritually fruitful without ascetic discipline and humility.

Dear friends, let us stand with godly fear,[35] keeping and maintaining the practice of the virtues, not presenting any obstacles to our conscience, but watching ourselves with godly fear, until it, too, is freed with us, in order that we are united with it, and so that it may become our guardian, showing us everything that we must cut off. If we do not obey our conscience, then it will resign from us and abandon us to fall into the hands of our enemy who will no longer take pity on us. Just as our Lord has taught us, '*Come to terms quickly with your accuser while you are on the way* <*to court*> *with him, or your accuser may hand you over to the judge, and the judge to the guard, and you will be thrown into prison. Truly I tell you, you will never get out until you have paid the last penny*.[36] They describe the conscience as an accuser[37]inasmuch as it opposes us whenever we want to fulfill our fleshly desires, and, if we do not listen to it, our conscience hands us over to the enemy.

This is why Hosea mourned Ephrem saying, '*Ephrem is an oppressor, he tramples on justice . . . calling on Egypt, turning by force to Assyria*'.[38] Now Egypt is the heart, seeking to fulfill its own fleshly

32. Cf. Ps 6:4.
33. Cf. Ps 40:14–15.
34. Mark the Monk, *On the Spiritual Law* 69 PG 65:913; Barsanuphius, *Letters* 13 and 40; *Sayings* Poemen 201. See also Abba Dorotheus, *Instruction* 3:40–43.
35. OGtI c. 3.
36. Mt 5:25–26.
37. Abba Dorotheus, *Instruction* 3 and 13.
38. Ho 5:11, 7:11.

desires. As for going by force to Assyria, this means that whether we want to, or not, we serve the enemy. Let us, then, dear friends, watch out, so as not to fall into the hands of our fleshly desires, nor to be captured and led by force into Assyria, nor to hear the following bitter words: 'The king of Assyria came to the land of Israel and carried away Ephrem and Israel to Assyria. He placed them in Halah on the Habor, the river of Gozan, and they are there to this day.[39] Then the king of Assyria sent people from his own nation and made them live in the land of Israel, and each of them made an idol and worshiped it, and, behold, they too are there to this day.' All this occurred to Ephrem 'he was oppressed by his enemy and crushed in judgment'.

So, brothers, you now know what happens to those who follow their evil desires and trample down their own conscience. Let us not envy them, friends, but let us envy all the saints who did not obey sin until death, preferring to obey, rather, their holy conscience and inherit the heavenly kingdom. Each of them was perfected in purity in their own generation, and their names cannot be extinguished for all future generations.

Let us take dear Jacob as an example,[40] for in everything he obeyed his elders in God, and, receiving the blessing, wanted to go as far as Mesopotamia to become the father of sons. He did not wish to become a father from the daughters of Canaan who quarreled with his parents. He took his rod and his bottle of oil, and came to the place called Bethel, which means 'House of God'. He slept there, and during the night saw in a vision a kind of ladder[41] reaching down from heaven to the earth, and the angels of God ascending it, while the Lord was standing at the very top. This is precisely a symbol of someone beginning to serve God for, in the beginning, the way of the virtues is revealed to that person, but, if he does not toil,

39. Cf. 2 K 17:6, 23; 18:11.

40. Cf. Gn 28:1–15.

41. For the notion of the soul's ladder in monastic sources, cf. Theodoret, *History of the Monks in Syria* 27 PG 82:1484 and John Climacus, *Ladder*. For Abba Isaiah's own ladder of virtues, see *Discourse* 16, below. See also Gregory Nazianzus, *Oration* 43 PG 36:529; John Chrysostom, *Homilies on John* 83 PG 59:454; and Barsanuphius, *Letter* 85.

he cannot reach God. Jacob arose and made a covenant with God that he would be his servant, and God strengthened him, saying, '*I will be with you, protecting you*'.[42] Then Jacob went to Mesopotamia to marry a wife there, and when he saw Rachel, the daughter of his mother's brother, he loved her and worked seven years for her. Yet, she was not given to him until he first wedded Leah. Rachel became barren until he worked another seven years for her. Listen to why this occurs.

Mesopotamia is so named because it lies between two rivers: the first is called Tigris, the second, Euphrates. The former leads to a place opposite Assyria; the latter is not near any enemy territory, but receives its name from its breadth. The Tigris symbolizes discernment, the Euphrates, humility. Leah is to be understood as a symbol of ascetic discipline, Rachel, of genuine vision. So these things occur to someone who is in Mesopotamia: through discernment he acquires ascetic discipline, because this is what resists the Assyrian enemy; and through humility he comes to genuine vision. Rachel, however, bore Jacob no children until Leah gave birth to all her children and Jacob had completed seven further years of service for Rachel.[43] The reason for this is that, unless you go through the entire scope of the practical stage, genuine vision is not free to be yours. Both of them were women, yet Jacob loved Rachel more than Leah, because Leah's eyes were weak, while Rachel was extremely beautiful.[44] This is the meaning of these words: that his first wife had weak eyes signifies the monk in the ascetic life who is yet unable to receive the glory of genuine vision, for the enemy is still confusing his ascetic work with ostentatiousness.

Do not, however, dwell on this, for even if Leah waits a while to give birth, she still offers her maid, Zilpah, to her husband. Then she adds even more to the births that she has given, and she names the child Asher, which means fortune.[45] When Leah ceases to give birth, then God remembers Rachel.[46] This means that if the ascetic

42. Gn 28:15.
43. A metaphor for the relationship between 'theory' and 'practice.' Cf. Gn 29:31–35.
44. Cf. Gn 29:17f.
45. Cf. Gn 30:9–13.
46. Cf. Gn 30:22f.

discipline controls the senses, so that they are freed from the passions, then genuine vision reveals its own glory to the intellect, for even though the sons of Leah were of assistance to Jacob, yet he loved Joseph more than all of them. That is to say, even while ascetic discipline protects us from the enemy, nonetheless, genuine vision unites us to God. Having seen Joseph, he wanted to go home to his parents, because he saw that he gave birth to the king of his brothers. Further, it says, when Jacob crossed all the streams of the river Jabbok and was left alone on the other side,[47] he received the grace of the blessing, as God said to him, '*You will no longer be called Jacob but Israel*'.[48] He was called Jacob because he prevailed over the enemy until he was made worthy of the blessing and saved his senses that were in the hands of the enemy. When the senses were liberated, his name was changed to Israel, which means an intellect that sees God. If the intellect reaches the point of beholding the divine glory, the enemy fears it, so that even if Esau comes in bitterness to encounter him, Jacob's humility extinguishes his evil,[49] and he no longer struggles against him, but rather surrenders himself to God. Even if the enemy vies against this person, seeing the great glory that he has achieved, it cannot cause him any harm, for God himself assists him, as it is written, 'Return to the land of your birth, and I will be with you'.[50] Thus, he came to Salem and bought a field there, and he built an altar to the Lord who heard him in the day of his sorrow. Now the name Salem means peace. This signifies that if a person wages war with God on his side, then he finds peace and sets up an altar on twelve stones. All this came upon Jacob from the toil of his service and all that he acquired in Mesopotamia.[51]

Our beloved Moses was a similar person, for he led his people out of Egypt, saved them from the hand of Pharaoh, crossed them over the Red Sea, and witnessed the death of all his enemies. He sent Joshua to conquer Amalek while he stood at the top of the mountain, with Aaron and Or, supporting his hands so that they

47. Cf. Gn 32:22f.
48. Gn 32:28.
49. Cf. Gn 33:1–4.
50. Cf. Gn 32:9.
51. Cf. Gn 33:18–20.

may not be lowered from the shape of a cross, and Joshua returned with joy after having conquered Amalek. Then he built an altar on twelve stones beneath the mountain, and he named that place 'The Lord is my refuge', 'for God secretly fights against Amalek <that is when he set up an altar on twelve stones> from generation to generation'. The name Amalek means boredom, for if a person begins to flee his desires and to abandon his sins, seeking refuge in God, boredom is the first enemy to attack him, wanting his sins to return to him. Meditation upon God wipes away boredom and that which brings about meditation is abstinence. That which guards abstinence is ascetic discipline. It is through these that Israel is liberated. Then, a person offers thanks to God, saying, 'I cannot do it <alone>, but you are my helper from generation to generation'.[52]

Such a one, also, was the great prophet Elijah,[53] for he was unable to destroy all the prophets of shame who opposed him until he had first purified the sacrificial altar that was built on twelve stones. He placed the wood around the altar and drenched it with water, after which he laid the holy sacrifice upon it. It was then that God became a fire for him, consuming the altar and all that lay upon it, and it was only at that point that he acquired boldness against his enemies. When he destroyed them, so that not even one was left, he gave thanks to God, saying, 'It is you that are responsible for all these things'. As it is written, 'He placed his head between his knees',[54] for, if the intellect stands diligently over its senses, it acquires immortality, and immortality brings it to such glory as God reveals to it. If the servant of Elijah is attentive, so that none of the seven passions[55] is seen to be aroused, then he sees a small cloud in the shape of a human drawing water from the sea, and this

52. Cf. Ex 17:8–15.
53. Cf. 1 K 18:31.
54. 1 K 18:30–46.
55. The normal number of sins or passions in monastic thought is eight: cf. Evagrius, *On Evil Thoughts* PG 79:1100–1133, *Praktikos* 6, and *On the Eight Evil Thoughts* PG 40:1272–1276. See also John Cassian, *Institutes* 5:1 and *Conferences* 5:2–3. Gregory the Great speaks of 'seven deadly sins' in his *Morals* 31:87 PG 76:621, which is the number more commonly encountered in the Middle Ages. Abba Isaiah speaks of 'seven passions' here, and of 'seven demons' in *Discourse* 18. See also his reference to 'mortal' sin in *Discourse* 9.

is the rest of the Holy Comforter. Immortality is having a healthy ascetic discipline, and not returning to those things for which you have asked forgiveness. If God accepts our ascetic discipline so that everything that we do is protected from the enemy, then it cannot even approach us, seeing that its will is nowhere to be found in us. The enemy leaves us of its own accord, as it is written, '*You must call on the name of your god, and I shall call on the name of mine, the god who answers with fire is indeed the Lord God*'.[56] This means that whenever the enemy sows a seed in a person who is unwilling [to cooperate], it cannot achieve what it desires, for it does whatever it can, but our God does not hear it, precisely because one's heart does not desire the enemy's will, being aligned instead to the will of God. Just as it says, '*You will call on the name of your god, and I will call on the name of the Lord, my God*'. Since their will was not in agreement with God's, he did not hear them at all.

These words may be applied not only to the above examples, but also to all those who follow the will of God and fulfill his commandments. Although these words are a symbol for those people, they have also been written for our counsel, since we follow in the footsteps of those who have struggled to acquire immortality.[57] This immortality is what guarded them from every arrow of the enemy, for they were thrown into God's protection, praying for his help and not trusting in any of their own ascetic labors. God's protection became like the walls of a city for them, for they knew that without the help of God they could do nothing, and so they humbly said with the Psalmist, '*Unless the Lord builds the house, the masons labor in vain*'.[58] If God sees[59] that the intellect is subjected to him with all its strength, and that it has no other assistance but him alone, he empowers it, saying, 'Do not be afraid, my child Jacob, little Israel';[60] and, again, 'Do not be afraid, for I have redeemed you and called you by your name; you are mine. Should you pass through the sea, I am with you; or through rivers, they will not

56. 1 K 18:24.
57. Cf. Co 10:11.
58. Ps 127:1.
59. OGtI c. 4.
60. Cf. Is 41:14.

overwhelm you. I am the Lord your God, the Holy One of Israel, your Savior.[61]

Therefore, when the intellect hears this boldness,[62] it becomes daring before the enemy and says, '*Who is my enemy? Let him attack me. Who is my accuser? Let him approach me. Behold, the Lord is my helper, who can do me any evil? Behold, all of you will grow old as clothes, and you will be consumed as cotton by moths.*[63] Our God is powerful, and we will be with those who are humble and protected by their humility, which becomes a helmet for them, protecting them from every arrow of the enemy, through the grace of God, for his is the power and the glory and the might to the ages of ages.

Amen.

61. Cf. Is 43:1–3.
62. OGtI c. 5; and Mark the Monk, *To Nicholas* PG 65:1032.
63. Is 50:8–9.

5

Faithful Commandments for the Edification of Those who Wish to Live Peacefully Together

When traveling together on foot, be very careful of the thoughts of the weakest among you, whether it concerns the need to sit for a while, or to eat a little earlier.

If you go out together in order to work, let each one of you pay attention to himself and not his brother, neither counseling nor commanding him.

If you happen to be working inside your cell, or building something nearby, or doing any other thing, let the one actually doing the job do as he pleases. And if he says, 'Please be so kind as to teach me <how to do this> because I do not know', and there is someone else around who does know, let him not be cruel and say that he does not know, for this is not godly humility.

If your brother does something in any old way and you happen to see him, do not say to him, 'You have ruined it'. But if he says, 'Please teach me', and you do not teach him but keep silent, you have no love of God within you because you are cruel.

If a brother cooks something and it does not turn out well, do not say to him, 'You have cooked badly'—as this will mean death for your soul—but examine yourself, thinking that, had you heard this from someone else, you would feel very sad, and then you will find rest.

When you are chanting together and one of you errs in a word, do not hurry to correct and upset him. If the word has passed, then it is over. But if he says, 'Please tell me what was wrong', tell him.

If you are eating something in the refectory and one of you does not like the food, he should not say, 'I cannot eat', but should force himself to eat for the sake of God, even unto death, and God will give him rest.[1]

If you are working together and one of you breaks the fast as a result of faintheartedness, let no one rebuke him, rather, be happy for him.

If other brothers visit your community, do not in any way wish to ask questions that cause damage and lead you to captivity when you are in your cell. Moreover, if your visitor cannot control himself and happens to tell one of you some of these harmful things, then the one who hears this should be silent until the captivity <of his thoughts> leaves him, so that they do not fill the brothers' hearts with a mortal germ.

If you need to go out of the monastery for something, do not ask anyone about anything that does not belong to you, in case you do not return to your cell safely. Even if you should hear something involuntarily, when you return, do not announce it to your brothers. If you leave the monastery, do not, under any circumstance, behave in a bold way wherever you may happen to go, lest others do not benefit from your example, especially from your hidden and apparent silence,[2] for all the passions develop in weak people on account of their idleness of heart, inasmuch as they do not see their own sins. However, God's help, and your hope, meekness, conscience, as well as the riddance of your will and violence of yourselves in all matters, are all found in humility. Pride, strife, thinking that you know better than your brother, trampling on the conscience, not caring that your brother is upset with you, saying, 'What's wrong with me?', are all found in hardheartedness.

1. Barsanuphius, *Letter* 525.
2. Evagrius, *Chapters on Prayer* 42.

If you are performing your manual labor and your brother enters your cell, do not think at all that you may have completed more than he, or he more than you.

If you are serving a sick brother, do not challenge him in secret, wishing to do more than he.

If your brother is working with something and breaks what he is making, do not say anything to him unless he says to you, 'Please teach me, brother', and then if you know but do not tell him, it is to your <spiritual> death. If you are carrying out your manual labor, no matter what this is, do your utmost not to find out how much you or your brother has completed during that week, for this is foolish. If you are going off in order to work with your brothers, do not let them know how much more you have done than they, for whatever work a person completes in secret, this is what God asks from him.

If your brother says something to you out of narrow-mindedness, endure it with joy. And if you examine your thoughts according to God's judgment, you will find that you are indeed a sinner.

If you are living with others and your thoughts wish to bind you to the food, say to them, 'This weak person here is my master.' If you wish to be overly abstinent in every way, find yourself a small cell alone, and do not upset your brother who is weak.

If a brother visits you as a guest and you have previously heard that he likes looking after his appearance, do not interrogate him with words until his weakness is manifested. Guard yourselves from doing anything that you know will upset your brother, should he find out. If you wish to have something and need to use it, do not grumble against your brother, thinking, 'Why did he not think of giving it to me alone?' Say in boldness and simplicity, instead, 'Please give me this, for I need it'. This is holy purity of heart. If you do not ask for it while grumbling and blaming him in your heart, then yours is the judgment.

If a passage of Scripture should come up in your conversation, then the one who knows the passage and understands it should do his best to humble his own will before his brother, in order to give rest gladly to his brother. And the reason for this is to humble oneself before your brother. The one who watches out for the judgment of the trial that he is to attend does his best so that his mouth is not sealed as to have no defense to offer at that terrible time.

Do not seek to examine the works of these times, lest you become like a group of esoterics where each comes to empty the contents of one's stomach, and the stench is indeed great. Rather, become, in purity, an altar of God, continually having the inner priest[3] making sacrifices, both in the morning and in the evening, in order that the altar is never left without sacrifice. And always force yourselves to pray continually before the Lord,[4] so that he might grant you simplicity and integrity, and take from you their opposites, namely, craftiness and demonic wisdom, curiosity, self-love and evil-heartedness, for these sins dissolve the ascetic labor of those who practice them. Finally, if a person knowingly fears God, and his senses are subjected to his conscience in a godly manner, God himself will secretly teach him much more than all the above. If, however, the master of the house is not there, then that wretched person has his house at the disposal of anyone, and whosoever wishes, says anything he wants to him, because the heart is not under his control but under the control of the enemy.

If you want to go out for a short while in order to work, let no one slight another and go out alone, leaving his brother to suffer in his conscience within his cell, but let him say with love, 'Do you want to go there together?' If your brother is not ready to go at that time, or if his body is weak, do not argue, saying, 'We need to go out now', but wait a while and return to your cell with loving compassion. Take care not to contradict your brother at all, lest you upset him. If you are living with your elder or brother, then you should not be aware at all of what someone else is doing in another house; this will bring peace and obedience. If you are living with your elder or brother, do not find yourself in some secret friendship, or secretly exchanging letters about something, without wanting your brothers to know, because in this way you will destroy both yourself and them. If you are living with an elder, do not wish

3. Cf. Gregory of Nyssa, *On virginity* 24 PG 46:413.
4. Evagrius, *Chapters on Prayer* 30; *Sayings* Agathon 9.

to perform an act of charity for a poor person unless you ask him first, and certainly do not perform it in secret.

If you are asking <your elder> about your thoughts, do not ask after doing something, but reveal that with which you are struggling at this very moment, whether it concerns your flight from the world, or else learning your manual labor, or changing the manual labor, or living with someone, or leaving your brothers. Ask freely before you do anything, whether it concerns the weaknesses of the soul, or the passions of the body that still drag you down. Do not ask about these matters as if you have not experienced them but ask about the passion saying, 'I have already suffered this', in order that you may be healed with regard to the passion. Moreover if you are asking about your thoughts, do not be a hypocrite and say one thing when you mean another, or <express it> as if someone else did it, but tell the truth and prepare yourself to do whatever you may be told, otherwise you are only mocking yourself and not the elders whom you approach. If you are asking your elders about spiritual warfare, do not listen to your own thoughts instead of the elders' advice, but first pray to God saying, 'Be merciful to me, and grant the elders to tell me whatever you will'. Whatever the elders in fact tell you, carry it out faithfully, and God will give you rest.

If you are living with brothers and for whatever reasons are not happy with their behavior or manual work, or because of a relationship, or something else, or because you simply cannot tolerate them, or because of boredom, or a desire to be more silent, or because you cannot bear the yoke [of monasticism], or cannot do what you want, or because you lack what you need, or perhaps you wish to commit yourself to a greater ascetic discipline, or because you are ill and cannot endure the work, or whatever other reason is convincing your heart to go, see to it that you are not persuaded to leave. Do not put down the yoke and depart in sorrow, or secretly in grief, or forget the brotherhood prevented by evil in the middle of a period of blame. Rather, wait for a time of peace, so that your heart may find rest wherever it goes. Then, throw the blame on yourself, neither slandering the brothers with whom you live, nor obeying your enemies and turning their benefits into wrongdoings, nor again avoiding disgrace and wanting your brother's disgrace to cover your own, thereby being led to fall into sin by your enemies wherever you later happen to dwell.

If you go somewhere else to live, do not wish to choose a cell hastily in which you will live. First learn the ways of that monastery, in case that place becomes an obstacle for you, whether as a result of worrying, or seeking honors, glory, or rest, or even causing a scandal to your friends. If you are wise, you will understand in just a few days whether everything there will lead to your <spiritual> death, or life.

If you offer your cell to your brother to stay a few days, do not subject your brother to your authority. If you are offered a cell in which to stay a few days, neither destroy, tear down, nor construct anything, unless you first ask the owner who gave the cell whether he is happy with this, or not. Otherwise, it <shows> a lack of gratitude on your part. If you are living with, or visiting someone, and receive an order from him, for the sake of God keep the order and do not disregard it, nor disobey it, either in secret or in the open.

If you are silent in your cell and have promised yourself not to eat food or anything else during mealtime, should you happen to go out, take care not to say to anyone while seated at the table, 'Excuse me, but I am not eating this', otherwise all your ascetic labor is handed over to your enemies in vain, for your Lord and Savior said, 'Do it in secret, so that your Father <who sees in secret> will reward you openly'.[5] He who loves his ascetic labors takes care of them in order not to lose them.

If you are living in community, whatever manual work you are doing, whether inside or outside, should your brother invite you somewhere, do not say, 'Please wait until I finish this little piece', but obey immediately. If you are doing some work together, do not retain every mistake you have seen from others outside and then find yourself telling your brothers in the community about it. If you are wise, <you will understand that> this brings death to your soul. If there are brothers who are living with you and have worked during the whole day, allow them to rest before it is time to eat. Do not pay attention to yourself, rather, watch for the judgment of God.

5. Cf. Mt 6:4.

Hold God before your eyes in whatever work you are doing. If you should go somewhere to stay, either alone or with others who were there before you, and happen to see there crafts or works which may be damaging, or harmful, or perhaps not even monastic, do not open your mouth to criticize them. If you do not like them, just move to another place and guard your mouth from slandering them. Otherwise, this will <lead> to your <spiritual death>.

If you are weak in regard to passions, guard yourself against allowing someone to tell you the passions of his thoughts in confidence, for this act will prove a loss for your soul. If someone says something that causes laughter, take care not to allow your voice to be heard loudly, because this is a sign of foolishness and lack of godly fear, revealing the absence of watchfulness within you.[6]

Since suffering has come over the whole world in our times, do not be disturbed by whatever you hear, but say within your heart, 'These hardly compare with the place where we will go for our sins!' Perform acts of love for the sake of God. Read <the Scriptures> that you may observe this: it is no small thing for a faithful person to be so close to completing a task.[7] If, then, you keep these things in simplicity and in knowledge, you will go away with joy to the resting-place of the Son of God. But if you do not keep them, you will labor here, and, when you die, you will be led to the place of hell, in accordance with the Scriptures. It is for all the above-mentioned that our Lord Christ came. Our hardheartedness, however, blinds us on account of our heart's desires because we love these more than God and we do not have the same love for him as we do for the passions.[8]

Behold, I have forced myself to write down these things as well for you, since my first writings[9] were insufficient for you. So do please try, at least from now on, not to remain in the condition of your

6. Athanasius, *Sermon on Renunciation* 4, PG 28:1412; *Sayings* John the Dwarf 7 and 9; Barsanuphius *Letter* 570. See also Evagrius, *Letter on virginity*, 563 and 565.

7. Cf. Mt 24:15–22.

8. Cf. John Climacus, *Ladder* Step 30; and Anastasius of Sinai, *Question* 135 PG 89:788.

9. An allusion to other, earlier writings of Abba Isaiah. On the common life, see also Basil, *Long Rules* 7, 24, 35, 37 and 42; and Cassian, *Conference* 19.

uncircumcised hearts, but help yourselves for the few remaining days <of your life>. If you keep these things, you will acquire humility, peace, patience, cutting of the will, and love. But if you do not keep them, and, instead, envy, contention, strife, pride of heart, blaming, grumbling, or disobedience prevails among you, then you are wasting your time, and you will truly go away to hell when you die.

Therefore, dear friends, love your brothers with holy love, and hold your tongue, not letting out of your mouth any random word of strife that might offend your brother. Our Lord God is powerful enough to give each one of you the ability to carry out and keep these commandments, so that we may find mercy through his grace, together with all the saints who have pleased him, for his is the glory, honor, and worship, now and ever, and to the ages of ages. Amen.

6

On Those who Desire to Lead a Life of Good Silence that They May Take Care to Reject Those who Rob Their Soul, so as Not to Waste Their Time in Captivity and Bitter Slavery, for They Convince Their Heart to Do Improper Things and Forget Their Sins

ENJOYING THE FUTILE QUESTIONING of Scripture gives rise to hatred and contention, whereas weeping over one's sins brings peace. For a monk, sin means to sit in his cell and forget his sins, giving himself to the futile questioning of Scripture. Whoever wonders in his heart, 'How does Scripture put it, this way, or that?' before he has taken control of himself, has a futile heart and has fallen into great captivity. Whoever is alert, in order not to be taken captive, always loves to surrender himself before God. Whoever seeks out a likeness of God is being blasphemous to God, but whoever seeks to honor God loves purity in godly fear. *Whoever keeps the words of God has come to know God*[1] and obeys him for his own benefit.

1. 1 Jn 2:3.

Do not seek the sublime gifts of God while still praying to him for help in order that he may come and save you from sin, for, if the place <of the heart> is undefiled and pure, the divine gifts come of themselves. Whoever depends on his own knowledge but still possesses his own will only gains hatred, and those who hear sorrow in their heart simply cannot be of the Spirit. Whoever considers the words of Scripture and practices them according to his own knowledge, thinking intently to himself that this is how reality is, is ignorant of God's glory and wealth. Whereas one who considers them and says, 'I do not know what they mean, for I am human', offers glory to God. In this person the wealth of God abides in accordance with his capacity and understanding.

Do not seek to exercise your mind with anyone else except your elders, lest you attract sorrow into your heart. Guard your tongue, in order that you may consider your neighbor honorable. Teach yourself to speak[2] knowingly the words of God, and falsehood will flee from you.[3] The love of human glory gives rise to falsehood. But humbly overcoming this produces greater godly fear in your heart. Do not seek to make friends with those who are glorified in this world, lest the glory of God becomes dimmed inside you. If someone slanders his brother to you, abusing him in order to reveal his evil, do not wish to take sides against him lest you are overtaken by that which you do not want. Simplicity[4] and disregard of oneself purifies the soul from evil. Whoever walks in a crafty way with his brother will not escape sorrow of heart. Whoever says one thing, but in his heart wickedly means another,[5] lives his entire monastic life in vain. Do not become attached to any such person, lest you become defiled by his impure germ. Instead, walk with those who are guileless, so that you share in their glory and purity. Do not show wickedness to anyone, lest you perform your ascetic labor in vain. Purify your heart with regard to everyone, so that you may behold God's peace within you, for, just as when one is bitten by

2. John Climacus, *Ladder* 12.
3. John Climacus, *Ladder* 12.
4. Evagrius, *Chapters on Prayer* 57 and 85.
5. Evagrius, *Chapters on Prayer* 57 and 85.

a scorpion its poison passes throughout his entire body and harms his heart, such is the <effect of> evil enacted in the heart against your neighbor, for its poison pricks the soul, and the whole person is in danger as a result of the wickedness. Yet, whoever cares about his ascetic labors, lest they are lost, rapidly shakes off this scorpion, namely wickedness and evil.

7

On Virtues[1]

THERE ARE THREE VIRTUES which are always provided for and required by the intellect: a natural impulse, courage, and resoluteness.

There are three virtues which, when it is seen to possess them, the intellect believes that it has reached immortality: discernment, that is, separating one thing from another, foreseeing everything before its time, and not being persuaded by some foreign thought.

There are three virtues which bestow light on the intellect at all times: knowing no evil against anyone, doing good to those who wrong you, and enduring calmly the things which come your way.[2] These three virtues give rise to another three which are still greater: knowing no evil against anyone gives rise to love, doing good to those who wrong you produces peace, and enduring calmly the things which come your way brings meekness.

There are four virtues which purify the soul:[3] silence, keeping the commandments, <spiritual> constraint, and humility.

The intellect always needs the following four virtues: praying to God by constantly prostrating oneself before him, surrendering before God, being unconcerned with everyone in order not to judge, and being deaf to the passions which speak to it.

1. On virtues see also Gregory of Nyssa, *Hymn* 1.2.9, PG 37:667ff; and *The Life of Moses* 2.287–90; Pseudo-Macarius, *Homily* 40:1–2; Dorotheus of Gaza, *Instruction* 14; and Symeon the New Theologian, *Catechesis* 4.

2. See also *Discourses* 7 and 17.

3. John Climacus, *Ladder* Step 15.

Four virtues fortify the soul, allowing it to breathe from the disturbance of the enemy: mercy, freedom from anger, long-suffering, and shaking off every seed coming from sin. Resisting forgetfulness protects all of these.

There are four virtues which, after God himself, assist the beginner: constant study, resoluteness, vigil, and disregard of oneself.

Four things defile the soul: not guarding one's sight when traveling in the city, having intimate friendship with a woman, befriending those who are glorious in this life, and loving to converse with one's natural parents.

Four things increase fornication in the body:[4] sleeping too much, eating to satiation, talking frivolously, and decorating the body.

Four things darken the soul: hating one's neighbor, despising, envying, and grumbling against him.

Four things render the soul barren: moving from place to place, liking distraction, loving material things, and miserliness.

Four things increase anger: bargaining, insisting on one's will, wanting to teach others, and considering oneself prudent.

Three things are difficult[5] for us to acquire and these protect all the virtues: mourning, weeping over our sins, and holding death before our eyes.[6]

Three things control the soul until it reaches a great stature and these do not allow the virtues to inhabit the intellect: captivity, reluctance, and forgetfulness. Forgetfulness fights against us until it brings our very breath to the point of anxiety; it is stronger than all the thoughts, giving rise to all evil, and continually taking down everything that we erect.

These are the works of the New Person and of the Old Person.[7] The one who loves his soul and does not want to lose it[8] keeps the ways of the New Person. The person who wants rest in this brief lifetime carries out and practices the ways of the Old Person but loses his soul. Our Lord Jesus Christ revealed the New Person in his own

4. John Climacus, *Ladder* Step 14.
5. John Climacus, *Ladder* Step 8.
6. *Sayings* Moses 14–15.
7. Cf. Ep 4:24f.
8. Cf. Mt 10:39.

body, saying, '*Anyone who finds his life will lose it; anyone who loses his life for my sake will find it*',[9] for he is the Master of Peace, and through him was the dividing-wall of hatred brought down.[10] He also said, '*I have not come to bring peace, but a sword*'.[11] Again, he said, '*I have come to bring fire to the earth, and how I wish it were already blazing*'.[12] This means that the fire of his divinity came upon those who followed his sacred teachings. Then they found *the sword of the Spirit*[13] and hunted down all the desires of their flesh, and so he gave them joy, saying, '*My peace I give to you;* <*my own*> *peace I give to you*'.[14]

Those, therefore, who sought to lose their soul in this life, cutting off their proper will, became like holy sheep for sacrifice to him. And when he appears in the glory of his divinity, he will call them to stand on his right, saying, 'Come, you that are blessed by my Father, inherit the kingdom prepared for you from the foundation of the world, for I was hungry and you gave me food',[15] and so on. Thus, those who have lost their soul in this brief lifetime have found it in the time of need, receiving a reward many times greater than they expected to receive. While those who fulfilled their desires looked after their soul, deceived by the vanity of their wealth and not keeping the commandments of God,[16] but thinking that they would live forever in this sinful age. This is why the shamefulness of their blindness will be revealed at the hour of judgment, and they will become like the goats that were cursed, hearing the terrible decision of the judge saying, '*Depart from me into the eternal fire* <and into the outer darkness> *prepared for the devil and his angels, for I was hungry and you gave me no food*',[17] and so forth. And their mouths will be closed, not finding anything to say, for they will recall their lack of charity and hatred of the poor. Then they will say, '*Lord,*

9. Mt 10:39.
10. Cf. Ep 2:14.
11. Mt 10:34.
12. Lk 12:49.
13. Ep 6:17.
14. Jn 14:27.
15. Cf. Mt 25:34–35.
16. See also Irenaeus, *Against Heresies* 4.12.5–13.3; Pseudo-Macarius, *Homily* 37; Symeon the New Theologian, *Catechesis* 5.
17. Mt 25:41f.

when was it that we saw you hungry . . . and did not take care of you?';[18] he will silence them saying, 'He who has done good to one of these that believes in me, has done it to me'.[19]

Dear friends, let us, therefore, examine ourselves whether each of us performs our commandments according to our ability, or not, for we are all obliged[20] to perform them according to our ability, the small among us in accordance with his slightness and the great in accordance with his grandeur. Those who placed their gifts in the treasury were, in fact, rich, but the Lord was more pleased with the two coins of the poor widow, for God pays attention to our intention.[21] Let us not allow room for boredom in our heart, lest envy[22] separates us from God. But let us perform our duties according to our poor means. Just as the Lord showed mercy to the leader of the synagogue and resurrected his daughter,[23] so he was also merciful to the woman with the issue of blood, who spent all her money on doctors before coming to know Christ.[24] Just as he healed the son of the centurion on account of his belief,[25] so he healed the daughter of the canaanite woman.[26] Just as he resurrected his dear friend Lazarus,[27] so he raised the only son of the poor widow on account of her sins.[28] Just as he did not overlook Mary, who anointed his feet with myrrh,[29] so he did not despise the sinful woman who anointed his feet with myrrh and with tears.[30] Just as he called Peter and John from their boat with the words, '*Follow me*',[31] so he called Matthew who was sitting down, collecting taxes.[32] Just as he washed the feet of the disciples, so he also washed those of Judas, making

18. Mt 25:44.
19. Cf. Mt 25:45.
20. Cf. Mark the Monk, *To Those who Think* 2 PG 65:929. See also, Lk 17:10.
21. Cf. Mt 12:41.
22. Literally, 'sorcery'.
23. Cf. Mt 9:25.
24. Cf. Mt 9:22.
25. Cf. Mt 8:13.
26. Cf. Mt 15:28.
27. Cf. Jn 11:44.
28. Cf. Lk 7:15.
29. Cf. Jn 12:3.
30. Cf. Lk 7:38.
31. Cf. Mt 4:19.
32. Cf. Mt 9:9.

no distinction between them.[33] Just as the comforter, the Spirit, came to the apostles,[34] so it also came to Cornelius <who spoke> with boldness.[35] Just as he obliged Ananias in Damascus for the sake of Paul, saying, '*This person is my chosen instrument*',[36] so he obliged Philip in Samaria for the sake of the Ethiopian eunuch,[37] for *there is no favor in God's eyes*[38] in respect of small and great, wealthy and poor, but he looks at our intention and our faith in him, as well as our fulfilment of his commandments and love for all people. This is precisely the seal of the soul upon death, as he said to his disciples, '*By this everyone will know that you are my disciples, if you have love for one another*'.[39] About what else, then, does he mean that they will know you, other than about the powers of the right and of the left? If the enemy sees the sign of love accompanying the soul, it keeps a distance from it on account of fear, and then all the holy powers rejoice with the soul.

Let us therefore, dear friend, struggle as much as we can to acquire this, lest our enemy overcomes us, for it was the Lord who said, '*A city built on a hilltop cannot be hidden*'.[40] About which other mountain is he speaking, if not this sacred saying? Let us then, dear friends, carry out our ascetic labor with diligence and knowledge, fulfilling his word that says, '*If you love me, you will keep my commandments*',[41] in order that our toil may resemble a safe and fortified city, both encouraging and protecting us in his word from the hand of all our enemies, until we encounter him. All of our enemies are scattered by his holy word if we find such boldness that is the mountain from which the stone was broken without hands, for he smashed the golden and four-sided idol, which was made out of silver, bronze, and iron metal. As the apostle wrote, '*Put God's armor on, so that you may be able to resist the devil's wiles, for our struggle is not against*

33. Cf. Jn 13:8.
34. Cf. Ac 2:4.
35. Cf. Ac 10:44.
36. Ac 9:15.
37. Cf. Ac 8:27.
38. Rm 2:11.
39. Jn 13:35.
40. Mt 5:14.
41. Jn 14:15, 23.

human enemies, but against the sovereignties and powers who originate the darkness in this world, the spiritual forces of evil in the heavens'.[42] These four rulers are the four-sided idol, which is hatred, and they were abolished by the holy word of God, as it has been written, because the stone which smashed the idol became a great mountain and filled the whole earth.

Brothers, let us run and take shelter in him, so that he may be our refuge and save us from these four wicked authorities, in order that we, too, may hear the joy with all his saints who gather to him from the four ends of the earth, for each of them will hear his own beatitude, according to his deeds. His holy name is powerful and it can be with us and encourage us in his work, not allowing our heart to be deceived by the forgetfulness of the enemy, but protecting us, according to our ability, in order to endure those things which come upon us[43] for his holy name, that we may find mercy together with those who have been accounted worthy of his beatitudes, for to him belongs all glory, <honor, and worship, to the Father and the Son and the Holy Spirit, now and always, and> to the ages of ages. Amen.

42. Ep 6:11–13.
43. See also *Discourse* 17.

8

Sayings

ABBA ISAIAH SAID, 'Lately I see myself as a wandering horse that has no master; whoever finds it sits on it and, when he leaves it, someone else takes it and sits on it'.

Again he said, 'I am like someone who has been captured by his enemies who have bound him and thrown him into a filthy pit; if he calls out to his lord, they cut him down with blows in order to silence him'.

Again he said, 'I am like a little sparrow whose leg is held by a child; if he relaxes his hold, it immediately flies upward, thinking that it has been set free. If the child holds it down, again it is brought down. This is how I see myself. I say this because one should not be carefree until one's last breath.'[1]

Again he said, 'If you give someone something that he desires and let him keep it, you have imitated the nature of Jesus. If, on the other hand, you ask for it back, you have imitated the nature of Adam. If you accept interest, however, you have contravened even Adam's nature.'

Again he said, 'If someone accuses you of doing something you either did or did not do and you remain silent, you are conforming to the nature of Jesus. But if you reply, "What have I done?", this is not according to his nature. If you argue point by point, then this is contrary to nature.'

1. On continual watchfulness, see Athanasius, *Life of Antony* 3–5; Evagrius, *Chapters on Prayer* 48, 137 and 149; *Sayings* Ammoe 4, John the Dwarf 27, Cronius 1, Poemen 14, 43, 135, 137 and 165; and John Climacus, *Ladder* Step 28.

Again he said, 'While you are performing your duties, if you act in humility, as if you were unworthy, your work is acceptable to God. But if it should rise in your heart that you remember another person who is sleeping or idle, your toil is in vain.'

Again he said, concerning humility,[2] 'It has no tongue in order to speak against someone for being careless, or someone else for being contemptuous; nor does it have eyes with which to notice another's faults; nor, again, does it have ears to hear that which does not benefit the soul. Neither does it have anything against others, except one's own sins. Instead, it renders one peaceful with all people for the sake of God's commandment, and not merely some friendship. For, if one fasts six days out of seven and is entirely given to great toils and commandments, all of that person's toils outside this way of humility are in vain.'

Again he said, 'If one acquires a vessel for personal use and cannot find it when necessary, the acquisition is in vain. In the same way, the person who says, "I fear God", yet when the time of need arrives—if he is found at a time of vain talk, or anger, or arrogance, or of teaching others about matters he has not reached, or of people-pleasing, or of seeking a reputation among people, and of similar passions—he does not find the fear of God and all of his toils are in vain.'

Again he said, 'If our Lord Jesus Christ had not first healed all the passions of humanity for which he came into the world, he would not have ascended the cross, for before the Lord came in flesh, humanity was blind, dumb, paralyzed, deaf, leprous, lame, and dead on account of everything that was contrary to nature. When, however, God had mercy on us and came into the world, he raised the dead, made the lame walk, the blind see, the dumb speak, the deaf hear, and resurrected a new person, free of all illness. Then he ascended the cross. They hung two thieves beside him, the one on the right glorified him and appealed to him, saying, "*Remember me, Lord, in your kingdom*",[3] but the one on the left blasphemed him. This means that before the intellect comes to its senses from carelessness,

2. John Climacus, *Ladder* Step 25.
3. Lk 22:42.

it is with the enemy, and if our Lord Jesus Christ resurrects it from its carelessness, granting it to see and discern all things, it will be able to ascend the cross.[4] Then the enemy continues to blaspheme with heavy words, hoping that the intellect will perhaps slacken in its toil and again return to the state of carelessness. This is symbolized by the two thieves whom our Lord Jesus Christ separated in the friendship. The one reproached him, in order perhaps to make him lose hope, but the other was patient in his request until he heard the words, "*Today you will be with me in paradise*".[5] The latter "stole" his way into paradise, and ate of the tree of life.'

Again he said concerning Holy Communion,[6] 'It is called union with God. Therefore, as long as we are conquered by passions—whether by anger, or envy, or popularity, or vainglory, or hatred, or any other passion—we are estranged from God. Where, then, is our union with him?'

Again he said, 'If we perform our duties and after completing them remain disturbed by them in our heart, all of our ascetic disciplines are in vain, for God does not accept them'.

One of the elders asked him, 'Father, when do the passions not strike?', and he replied, 'When it rains on the earth that bears seed, there is growth, but if there is no seed, how will it grow?[7] However, if one struggles to uproot that which is contrary to nature from his heart, they will not disturb him,[8] for God desires us to be in all things like him, and it is for this reason that he came and suffered, in order to change our hardened nature, and to cut off our willfulness and the false knowledge that dominated our soul, for, indeed, the irrational animals retained their own nature. Humanity, however, changed its proper nature. Now, therefore, in the same way that beasts are obedient to humanity, a person ought to be obedient to his neighbor for the sake of God, for this is the reason why the Lord

4. Cf. Mark the Monk, *To Nicholas* 7, PG 65:1040 and Barsanuphius *Letters* 48 and 156.

5. Lk 22:43.

6. Sacraments are an important part of palestinian and gazean monasticism. See also *Discourse* 16.

7. Regnault begins a new saying here but there is no reason for this, at least according to the Augustinos and Chitty editions.

8. Literally, 'impel him'.

came. So, consider how superior the beasts are to you, depending as they do on the credit of your knowledge. If I wish to return to the level of nature, then, just as the beasts do not have a proper will or knowledge, I too must behave likewise not only with my counselor and companion, but also with my enemy. This is the will of God.

Whosoever wishes to discover peace in the cell and not to be taken advantage of by the enemy, keeps away from people in all matters, in order not to blame, or flatter, or justify, or bless anyone, or justify himself, or upset anyone for any reason, or notice anyone's weakness, or allow the slightest thought of anger in the heart against anyone, or release one's knowledge on an ignorant person or one's will on a foolish person. Then, one will come to know oneself and understand what is harmful, but one who trusts in his own righteousness and holds onto his own will is unable to avoid the enemy, or to find any rest, or even to know what he lacks, and when this person leaves his body, it will be difficult to find mercy. Finally, what is important is to wait upon God with all your heart and all your strength,[9] to be compassionate with all people, to be full of compunction and pray to God for his help and mercy.'

Again he said, about teaching one's neighbor the commandments of God, 'How do I know that I have been accepted by God in order to say to someone else "do this or that", when I am personally in need of repentance for my sins?' The one who has fallen into sin is in need of repentance and may never feel secure. Since you do not know if you have received forgiveness, what you do know for certain is that the sin has been committed and that mercy belongs to God, for you cannot be carefree in your heart until you face God in judgment. Now, if you wish to know whether you have received forgiveness for your sins, the sign for this is as follows. If there is no movement in your heart from the sins you have committed, or, if when another person speaks to you about these sins you no longer recognize them, then you know you have received mercy,[10] but if they are still active inside you, master them and weep over them, for if you are careless in regard to these sins, they will cause you fear and trembling and pain until you meet God at the judgment-seat.

9. Mark the Monk, *On those who think* 90 PG 65:944.
10. Barsanuphius, *Letter* 239.

If a person asks you to teach him, give your soul to him until death, telling him about the way that leads to freedom, but if he returns, saying the same things, without any progress in those matters of which you spoke to him, you will know that he has not listened to you. Keep away from him, then, because you will lose your soul, for it is a great thing for a person to leave his own will and right, even when he thinks that it is according to God, and to keep the word of the one teaching him according to God.

Abba Nistheros, the one of God, who saw the glory of God, although he had his sister's sons living with him, never gave them any orders, but allowed the proper will of each, whether they became good or evil, not being concerned with them.[11] And he used to say about Cain and Abel, who had neither the Law nor the Scripture, 'Who taught them to do this or that?' Unless God teaches us, we toil in vain.'

Again he said, 'If someone speaks useless words to you, do not wish to listen to them lest your soul is destroyed. In order not to grieve him, do not be embarrassed in front of him. Moreover, do not tolerate what is being said, thinking to yourself, "I will not accept the words in my heart". Do not believe this, for you are not greater than the first-formed,[12] whom God created with his own hands, whom the evil conversation did not edify. Just leave, and do not wish to listen. In addition, watch that you do not leave in body while still wishing to find out what was said. Even if you hear a little of the conversation, the demons will not cease to haunt you with the words you heard, but will kill your soul. When I say leave, I mean leave altogether.'

Again he said, 'From what I can see, profit, honor, and peace are a struggle for humanity until death'.

Again he said, 'Teaching one's neighbor brings about distortion of the soul. Wanting to guide one's neighbor on the right way brings about great destruction of the soul, for as long as you are teaching

11. Not a known recorded saying of Abba Nistheros. Cf. *Sayings* Poemen 131 and Nistheros 2. Abba Poemen and Barsanuphius speak only of one disciple named Nistheros. Cf. Barsanuphius, *Letter* 661. See also John Climacus, *Ladder* Step 10 on the content of this saying.

12. That is, Adam.

your neighbor to "do this or that", imagine that you are holding a hoe with which, while destroying your own house, you wish to build your neighbor's.'

Again he said, 'Woe to the soul that has sinned after Holy Baptism,[13] for that person cannot be carefree, since he is in the state of repentance, if he has fallen in the flesh, or stolen, or committed one of the other sins, or looked on somebody passionately, or even tasted food secretly, looking around to see if he had been caught, or been curious to see what is inside a cloak left by someone. Whoever does these things insults Jesus.'

Someone asked him, 'Is it really a matter of such precision, Father?'

He answered, 'It is just as serious as someone who has dug a trench along a wall and is cheated by the enemy in regard to the payment. If you are successful in one, you will also be in the second, for if you fail in small matters, you will also fail in significant ones.'[14]

Again he said, 'Even if someone performs great wonders and hearings, and *possesses all knowledge*,[15] and raises the dead, he cannot be carefree if he has fallen into sin, because he is in the state of repentance.[16] Even if he is leading a life of great ascetic discipline, should he see someone entirely in sin or carelessness and show contempt toward that person, then all his repentance is in vain, for he has rejected a member of Christ's body by passing judgment and not leaving it for God the Judge.'

Again he said, 'We are all as if in surgery. One has a pain in the eye, another in the hand, a third in the veins, and whatever other diseases exist. Among these, some wounds are already healed, but when you eat something harmful, they return once again. This is what occurs to a person who is in repentance and yet judges or shows contempt toward others, because he must again return to repentance. Since those in surgery have different illnesses, if someone cries in pain with regard to his own suffering, let no one else ask, "Why are

13. John Climacus, *Ladder* Step 5.
14. Cf. Mt 25:21, 23.
15. 1 Co 13:2.
16. John Climacus, *Ladder* Step 5.

you crying out?" Is not each of us concerned with our own pain? Therefore, if the pain of my own sin is before me,[17] I would not look at the sin of another, for everyone that lies in surgery observes the precautions of his own doctor, taking care not to eat whatever harms his wound. Nevertheless, woe to the soul that does not wish to escape all sin, for it will face many tribulations from those who envy and encounter it, because it will need much long-suffering and gratitude in all things. When the <Hebrew> people were in Egypt, they ate and drank in abundance, but they were enslaved to Pharaoh, and when the Lord sent them assistance, namely Moses, in order to deliver them from Pharaoh, then they were oppressed and distressed. Throughout all the plagues God sent upon Pharaoh, Moses did not grow confident when he saw their destruction, until the time came when God said to him, "I shall send one last plague upon Pharaoh", and you will say to him, "Release my people, or I will strike dead your firstborn".[18] It was then that Moses grew confident. God said to him, "Whisper to my people in their ears, that everyone is to ask his neighbor and every woman is to ask hers for vessels of silver and gold, and for clothing: load them on the backs of your children, and plunder the Egyptians".[19] They lived on these goods until they built the Ark of the Covenant.'

So he said, 'This was the interpretation of the elders: the gold and silver vessels, and the clothing, are the senses which serve the enemy. The meaning of this, then, is as follows: if a man removes these from the enemy in order that they may bear fruit for God, divine protection comes upon him. The cloud did not cover the Ark so long as it was unfinished, but only when it was completed. Likewise, in the case of the temple that was built, while it remained incomplete, the cloud did not cover it. When it was finished, however, and the blood and fat of the whole-burnt offerings were brought inside, God smelled its fragrance, and the cloud covered the building. This means that unless a person loves God with all his

17. Cf. Ps 51:3.
18. Cf. Ex 11:1f.
19. Cf. Ex 11:2, 35–36.

strength and with all his mind, and cleaves unto God with all his heart, the protection of God's peace does not come to him.'

Again he said, 'Unless the senses have been alleviated of all disease,[20] if the intellect wishes to ascend the cross, the wrath of God falls on it, for it has assumed something beyond its limitation, not having first cured its senses. If defilement is at work inside you and you consent to it, procuring that which gives rise to it and not grieving over it with pain of heart, this is contrary to Adam's nature. If your heart has by nature[21] overcome sin and has been removed from its cause, and if you have placed punishment before you with the knowledge of your helper who should stay with you, and if you do not upset him in any way but weep before him saying, "Your mercy alone can deliver me, Lord; it is impossible for me to escape their hold without your help", and if you also take care in your heart that you do not upset your teacher according to God, this is the way of Jesus, in accordance with his nature, and he will guard you from every evil. Amen.'

20. Isaac of Nineveh, *Homily* 30, 141f.
21. OGtI c. 6.

9

Commands for Those who have Renounced <the World>

If you have renounced the world and offered yourself to God for repentance, do not allow your thought to trouble you concerning past sins, supposing them not to be forgiven, nor disregard his commandments, or else not even your past sins will be forgiven.

Keep these <commands> until death, and do not despise them.

Do not eat with a woman.

Do not maintain friendships with younger people.[1]

Do not, as a younger monk, sleep with anyone on the same mat, except with your brother, or your abba, and even then with fear and not with disrespect.

Do not look at yourself with disrespect while putting on your clothes.

If you need to drink wine, take up to three glasses,[2] and do not break this rule for the sake of friendship.

Do not stay in a place where you have sinned before God, and do not neglect your duties, lest you fall into the hands of your enemy.

Compel yourself to study the Psalms, because this protects you from captivity and defilement.

1. Isaac of Nineveh, *Homily* 7, 67f.
2. *Sayings* Sisoes 2 and Xoios 1. Cf. Barsanuphius, *Letter* 82.

Learn to love all forms of suffering, and your passions will be humbled.

Take care not to measure yourself in any way, and you will cease mourning over your sins.

Guard yourself from falsehood, for this expels the fear of God from you.

Do not reveal your thoughts before everyone,[3] lest you scandalize your neighbor.

Reveal your thoughts to your fathers,[4] in order that the grace of God may protect you.

Force yourself to perform your manual labor, and the fear of God will dwell in you.

If you see an offence that is not mortal,[5] do not scorn your brother, lest you fall into the hands of your enemy.

Guard yourself in order that you may not be captured by your sins, lest they are renewed within you.

Love humility, and it will protect you from your sin.

Do not be contentious, lest any wicked thing dwells in you.

Give your heart to the obedience of your fathers, and the grace of God will dwell in you.

Do not try to be wise on your own, lest you fall into the hands of your enemy.

Accustom your tongue to say, 'Forgive me', and humility will come upon you.

When sitting in your cell, continually observe these three things: your manual labor, your study, and your prayer.

Think to yourself daily, 'I only have this day to do something in this world', and you will not sin before God.[6]

Do not be gluttonous when eating, lest your past sins are renewed within you.

Do not be slothful in any work, lest the enemy's power attacks you.

3. Isaac of Nineveh, *Homily* 7, 67f.

4. *Sayings* Rufus 2; John Chrysostom, *To Theodore* 2.4 PG 47:313; Barsanuphius, *Letters* 554, 694, and 703.

5. Cf. *Discourse* 4.

6. Athanasius, *Life of Antony* 19–20.

Force yourself in your study, and you will quickly receive divine rest.

Just as a house that is destroyed outside a city becomes a place of stench, the soul of a cowardly beginner becomes the dwelling-place of every dishonorable passion.

Compel yourself to much prayer with tears,[7] in order that God may have mercy on you and strip you of the old, sinful person.

Enjoin yourself to all of these things, for ascetic discipline, poverty, detachment, suffering, and silence give birth to humility, and humility in turn forgives every sin.

Our good God and master is powerful, and can strengthen us to study and carry out these rules, that we may find mercy with the holy ones who have kept his commandments. Amen.

7. Pseudo-Athanasius, *On virginity* 16–17 PG 28:272; Evagrius, *Chapters on Prayer* 6.

10

Another Discourse

GOD SHOWED SAINT PETER THE APOSTLE that he should not consider anyone as common or unclean.[1] Since his heart was sanctified, everyone has been sanctified. For the person whose heart lies in the passions, however, no one has been sanctified, but rather that person considers everyone as in accordance with the passions in his own heart. Even if someone were to say that such and such is a good person, he would immediately become angry in his heart. Therefore, guard yourselves against blaming anyone either by word of mouth or in your heart.

While a person is careless about himself, he thinks in his heart that he is a friend of God. Yet, if he has been freed from the passions, he is ashamed to raise his eyes to heaven before God, considering himself unworthy of even living. Indeed, if he has been seized by the mercy of God, then he sees himself as greatly estranged from God.

A certain person had two servants. He sent them out into his field to harvest the wheat, ordering them each to harvest seven measures daily. Now one of them did his best to fulfill his lord's command but he was unable to do so because the task exceeded his ability. The other proved to be lazy, saying to himself, 'Who can do so much work each day?' He carelessly neglected his duty and, instead, slept for one hour, lay down for another, yawned for a third, and *turned here and there like a door on its hinges*,[2] wasting the whole day. When it

1. Cf. Ac 10:28.
2. Pr 26:14.

was evening, they appeared before their master who differentiated between the two, recognizing and receiving the work of the earnest slave, even though he did not fulfill the command. As for the lazy and negligent slave, he was thrown out of the house.

Therefore, let us also not grow weary in any of our exhaustive ascetic discipline but let us do our best, working with all our soul, and I believe that God will receive us with his saints.

Nonetheless, a person must pray a great deal before God, with great humility of heart and body, not considering himself as doing any good through any of his works, feeling neither convinced by compliments nor sad on account of blame, but instead allowing the remembrance of his sins to make peace in his heart with his enemies. He should not permit any bitter word from his mouth to be spoken against anyone and should not blame anyone, even before good people who love him.

Finally, a monk must close all gates to his soul,[3] guarding all his senses so that they may not bring death to his soul, and protecting himself from those who address worldly words to him. Truly blessed is the person who busies himself with his own sins.

3. OGtI c. 7.

11

On the Grain of Mustard Seed

THE PARABLE OF THE GRAIN OF MUSTARD SEED is a mystery, as the Fathers have said, and we are called to imitate its example. It is written, '*The kingdom of heaven is like a grain of mustard seed, which a person took and sowed in his field. It is the smallest of all seeds, but when it has grown it is the greatest of herbs and becomes a shrub, so that the birds of the sky come and make nests in its branches.*'[1]

This, then, is the grain of mustard seed, and these are its virtues which we are called to imitate in every way. When it says, '*it is the smallest of all seeds*', it is referring to humility, that we must be subjected to all people. Its growth signifies meekness and long-suffering. Its redness means purity, not having any stain in the flesh. Its sharp twigs[2] are the hatred of the passions, for such hatred is bitter for those who still desire worldly things. Its sweetness, which is only activated when it is mashed or threshed, signifies endurance. Its thresher is stung in the eyes on account of its powerful affliction. It is used to pickle dead things in order that they do not stink. Let us understand this and do likewise, dipping in it the dead parts of our soul so that they are not exposed to stench or worms.

This is why the Lord Jesus became human, in order that we may be concerned with endeavoring to behave as he did, searching ourselves as best we can in accordance with his example, asking whether or not we are like that seed, its condition and humility,

1. Mt 13:31.
2. Barsanuphius, *Letter* 156.

its sweetness and bitterness and taste. His mercy will strengthen us according to his will, for his is the glory, of the Father, and the Son, and the Holy Spirit, to the ages of ages. Amen.

12

On Wine

THE EXAMPLE OF WINE IS YET ANOTHER MYSTERY symbolizing a person's nature that desires to encounter God in purity by preserving its work intact in order that God may receive it with joy.

The cask that has been pitched gently is an image of bodily purity that is healed in every member of the shameful passions, for, just as it is impossible to pour wine into a cask that has not been entirely pitched over, or has a crack, it is impossible for a person serving even one pleasure to serve God. In the same way, let us search ourselves, for we cannot please God if we have any hatred or enmity, for these things prevent us from repenting.

Wine is boiled in its early stages; this is an image of youth, because it is unsettled until it matures and ferments.

There can be no wine unless one adds chalk and a measure of leaven. The same is true of youth that cannot progress in its individual will unless it receives the leaven from its spiritual fathers who can show it the right way, until God blesses it in order for it to be able to see.

They leave the wine inside the house until it ferments. Likewise, without silence, endurance, and much spiritual discipline, it is not possible to settle.

If it is left among seed and fruit, it becomes vinegar. If left among relatives or other people who do not share the same discipline and struggle, a youth's nature loses the ways received by its spiritual fathers.

They put earth around the wine cask so that it does not take in air and is ruined. So also with youth, unless it acquires humility in all things, all of its ascetic discipline is in vain.

If people taste the wine frequently, it takes in air and loses its taste. The same often occurs with a person who reveals his ascetic labor, for vainglory destroys his every achievement.

If people leave the cask lid open, the dread mosquitoes destroy the wine. The same is also true of talkativeness, laughter, and vain chatting.

If they leave the wine in the open air, it loses its form and taste. Likewise, pride destroys our every achievement. Instead, wine is hidden in the cellars, and is covered with padding. This is like keeping silence and not reckoning oneself worthy, for it is impossible to preserve one's achievements without silence and humility.

All of this is done to the wine until it satisfies the farmer and he is pleased with the result. Likewise, one has to acquire all these virtues until his ascetic labor is pleasing to God. Just as it is impossible to trust the quality of a wine unless it is opened and tasted, it is impossible for someone to grow confident in his heart, for he is forever fearful of encountering God who will see if his work is perfect. Again, just as when the cask perspires, the wine flows out onto the earth without the master's knowledge, if he is not careful, so also a small and minute detail can destroy one's ascetic labor, if one is careless.

Therefore, let us do our best, my brothers, to protect ourselves from those who harm us, and on that day we shall receive God's mercy and grace, when we say to him, 'We have done all that we could, according to our limitations, to guard our words with our conscience, but yours is the power, the mercy, the assistance, the protection, the forgiveness, and the tolerance, for what am I in the hands of the wicked ones from whom you saved me? I have nothing to give you, for I am sinful and unworthy of your gifts. You have protected me from the hands of my enemy. You are my Lord and my God, and yours is the glory and mercy <and the protection, and assistance, and dominion>, to the ages of ages. Amen.'

13

On Those who have Struggled and Reached Perfection

THESE ARE THE SIGNS WHICH OUR LORD JESUS performed before ascending the cross, for he says, '*Go and tell John what you have heard and seen. The blind receive their sight, the lame walk, the lepers are cleansed, the dead are raised, the poor have good news brought to them, and blessed is anyone who takes no offense at me.*'[1] Since John baptized the Lord Jesus, this word assumes a symbolical meaning, because the one who is baptized must confess the significance of his action. *The signs performed by the Lord Jesus were many.*[2] However, the phrase '*the blind receive their sight*' refers to the blindness of someone who attends to the hope of this world. If this person renounces it and beholds the expected hope <of the future world>, then he receives his sight. Similarly, the phrase '*the lame walk*' signifies that someone desiring God but loving the fleshly cares of the heart is, in fact, lame. If this person renounces these and loves God with all his heart, he is able to walk. Likewise, the phrase '*the deaf hear*' refers to the person who is distracted <by worldly cares>, who is deaf on account of captivity <to such thoughts> and forgetfulness. If he acquires stillness in knowledge, he is able to hear. Again, the phrase '*the lepers are cleansed*' has the following meaning. Since it is written in the law of Moses that 'an unclean person will not enter

1. Mt 11:4–6; Lk 7:22–23.
2. Jn 20:30.

the house of the Lord',[3] this includes whoever holds enmity, or hatred, or envy, or slander against his neighbor, but if this person renounces these, he is cleaned. Therefore, if the blind person sees, the lame walks, <the deaf hears,> and the leper is cleansed, anyone who dies spiritually on account of these, at a time of negligence, may be raised from the dead and renewed, proclaiming the good news to his senses which have been impoverished through a lack of holy virtues, and declaring that this person is now able to see, and walk, and be cleansed. This is the confession that you have offered to the one who baptized you.

By baptism I mean humble endurance of suffering, and silence, for it is written about John that, '*He wore clothing of camel's hair, with a leather belt around his waist*', and lived in the desert.[4] This is the sign of endurance: first it cleanses a person, and, if he labors, then he acquires it. When one acquires it within, he is able to ascend the cross in stillness.[5]

The cross is a sign of future immortality, which is achieved only after shutting the mouths of the Pharisees and Sadducees. The latter symbolize faithlessness and hopelessness, while the former symbolize craftiness, hypocrisy, and vainglory. As it is written, '*after that, no one dared to ask Jesus any question*',[6] and so, he sent Peter and John to prepare the Passover.[7] This means that, if the intellect sees that it is not dominated by anything, it is prepared for immortality, gathering its senses together and uniting them, nourishing them through an inseparable communion.

Again, Jesus prayed, '*If it is possible, let this cup pass from me* at this time'.[8] These words refer to us. If the intellect desires to ascend the cross, then it requires much prayer and many tears in order to be subjected before God at all times, and it must request assistance from his goodness in order to be strengthened and preserved, until

3. Cf. Lv 15:31; Nm 5:3.
4. Mt 3:4, 1.
5. On the imitation of Christ see Basil, *Long Rules* 3, 5 and 7; Pseudo-Macarius, *Homily* 43:1–2; and Symeon the New Theologian, *Catecheses* 20 and 27. See also *Discourse* 8.
6. Mt 22:46; Mk 12:34.
7. Cf. Lk 22:8.
8. Mt 26:39.

he raises it in holy and invincible newness of life. The time of the cross is one of great danger. In prayer, it needs the presence of Peter, John, and James, namely of a healthy faith, a courageous heart of hope, and a love for God.

So this is what happened for our sake to our master himself, to our good Lord and God Jesus, who became an example for us in everything, as the apostle said, '*So that <we may> know him, and the power of his resurrection, and the sharing of his sufferings by becoming like him in his death, if somehow <we> may attain the resurrection from the dead*'.[9] The bile that God tasted[10] for us concerns us; we may lose every evil desire that is within us by shutting our mouths and not allowing it to come outside and become enacted. The vinegar that he tasted[11] for us again concerns us; we may extinguish every willfulness and every vain disturbance. The fact that they spat on him[12] for our sake concerns us; we may extinguish our need for popularity and all worldly glory. The crown of thorns which was woven and placed on his head[13] is symbolical for us; we may bear our blame at all times, calmly enduring insolence. The staff with which his head was beaten for our sake is symbolical for us; always having humility as our helmet, we may extinguish every pride of the enemy. That '*Jesus was handed over to be flogged before being crucified*'[14] is symbolical for us; we may despise all human rebuke and ridicule. That '*they divided his clothes among them, casting lots*'[15] is symbolical for us; just as he remained calm throughout, we, too, must overlook everything in this world before ascending the cross. According to the words of the apostle, '*You cheerfully accepted the plundering of your possessions, knowing that you yourselves possessed something better and more lasting in heaven*'.[16] These are the things that we do in order to ascend the cross with him. If you do not do as he did, in accordance

9. Ph 3:10–11.
10. Mt 27:34.
11. Mt 27:48.
12. Mt 27:30.
13. Mt 27: 29.
14. Mt 27:26; Mk 15:15.
15. Mt 27:35; Mk 15:24.
16. Heb 10:34.

with your human ability, you will not be able to ascend and mount the cross.

The fact that '*it was the sixth hour*'[17] when he was crucified for our salvation by harshness of heart is symbolical for us; we may be strengthened against all despair and faintheartedness. For it is written, '*Through the cross he has put to death the hostility in us*'.[18] When it says, '*It was the ninth hour, and Jesus cried out with a loud voice: Eloi, Eloi, lama sabachthani*',[19] it is symbolical for us; after enduring distress until the passions have been extinguished, we may then in all humility feel bold and cry out to God.[20] The phrase '*at the setting of the sun Jesus breathed his last*'[21] is symbolical for us; when the intellect is liberated from all visible and worldly hope signifies that sin has died within you. The phrase '*the curtain of the temple was torn in two, from top to bottom*'[22] is symbolical for us; when the intellect is freed, the barrier that separates it from God is lifted. The phrase '*the rocks were split and the tombs were opened*'[23] is symbolical for us;[24] when this death comes upon us, all heaviness, blindness, and things closed in the soul are broken, while the senses that kill and give rise to death are made whole and arise invincible.[25]

The fact that he was wrapped in a clean linen cloth and covered with fragrances is symbolical for us; after this death we are wrapped in holiness and given the rest of immortality. The phrase '*they placed him in a new tomb in which no one had been buried*',[26] and rolled a great stone to the door'[27] is symbolical for us; when the intellect is liberated from all these things and reaches the sabbath day of rest,[28] it is in another, new age and considers new things, attending to matters not corruptible but incorruptible.

17. Mk 15:33.
18. Ep 2:16.
19. Mk 15:34.
20. OGtI c. 8.
21. Cf. Mk 15:33, 37.
22. Mk 15:38.
23. Mt 27:51–52.
24. OGtI c. 8.
25. Cf. Rm 7:5.
26. Jn 19:14.
27. Cf. Mt 27:60.
28. OGtI c. 10.

Thus, '*wherever the corpse is, there the vultures will gather*',[29] and the fact that 'He was resurrected in the glory of his father, and ascended into heaven, and sat at the right hand of the majesty on high'[30] is symbolical for us; according to the words of the apostle, '*So if you have been raised with Christ, seek the things that are above, where Christ is, seated at the right hand of God. Set your mind on things that are above, not on things that are on earth, for you have died.*'[31]

His honorable name is powerful and merciful, being a model in all things for the saints, taking care of our weakness so that we may in our poverty renounce our sinfulness and find mercy with his saints. Amen.

29. Mt 24:28.
30. Heb 1:3.
31. Col 3:1–3.

14

Acts of Mourning

WOE TO ME, WOE TO ME, for in no way have I been freed from Gehenna. Those who drag me toward it still bear fruit within me, and all its acts are alive within my heart. Those who overwhelm me in its fire are still active in my flesh, wanting to succeed. I have not yet learned from here my place of destination. The straight way is not yet prepared for me; I have not yet been liberated from the evil spirits in the air who will hinder me on account of their evil deeds that are within me. I have still not seen any redeemer coming to save me from these, for their evil still bears fruit within me. I have yet to know boldness in my relationship with the judge. I have yet to prove that I do not deserve death. I have not yet stopped committing wrong.

A criminal does not rejoice when he is locked in prison. He cannot do as he pleases because he is ironbound. He cannot teach another person because he is locked away in wooden stocks. He cannot recall what it is like to be at rest because he lives in pain. He does not enjoy his food because his neck is also bound. He does not think about committing further crimes, but weeps with painful heart because he has sinned entirely. He says about all the wrongs and punishments he faces, 'Yes, I deserve these', and is always considering what his end will be like. Examining the punishments of his sins, his heart is not concerned with judging others. The pain of the torments eats away at his heart. Alas, even thinking about them is bitter. He cannot encourage others not to despair. Worrying about food is not his concern. Instead, what concerns him is the mercy of those who can be merciful to him, but he does not even know the taste of their mercy on account of his sorrow that he has entirely sinned. When he is rebuked, he does not respond angrily.[1] He endures the pain, claiming that he deserves it. The joy of laughter is removed from him. He shakes his head sighing, remembering the judgment seat before which he will appear. When he hears a conversation, he does not say, 'That is right' or 'That is wrong'. His sense of hearing cannot accept anything, whether right or wrong. His eyelids flow with tears as a result of the pain that constrains him. If he comes from a noble family, he is even more sorrowful because of the shame that will come upon him on the day of judgment. As the place of judgment is being prepared for him, he does not notice whether the crowd that has gathered is good or bad. If others have been condemned with him, he does not notice them, or take counsel with them about what to do, for *each of them bears his own burden*.[2] As he is being dragged toward execution, his face grows dark. No one speaks upon his behalf for fear of torments; he confesses all that he has done and recognizes that he is worthily judged for his wrongdoings.[3]

How long will I behave as a drunkard, though without wine, and be carefree when I have these things before me? The hardness of my heart has dried up my eyes,[4] the drunkenness of care has dried out my head, and the distraction of my heart has caused me forgetfulness until the hour of darkness. The needs of my body have bound me, and my ruin is pushing me to abandon the journey. I no longer have a friend to speak for me, nor a gift to offer people. The reputation of my evil deeds prevents them from recognizing me. Even if I beg them, they pay no attention to me, for they can see that I have not yet stopped suffering. I cannot beg them with open heart, and the thorn of my sins has not yet started continually stinging my heart. The burden of my negligence has not yet fully weighed down upon

1. Cf. Si 20:1.
2. Ga 6:5.
3. John Climacus, *Ladder* Step 5 describes the 'prison' in the alexandrian monastery.
4. Mark the Monk, *On the spiritual law* 18 PG 65:908, and *On those who think* 196 PG 65:961.

me. I have not yet completely known the power of the fire, because I have been struggling not to fall inside it. A voice is heard in my ears, describing the hell that lies before me, because in truth I have not yet purified my heart.

The wounds have scarred my body, but there is no stench so that I may yet seek healing. I hide the wounds of the arrows from people and I cannot bear the doctor removing them. He has prescribed ointments for my wounds but I am not sufficiently strong-hearted to endure their astringency. The doctor is good. He seeks no compensation from me, but my reluctance prevents me from visiting him. When he comes to me in order to heal me, he finds me eating those things that worsen my wounds. He implores me to stop immediately, but the pleasure of their taste deceives my heart. After I have finished eating, I feel remorseful, but my remorse is not sincere. When he sends me food, saying, 'Eat in order that you may be healed', my bad habit does not allow me to accept it. In the final analysis, I do not know what I will do.

Therefore, weep with me, all my brothers who know me, in order that assistance beyond my strength may come to me and dominate me, that I may become his worthy servant, for his is the power, to the ages of ages. Amen.

15

On Detachment

BELOVED, LET US CARE FOR OURSELVES,[1] for '*the appointed time has grown short from now on*'.[2] One cannot care for one's soul so long as one is caring for the body. Just as one cannot at the same time look toward heaven and toward the earth, neither can the intellect care for the things of God and the things of the world,[3] for those things which will not help you after death are shameful for you to care about. You should think that God is watching you in everything that you do, that God can see through your every thought. Whatever you are ashamed to do before others, you should also be ashamed to think in secret, for '*the tree is known by its fruit*'.[4] Thus, the intellect recognizes its thoughts from its contemplation, and the rational soul is also recognized by its contemplation. Do not, therefore, consider yourself dispassionate so long as sin still seduces you. Whoever has been given freedom no longer gives regard to actions that are contrary to nature. So do not consider yourself as free so long as you irritate your master, for freedom does not come while your heart desires something worldly. *Take care of your body as a temple of God.*[5] Take care of it, knowing that you will be resurrected

1. Pseudo-Athanasius, *On discernment* PG 28:1410. The opening of this homily, although not by Athanasius, is identical to the present *Discourse*.
2. 1 Co 7:29.
3. On renunciation, see Basil, *Long Rules* 5, 6, 8 and 9, and *Short Rules* 2, 92, 94, 187–90, 234 and 237; Philoxenus of Mabbug, *Homily* 8; and Abba Dorotheus, *Instruction* 1:1–25 and 8:92.
4. Mt 12:33.
5. 1 Co 6:19.

and give account before God. Fear God, knowing that you will give account for all that you have done. Just as when your body is wounded, you care for it so that it may be healed, make sure that it is dispassionate[6] on the day of the resurrection of all. Each day ponder which passion you have conquered before you proceed to make any requests to God. Just as the soil cannot bring fruit without seed and water, neither can we repent without humility and bodily toil. Just as the seed grows with temperate seasons, we also mature with the commandments, and our intellect keeps the commandments. Faith in God and fear of God consists of not grieving one's conscience. If the pleasure of impurity is sown within you while you are sitting in your cell, take care to resist the thought, lest it takes control of you. Strive to remember God, that he is watching you, and whatever you are thinking in your heart is uncovered before him. Say, then, to your soul, 'If you are ashamed of being seen to sin by sinners who are like you, how much more ashamed should you be of God who watches the secrets of your heart?'

Through the discernment[7] of this thought, the fear of God is revealed in your soul. If you pursue the fear of God, you will become undisturbed and no longer violated by the passions, as it is written, '*Those who trust in the Lord are like Mount Zion; he cannot be moved forever, who dwells in Jerusalem*'.[8] The one who believes that there is judgment after death cannot judge his neighbor in anything at all, because he will himself give account before God about all his actions, as it is written, '*All of us must appear before the judgment seat of Christ, so that each may receive recompense for what has been done in the body, whether good or evil*'.[9] The one who believes that there is a kingdom for the saints will take care to preserve himself to the slightest, insignificant detail, so that he may become *a chosen vessel*,[10] for it is written, 'The

6. Cf. Basil, *Ascetic Sermon* 1, PG 31:872; and John Climacus, *Ladder* 29.

7. On discernment, see Basil, *Long Rules* 10, 43 and 49, and *Short Rules* 152; Cassian, *Conference* 2; Pseudo-Macarius, *On patience and discernment* PG 34: 865–89; Diadochus of Photice, *On Spiritual Knowledge and Discrimination: One Hundred Texts* 26–35; and Symeon the New Theologian, *Catechesis* 28. There are innumerable examples in both the Alphabetical and Anonymous Series of the *Sayings*.

8. Ps 125:1.

9. 2 Co 5:10.

10. Ac 9:15.

kingdom of heaven is like a net that was thrown into the sea and caught fish of every kind. When it was full, they drew it ashore, <sat down> and put the good into his holy kingdom, but threw the bad into Gehenna.[11] The one who believes that his body will, by nature, arise on the day of resurrection is obliged to care for and cleanse it from every impurity,[12] for it is written, '*He will transform the body of our humiliation that it may be conformed to the body of his glory, by the power that strengthens him*'.[13] A person in whom the love of God has dwelt can no longer be separated from God by anything worldly, for it is written, '*Who will separate us from the love of Christ? Will hardship, or distress, or persecution, or famine, or nakedness, or peril, or sword?*',[14] and God is powerful to enable us to be found among those whom nothing worldly can separate from the love of Christ, so that we may find mercy with them through the power of our Lord Jesus Christ, for his is the glory, together with the Father who is without beginning and the life-giving Spirit, now and always, and to the ages of ages. Amen.

11. Cf. Mt 14:47–50.
12. Barsanuphius, *Letter* 607.
13. Ph 3:21.
14. Rm 8:35.

16

On the Joy that Comes to the Soul that Desires to Serve God[1]

FIRST, I GREET YOU IN GODLY FEAR, and entreat you to be perfect in a manner that is pleasing to him, in order that your ascetic discipline may not be futile, but, rather, that it may be joyfully received from you by God.

A trader who makes a profit is joyful. Anyone who learns a skill well is joyful; he does not count the toil endured in the learning. A married man who has a wife that comforts and cares well for him is filled with joy in his heart upon seeing her.[2] A soldier, who ignores death in fighting for his king until victory, is promoted. Behold, these are the ways of this lost world, and such people are joyful when they succeed in their proper task.

How much joy do you suppose fills the soul when a person begins to serve God, and when that person completes the task? Upon his death, he will present his ascetic discipline, and the angels will rejoice with him when they see him rid of the powers of darkness. When the soul leaves the body, the angels journey with it. At that moment, all the forces of darkness come out to meet the soul, wanting to possess it and examining whether it has anything that belongs to them. Then it is not the angels who war against these forces, but the good works that have been achieved which fortify and protect

1. Possibly a letter to a brother. See Basil, *Long Rules* 17, and *Short Rules* 193.
2. Cf. Pr 31:11.

the soul from them, so that it may not be touched by them. If the good works are victorious, then the angels lead the soul, chanting in procession, until it meets God in gladness, and at that time it forgets every worldly labor and ascetic toil. Let us, therefore, do our utmost to work well during this brief lifetime, preserving our ascetic labor from every evil, in order that we may be saved from the hands of the evil spirits of this world, for they are wicked and lack compassion. Blessed is the person in whom nothing is found that belongs to them. His joy, gladness, rest, and crown will be exceedingly great, whereas all the affairs of this world subject to change, whether it is a matter of trade, or marriage, or the others that I mentioned.

Dear brother, let us do our utmost in tears before God, so that his goodness may be merciful to us and grant us strength that we may, in turn, wrestle against the evil spirits that come to meet us in regard to the deeds we have performed. Let us take care, therefore, with all sincerity of heart, and acquire within ourselves a desire for God that will save us from the hands of the evil ones when they come to meet us there. Let us learn to love the poor, because this may save us from avarice when it approaches us. Let us strive to make peace with all people, because this will save us when it approaches us. Let us acquire long-suffering in all things, for this will protect us against negligence when it approaches us. Let us love all people as our brothers, neither allowing any hatred against anyone to enter our heart, *nor returning evil for evil*,[3] for this will protect us from envy when it approaches us. Let us strive for humility in everything, enduring the words of our neighbor when he either hurts or rebukes us, and this will protect us from pride when it approaches us. Let us seek to honor our neighbor, never causing any harm by blaming, and this will protect us from slander when it approaches us. Let us overlook the needs and honors of this world, that we may be saved from jealousy when it approaches us. Let us train our mind in godly study, righteousness, and prayer, that these may protect us from falsehood when it approaches us. Let us purify our heart and

3. Rm 12:17.

body from sinful desire, that we may be saved from impurity when it approaches us.[4]

All these things occupy the soul when it leaves the body, and the virtues assist the soul, if the latter has acquired them. Which wise person would not give his life to be delivered from all this? Therefore, let us do our utmost. The power of our Lord Jesus Christ is great enough to assist us in our humility, for he knows that humanity is wretched, and has given us the opportunity to repent while still alive, until our last breath. So let your thought be concentrated on God, that he may protect you. Pay no attention to the needs of the world, falsely placing any hope in it, in order that you may be saved, for you will leave behind the things of this world, and move to the next. Whatever you do for the sake of God, this is what you will find as a sure hope at the time of need.[5]

Despise worldly words, in order that your heart may see God. Love continual prayer, in order that your heart may be illumined.[6] Shun laziness, and the fear of God will dwell in you. Distribute now with a generous disposition to someone who has a need, so that you may not be put to shame among the saints and their goods. Hate the desire of food, that Amalek may not hinder you.[7] Do not hurry through your duties, lest the beasts devour you. Do not love wine to the point of drunkenness, lest you become deprived of the gladness of God. Love the faithful, that they may have mercy on you. Desire the saints, that their zeal may consume you.[8] Remember the kingdom of heaven, in order that your desire for it may very gradually attract you. Think of Gehenna, so that you may despise its works. When you wake up each morning, remember that you will give account to God for your every deed. In this way, you will not sin against him, and fear of him will dwell in you. Prepare yourself to encounter him, and you will do his will. Question yourself on a

4. Cf. Mark the Monk, *To Nicholas* 4 PG 65:1036 and Barsanuphius, *Letter* 214.
5. Cf. 2 Th 2:16.
6. *Sayings*, Poemen; Mark the Monk, *On those who think* 107 PG 65:945 and *To Nicholas* 6, PG 65:1037.
7. Cf. Jg 7:4.
8. Cf. Ps 69:9.

daily basis here about what you lack, and you will not toil at the time of need when you die. Let your brothers see your deeds, and your zeal will consume them too.[9] Examine yourself daily as to which passion you have conquered, and do not put your trust in yourself, for mercy and strength belong to God. Do not consider yourself to be faithful, even until your last breath. Do not think highly of yourself, or that you are good, for you can never trust your enemies. Do not be confident while you are still living, until you pass beyond all the powers of darkness.

Brother, be vigilant against the demon[10] that brings you sadness,[11] for its spoils are many, until it renders you powerless. On the other hand, godly sadness is joy[12] and consists of seeing yourself standing in the will of God. The demon that tempts you, saying, 'Where can you flee? You have no repentance', belongs to the enemy who is trying to make you lose self-control, whereas godly sadness does not attack you, but says, 'Do not be afraid; try again', for it knows that humanity is weak, and strengthens us. Let your heart be wise in its thoughts, and you will not be burdened by them, for the one who fears them is weakened by their weight. One who fears their action clearly proves themselves to be unfaithful to God. Not measuring oneself, and allowing oneself to remain unknown, reveals that a person is not spending time with the passions or doing their will, but, rather, is doing the will of God. One who wants to have a word to say on many subjects shows that there is no fear of God in him, for the fear of God is the soul's protection and assistance, watching over the inner, governing intellect, in order to destroy all its enemies. The person who seeks godly honor takes the time to drive impurity away from himself. Knowledgeable care is what cuts away the passions, for it is written, '*Care will come upon a wise*'.[13] One who has fallen ill is also the one who knows health. One who

9. Cf. Ps 69:9.

10. Evagrius, *Praktikos* 15, 23, and 27. Demons are interchangeable with passions in the Evagrian tradition: cf. *Praktikos* 58 and *On the eight evil thoughts* PG 40:1272–76.

11. John Climacus, *Ladder* Step 5.

12. Cf. Diadochus, *Century* 27, 37, and 100; and John Climacus, *Ladder* Step 7.

13. Pr 17:12.

is crowned receives this honor because he has overcome the king's enemies.

There are passions and there are virtues, and if we are discouraged, it is obvious that we are traitors. A courageous heart is, after God, the soul's helper, just as boredom assists evil. The strength of those who wish to acquire the virtues is that, if they fall, they will not be discouraged, but will try again.[14] The instrument of the virtues is ascetic discipline in knowledge. The fruits of the passions result from negligence. Not judging one's neighbor is a protection for those who struggle in knowledge, but blaming one's neighbor destroys this protection in ignorance. Taking care of one's tongue[15] is the sign of a person who practices the virtues. Not controlling one's tongue shows that a person has no inner virtue. Charity in knowledge gives birth to foresight, and leads to love, but lack of charity shows that a person has no inner virtue. Goodness gives rise to purity. Distraction gives rise to passions, and hardheartedness gives rise to anger. Discipline of the soul is hatred of distraction, and discipline of the body is poverty. The fall of the soul is loving distraction, and its rise is silence in knowledge. Excessive sleep disturbs the passions within the body, and vigil in measure is the heart's salvation. Too much sleep thickens the heart, but vigil in measure refines it. It is better to sleep in silence and knowledge, than to keep vigil with idle talk. Compunction calmly expels all evil. Not offending your neighbor's conscience gives rise to humility. Human glory very gradually gives rise to pride. Loving to boast expels knowledge. Self-control in food humiliates the passions. Desire of food stimulates them without any trouble. Adorning the body is the destruction of the soul, but caring for it with godly fear is good. Being careful about God's judgment gives rise to fear in the soul. Trampling on one's conscience shakes off the virtues from the heart.[16] Love for God expels negligence, and fearlessness arouses it. Guarding one's mouth awakens the intellect to God, if it is silent in knowledge,[17]

14. Palladius, *Lausiac History* 22; John Climacus, *Ladder* Step 5.
15. John Climacus, *Ladder* Step 22.
16. John Climacus, *Ladder* Step 5.
17. Barsanuphius, *Letters* 554 and 652.

but loquacity begets boredom and madness. Dismissing your will before your neighbor signifies that the intellect is looking to the virtues, but holding onto your will before your neighbor signifies ignorance. Study, with godly fear, protects the soul from passions, but talking in a worldly manner darkens it from virtues. Love of matter troubles the intellect and the soul.

A person who performs his ascetic labor but does not protect <himself> is like a house without doors or windows, into which any reptile that wants can enter. Human honor eats away the heart that is convinced by it, like rust, which eats away at iron. Just as a knife caught up in a vine destroys the fruit,[18] so also vainglory destroys a monk's labor if he is convinced by it.[19] The first of the virtues is humility, and the first of the passions is gluttony. The end of the virtues is love, and the end of the passions is self-justification. Just as a worm eats away at wood and destroys it, evil in the heart darkens the soul. Surrendering one's soul before God gives rise to calm endurance of insolence, and its tears are protected from everything human. Not blaming oneself also brings the inability to endure anger. Conversing with secular people disturbs the heart and shames it in prayer to God, so that it has no confidence. Loving the needs of the world darkens the soul; totally ignoring them brings knowledge. Loving ascetic labor is a way of hating the passions; laziness brings them back without any trouble. Do not bind yourself to a particular way of life, and your thoughts will be at peace within you. Do not trust your own strength, and God's assistance will come to you. Do not show hatred against anyone because your prayer will not be accepted.[20] Be at peace with all, so that you may be confident in prayer. Guard your eyes, and your heart will see no evil. One who looks at another with sensual pleasure is committing adultery. Do not wish to hear about any harm to someone who has hurt you, lest you return the evil in your heart. Guard your ears, so that you do not bring spiritual warfare upon yourself. Work on your manual

18. Cf. Na 1:10.
19. This passage is indicative of Abba Isaiah's environment: near a coastal city, with surrounding vineyards.
20. Barsanuphius, *Letter* 127.

labor, so that a poor person may find bread,[21] for idleness is death and destruction for the soul. Continual prayer destroys captivity, but ignoring it, even a little, is the mother of forgetfulness. One who keeps death nearby in his expectation does not sin much, but one who expects to live a long time will be entangled in many sins. When a person is prepared to give an account to God for all his deeds, God himself will take care to purify his every way from sin, but the person who pays no attention and says, 'It will be some time before I die', dwells in evil. Each day, before you do anything, remember and always consider where you are and where you must go when you die, and you will not neglect your soul for even a day. Think of the honor received by all the saints, and their zeal will attract you very gradually. Ponder also on the punishments received by sinners, and you will always be guarded from evil. Take counsel at all times with your elders, and you will live all your life in peace.

Observe yourself, in order to see if the thought pricks you that your brother is upset with you; do not overlook this thought, but show penitence toward him, with a sad voice, until you persuade him. Watch that you are not hardhearted against you brother, for we are all forced by hatred. If you are living with other brothers, do not command them to do anything, but labor with them so that you do not lose your reward. If the demons trouble you about food, clothing, or great poverty, suggesting that you utter rebukes, in no way respond to them, but surrender yourself to God with all your heart, and he will grant you rest. Take care not to neglect performing your duties, for these bring illumination to the soul. If you have done good things, do not take pride in them, and if you have done many evil things, let not your heart be immensely saddened, but stand firm in your heart so that you are no longer persuaded to do such evil, and if you are wise you will be protected from their desire and pride. If you are bothered by fornication, continually afflict your body with humility before God, do not allow your heart to be convinced that your sins have been forgiven, and you will find rest. If jealousy afflicts you, remember that we are all members of Christ, and that our neighbor's honor and reproach

21. Athanasius, *Life of Antony* 3.

belong to all, and you will find rest. If gluttony or the desire for food is your spiritual warfare, remember its stench, and you will find rest. If slander against your brother afflicts you, remember how sorry he will be if he hears such things, and you will immediately run to dissuade him, and find rest. If pride dominates you, remember that it will destroy all your ascetic labor and that there is no repentance for those who yield to it, and you will find rest. If contempt against your neighbor attacks your heart, remember that it is for this reason that God puts you in the hands of your enemy, and you will find rest. If bodily beauty attracts your heart, remember its stench, and you will find rest. If the enjoyment of women is sensually most pleasing to you, remember where those women who have already died have gone, and you will find rest.

All things are abolished by discernment, when it gathers and considers them, but it is impossible for discernment to come to you, unless you cultivate its ground, beginning with silence. Silence gives birth to ascetic discipline. Ascetic discipline gives birth to weeping. Weeping gives rise to fear of God. Godly fear begets humility. Humility begets foresight. Foresight begets love. Love renders the soul diseased free and dispassionate.[22] Then, and only after all this, a person knows that he is far from God. So one who wants to receive all these honorable virtues must not care about what all the other people think but must be prepared for death. Whenever he prays, he must understand what it is that separates him from God, so that he may abolish it and hate all contact with it, and the goodness of God will grant him these virtues quickly. Know this also, that anyone who eats and drinks indifferently, and is attached to something worldly, will not reach or ever acquire these virtues, but is deceiving himself.

I entreat everyone who wants to offer repentance to God, therefore, to refrain from too much wine, for this renews all the passions[23] and expels the fear of God from the soul. Nevertheless, ask God, with all your strength, to send you his fear, in order that, through your strong desire for him, he may destroy all the passions that

22. Abba Isaiah reveals his own list or 'ladder' of eight virtues: silence, ascesis, weeping, fear of God, humility, foresight, love, and dispassion.

23. Barsanuphius, *Letter* 508.

array against your wretched soul, wanting to separate it from him in order to claim it. This is why the enemy does its utmost to struggle against us.

Therefore, brother, as long as you are in the body, do not pay attention to leisure,[24] and, if you see a time of rest from the passions, do not trust yourself, for they shrewdly withdraw for a while, so that a person might relax his heart, thinking that he has found rest, and then suddenly they leap inside the wretched soul and seize it like a bird,[25] and, if they are stronger than it in regard to any sin, they humiliate it mercilessly, rendering the struggle still more difficult than that for which he had earlier prayed for forgiveness.

Let us, therefore, stand in godly fear, and let us protect the practice <of our virtues>, preserving all the virtues that prevent the evil of the enemy, for the labor and toil of this brief life not only protect us from evil, but even prepare crowns for the soul before death.[26]

Our teacher, our holy Lord Jesus, saw their great mercilessness and took pity on the human race, commanding with a strict heart, '*Keep awake at all times, for you do not know at what hour the thief is coming*',[27] 'lest he come suddenly and find you asleep'.[28] In teaching his disciples, he commanded them, '*Be on guard so that your hearts are not weighed down with dissipation, and drunkenness, and the worries of this life, and that hour catches you unexpectedly*';[29] and knowing that the evil demons outnumber us, and showing <them> that power belongs to him, so that they need not fear, he said, '*See, I am sending you out like lambs into the midst of wolves*',[30] but he commanded them not to take anything for the journey, for so long as they had nothing that the wolves wanted, they could not be devoured by them. When they returned healthy, having kept this command, he congratulated them, giving thanks to God the Father on their account, and, encouraging their heart, he said, '*I watched Satan fall from heaven like a flash of*

24. OGtI c. 11.
25. Cf. Lm 3:52.
26. OGtI c. 12.
27. Mt 24: 42–43.
28. Cf. Mk 13:36.
29. Lk 21:34.
30. Lk 10:3.

lighting. See, I have given you authority to tread on snakes, and scorpions, and over all the power of the enemy, and nothing will hurt you'.[31] So his commission entailed fear and the keeping of a command, and when this command was fulfilled by them, he gave them authority and power. These words do not only belong to those disciples, but to all who fulfill the commandments, for, having loved these entirely, he said, '*Do not be afraid, little flock, for it is your Father's good pleasure to give you the kingdom. Sell your possessions, and give alms. Make purses for yourselves that do not wear out, an unfailing treasure in heaven*'.[32] When they kept these words as well, he said to them, '*I leave you with my peace; my peace I give to you*';[33] and, convincing them, he said, '*Those who love me will keep my commandments, and I and my Father will come to them, and make our home with them*';[34] and, rendering them fearless of the world, he said to them, '*In the world you face persecution, but take courage; I have conquered the world*';[35] and, encouraging them not to lose heart in face of persecutions, he spoke to them, granting joy in their hearts, '*You are those who have stood by me in my trials, and I confer on you, just as my Father has conferred on me, a kingdom, so that you may eat and drink at my table*'.[36] He did not say these things to all, but to those who stood by him in trials. Who, then, are they that stood by Jesus in his trials, if not those who stood up to whatever is contrary to nature, until it was cut off? He told them these things as he was on his way to the cross. The one, therefore, who wishes to eat and drink at his table, will journey with him to the cross, for the cross of Jesus is abstinence from every passion, until it is cut off. The beloved disciple cut them away and dared to say, '*I have been crucified with Christ. It is no longer I who live, but it is Christ who lives in me*'.[37] Therefore, Christ lives in those who have abolished the passions. Exhorting his children, the apostle said, '*Those who belong to Jesus Christ have crucified the flesh with its passions and desires*'.[38] Further,

31. Lk 10:18.
32. Lk 12:32–33.
33. Jn 14:27.
34. Jn 14:23.
35. Jn 16:33.
36. Lk 22:28–30.
37. Ga 2:19–20.
38. Ga 5:24.

writing to his child Timothy, he said, '*If we have died with him, we will also live with him; if we endure, we will also reign with him; if we deny him, he will also deny us*'.[39]

Who, then, are they who deny him but those who carry out their fleshly desires, and insult their holy Baptism?[40] Through his name we received remission of sins,[41] and on account of jealousy, the enemy again overcame us through sin. Therefore, our Lord Jesus Christ saw how great the enemy's original evil was, and, additionally, offered us repentance, to our last breath, for were it not for repentance, no one would be saved. Knowing that we sin, even after Baptism, the apostle said, '*Thieves must give up stealing*'.[42]

As long, then, as we have the seal of holy Baptism, let us strive to abandon our sins, that we may find mercy on that day,[43] for he is at hand, and is coming, *seated on the throne of his glory, and all the tribes of the earth will be gathered before him*,[44] and each one of us will be revealed from the very torch that is in our hand. Thus, whoever does not have oil, his torch will be extinguished and thrown into the darkness. Whosesoever's torch is bright, will accompany him into the kingdom.[45] Let us, therefore, dear brothers, strive to fill our vessels with oil while we are still in this life, that our torch may shine and we may enter his kingdom. Now the vessel is repentance, and the oil inside it is the practice of all virtues. The bright torch is the holy soul. So, if the soul shines brightly through its good deeds, this is how it will enter the kingdom with him, and if the soul is darkened by its own evil, it will be sent to the darkness.

Therefore, struggle, brothers, because our *time is at hand*,[46] and blessed is he who is concerned about this, for the fruit is ripe, and it is the time of harvest. Blessed is he who has saved his fruit, for the angels will gather it in the eternal storehouse.[47] Woe to those who are

39. 2 Tm 2:11–12.
40. Mark the Monk, *On baptism* PG 65:1025.
41. Cf. Ac 2:38.
42. Ep 4:28.
43. Cf. 2 Tm 1:18.
44. Mt 25:31–32.
45. Cf. Mt 25:1–13.
46. Lk 21:8.
47. Cf. Mt 13:30.

the weeds, for they will inherit the fire. The inheritance of this world is gold, silver, houses, and clothing, and it is not simply that these things prepare us for sin, but we leave them behind when we die. However, God's inheritance is boundless, and '*no eye has seen, nor ear heard, nor human heart conceived*' it.[48] He has granted it to those who obey him in this brief life, and it is received through bread, water, and clothing given to those in need, and through loving kindness, purity of body, not rendering evil to one's neighbor, a guileless heart, and obeying the rest of his commandments. Those who keep these have rest in this age, and people will respect them. When they die, they will receive eternal joy, but the faces of those who carry out their sinful desires and do not repent—being distracted by sensual pleasure, enacting their evil through deceit, being vain in their talk, violent in their battles, fearless of God's judgment, unmerciful to the poor, and committing all the other sins—will be filled with shame in this age, and people will despise them. When they leave this world, reproach and shame will lead them to Gehenna.

God is powerful and makes us worthy to progress in his works, keeping us from every evil deed, in order that we may be saved *in the time of trial which will come upon the whole world*,[49] for our Lord Jesus *will not tarry*,[50] but will come, bearing the reward,[51] and he will send the impious to the eternal fire. To his own he will grant a reward, and these will enter with him and find rest in his kingdom, to the ages of ages.

Amen.

48. 1 Co 2:9.
49. Rv 3:10.
50. Heb 10:37.
51. Cf. Rv 22:12.

17

On Thoughts about Renunciation and Exile

BEFORE ALL ELSE, THE FIRST STRUGGLE IS EXILE; especially if you have fled alone, then the struggle is to leave your own and move to another place, bearing perfect faith and hope, as well as a stable heart with regard to your own desires, for thoughts will completely encircle you, frightening you about temptations, hardships in poverty, and illnesses, suggesting to you questions about how you will cope with these if you have no one who cares for, or knows you. God's goodness is trying you in order to reveal your effort and love for him. So when you are alone in the cell, they plant inside you unbearable thoughts of fear, saying, 'It is not only exile that saves a person, but obeying the commandments', bringing to your heart and saying, 'What then, are they not also servants of God?' They sow thoughts inside your heart regarding bad weather and bodily needs, until your heart is weakened through discouragement, but, if love and hope are found and remain in you, the evil of these things will not be activated. Therefore, your effort before God becomes clear; <it is> evident that you love him more than bodily rest. Those who endure the tribulation of exile are brought to the virtue of hope, and this hope protects them, at least partially, from fleshly desire, for you are not in exile for its own sake, but in order to prepare yourself, and have time to struggle against the enemy, so that you may learn how to reject each foe in its time, until you reach the rest of dispassion and are liberated as a result of being victorious at each battle, in its own time.

It is a great and honorable thing to conquer vainglory,[1] and to progress in knowledge of God, for one who falls into the shame of this evil passion of vainglory is estranged from peace, and becomes hardhearted toward the saints, and, at the end of his wrongdoings, falls into evil pride and into the concern for lies. You, the faithful one, however, should conceal your ascetic labors and take great care, by striving with heart and tongue, that your tongue does not remove these labors and surrender them to the enemy,[2] for the one who works to lay aside the bodily passions and all their weaknesses through repentance, has rendered his soul honorable for God as a blameless deposit, in order to be made worthy of becoming his temple. On the other hand, the one who loves human glory cannot attain dispassion, because envy and jealously dwell in him. Such a person has sold his soul to many temptations, and his heart is slaughtered by the demons because he can never find the time to obey all his commands. God reveals a person's sins to the one who has acquired humility so that he may know them, and, if compunction also plays a part in him so that both of these virtues remain in him, they will remove from his soul the seven demons[3] and nurture the soul from its own honor and from its holy virtues. Such a person is not worried about people's reproaches, for his own sins which are remembered become his armor, and protect him from wrath and recompense, and he endures what comes his way,[4] for what reproach can be attributed to such a person who, before God and before himself, has his own sins. Therefore, if you cannot bear the word of your neighbor, and return the wrong, struggle

1. On vainglory, see Evagrius, *Praktikos* 13; Cassian, *Institutes* 11; John Climacus, *Ladder* Steps 22 and 23; and Symeon the New Theologian, *Catechesis* 10. There are also many examples of overcoming vainglory in both the Alphabetical and Anonymous Series of *Sayings*.

2. Mark the Monk, *On those who think* cc. 135, PG 65:949 and 957.

3. See *Discourse* 4.

4. See *Discourse* 7. Cf. Mark the Monk, *To Nicholas* 3 PG 65:1033; and Barsanuphius, *Letters* 2, 163, 215, 278, 315, 574, and 823. See also Dorotheus, *Instruction* 7:83–84 (PG 88:1696), 10:110 (1724), and 13:138 (1761), and *Letters* 2, 9 and 10.

will arise in your heart, causing you great sorrow about everything you said. This captivity will completely overcome you, and make you praise those who live alone in silence, hardening your heart toward your neighbor, as having no love. Strive, instead, to acquire long–suffering, because it overcomes wrath, and love heals sorrow. Praying to God with fear protects both these virtues, for love and long-suffering bring natural wrath, and if these virtues remain in you, instead of directing your anger against your neighbor, you will direct it against the demons and be at peace with your neighbor, being filled with compunction and humility. The person who is, for the sake of God and for the peace of his own thoughts, able to bear[5]a harsh word spoken by a difficult and unwise person, will be called a son of peace,[6] and be enabled to acquire peace of soul, body, and spirit. If these three are all in agreement, so that those who war against the law of the intellect cease, and the captivity of the flesh is abolished, then that person will be called a *son of peace*, and the Holy Spirit will dwell in him, because it has become his and will not be separated from him.

Blessed are they whose ascetic labors are achieved with knowledge, for these labors have given them rest from every weight. These people have escaped the craftiness of the demons, especially those of cowardice who hinder us in every good work that we embark upon, by bringing the intellect to sluggishness when we try to lead a life in expectation of God. Their aim is to lead us away from this way through the ascetic toils. I think, however, that if we have love, patience, and self-control, the demons cannot do a single thing, especially if the intellect knows that laziness destroys everything and despairs it. If you have renounced all visible, material things, watch out for the demon of sadness lest, on account of great poverty and sorrow, you are unable to reach the great virtues which are not measuring yourself, enduring insolence, and not making a name for yourself in the order of this world. If you struggle to acquire these, they will prepare for you the crowns of the soul, for the poor are not

5. John Climacus, *Ladder* Step 25. This scholion is attributed to Abba Isaac but in fact belongs to Abba Isaiah.
6. Lk 10:6.

those who have renounced and given away this visible world alone, but those who have given up all evil and who hunger always for the remembrance of God. Nor is it they who appear to have sorrow that acquire dispassion, but those who are concerned with the inner person and who cut off their willfulness, who ultimately receive the crown of virtues. Therefore stand over your heart, watching your senses,[7] and if your memory is at peace, seize the thieves who try to break in secretly,[8] for one who is precise with his own thoughts knows about the commandments with warmth of heart,[9] you will understand those who disturb you and the reason for which they cause trouble, bringing you neglect and making you choose to move elsewhere without reason, and then regretting that choice as well. They disturb the intellect in order to render it distracted and idle. Yet those who know their wickedness remain untroubled, giving thanks to the Lord for the place that he has chosen for them to endure these temptations, for patience, long-suffering, and love is thankful for the ascetic toils and labors, but boredom and laziness, as well as the love of relaxation, seek the place where they will find glory. As a result, the senses are weakened from much human glory, and the captivity of the passions inevitably overpower them, and they loose their hidden self-control on account of distraction and satiation.

The saint also said that before the senses cease from being weak, if the intellect desires to ascend the cross, the wrath of God comes upon it, because it began something beyond its limits, not first having healed its senses. If your heart is distracted and you do not know how to control it, then it is your behavior that leads it to distraction, either willingly or unwillingly, inasmuch as it is contrary to the nature of Adam. If your heart by nature[10] hates sin and stays away from those things that cause sin, placing punishment before you in true knowledge, and if you are estranged from those things that

7. OGtI c. 12.

8. Athanasius, *Life of Antony* 43; Mark the Monk, *On baptism* PG 65:992; and Anastasius of Sinai, *Questions* 1 PG 89:329.

9. John Climacus, *Ladder* Step 12.

10. OGtI c. 6.

drag you <toward hell>, praying with knowledge to your Creator for his assistance, and grieving him in no way, but weeping before him, and saying, 'It is up to you to show mercy and redeem me, for it is impossible for me to avoid falling into their hands without your help', and if you are careful in your heart so as not to grieve him who teaches you in the way of God, these things are according to the nature of Jesus. If a person achieves everything,[11] but does not acquire obedience, humility and patience, then he deviates from the way that is according to nature. Give your whole heart to the obedience of God, praying to him in truth, and saying, 'Lord, I am before you, make me worthy of your will, for I do not know what is of benefit to me. You fight on my account, for I do not know their evil'. If you are practicing that which is according to the nature of Jesus, then he will not let you be led astray in any way.

However, if you obey one commandment and disobey another, you have not given yourself to obeying him, and he will not care about you, for just as a field is unable to disagree with a laborer who is trying to cleanse it from tares and sow in it natural seed—for it is not possible for natural things to grow with unnatural things, because the former will be stifled by the latter inasmuch as the tares are not as healthy—the same occurs if you are not purified from your fleshly desires, for you are unable to be preserved from sin, if you are first unable to protect yourself from its causes. These causes are as follows: faintheartedness is the evil mother of sin; boredom gives rise to willfulness; and willfulness and boasting give birth to despising. The heart that desires authority brings about a love for worldly conversation, a search for things that are of no use to you, a teaching of those who do not ask this of you, a wounding of one's neighbor, as well as many other evils.[12] Therefore, if anyone has either shown, or else wishes to show, progress, he should protect himself in true knowledge from these causes of sin, and these will, by themselves, become weak. Thus, one who struggles sees them and their bitterness; whereas one who neglects his struggle is preparing

11. John Climacus, *Ladder* Step 26.
12. Improper spiritual direction, or abuse of spiritual authority. See *Discourse* 8.

punishment for himself. One who fears bodily weakness[13] cannot attain the way that is according to nature. If, however, he falls down before God in all his ascetic labors, God is able to give him rest, for had Gideon not broken the water jars, he would not have seen the light of the torches.[14] In the same way, unless a person despises the body, he cannot see the light of divinity, for unless Joel, too, the wife of Chaber the Kennite, had broken the post of the tent, she would not have overturned the pride of Sisara.[15] Therefore, if the intellect is strengthened and prepared to follow the virtue of love that quenches all the passions of the soul and the body, by showing long-suffering and goodness,[16] by hating envy and pride, by not considering evil in the heart, and by not allowing anything that is contrary to nature to dominate the intellect, then the intellect resists that which is contrary to nature with the power of love until it is filled with that which is according to nature. If the genuine intellect dominates, it becomes the head of the soul and accepts nothing that is contrary to nature, for the intellect relates to the soul all the injustice contrary to nature that it has caused it, during the whole time that it was mingled with this world.

When our Lord Jesus showed mercy to his saints, he separated the thieves on the cross, for two thieves were crucified, and he was in their midst. The one on the left was troubled, seeing that his polluted friendship with the thief on the right was abolished, but the one on the right looked to Jesus in humility and fear, saying, '*Remember me when you come in your kingdom*'.[17] Thus, it becomes clear that they are no longer friends, and that the thief on the left cannot convince the other with his evil wiles.

Now those who have not yet reached this way fall and rise until they receive mercy, and they cannot be saved unless they receive mercy. In the same way, you should be concerned about understanding in fear and humility, just as the thief on the right, for

13. Mark the Monk, *To Nicholas* PG 65:1040, and *On those who think* 217–19 (PG 65:961).
14. Cf. Jg 7:19.
15. Cf. Jg 3:21.
16. Cf. 1 Co 13:4.
17. Lk 23:42.

humility brings about self-contempt. Thus when one is separated from the thief on the left[18] and knows with precision all sins that he has committed before God—because he cannot see his sins unless he is separated from them by a separation of bitterness—then when he has reached this point, he has found mournfulness, prayerfulness, and shamefulness before God, recalling the wickedness of their friendship with the passions.

God, however, is able to strengthen those who work in humility, for his is the honor and the glory, to the ages of ages. Amen.

18. OGtI c. 17. Cf. Nicephorus, *On sobriety and guarding* the heart in *Philokalia* 2, 239.

18

On Forgiveness

THE MOST HOLY APOSTLE COMMANDED his children, saying, '*The Lord is near. Do not worry about anything, but in everything, by prayer and supplication with thanksgiving, let your requests be made known to God*',[1] and '*Let the peace of God rule in your hearts*'.[2] In the Gospel according to Mark, the Lord says to the disciples, 'Forgive your debtors all their transgressions, and your Father will forgive you yours'.[3] This word of the Lord is fearful, for unless you see that your heart is pure toward all,[4] you can ask nothing from God. Instead you offer him insolence, inasmuch as you say to him who searches hearts, 'Forgive me my sins', when you are sinful and bear a grudge against your fellow human being. Such a person does not pray with the intellect, but ignorantly with the lips, for one who truly desires to pray with the intellect to God, in the Holy Spirit, and with a pure heart, searches his heart before praying, to see whether he is free from all anxiety before every person or not. If he is not, he deceives himself, because no one is listening to him, since the intellect is not praying but is simply <following> the habitual routine of daily prayer. However, the person who wishes to pray in a pure manner will first examine what is in his intellect. Is he saying, 'Have mercy on me', and at the same time showing mercy to another who asks for this, or is he saying, 'Forgive me', and at

1. Ph 4:5–7.
2. Col 3:15.
3. Cf. Mk 11:26.
4. Mark the Monk, *On the spiritual law* 26 PG 65:909; Barsanuphius, *Letter* 18.

the same time forgiving others? If you say, 'Do not remember the evils which I have committed, either voluntarily or by force', you too should not remember those of others. If it is a matter of force, then, you too should not hold something against another person. Unless you have managed to do these things, then you are praying in vain. According to all the Scriptures, God is not listening to you. Forgive me!

Again, he said in the prayer of <the Gospel according to> Matthew, '*And forgive us our debts, as we also have forgiven our debtors*',[5] and in <the Gospel according to> Luke, 'If you forgive others their trespasses, your heavenly Father will forgive you'.[6]

I have offered you all <the way> of love, so that whatever you want God to do to you, you may do first, and then you will be set free according to the measure that you have cleansed your heart toward the whole of creation, so as to remember no injury, then you are obliged to keep this way. God requires exactitude and not simply words. Every person binds himself to Gehenna, and looses himself, for nothing is stronger than the will which leads you either to death or life. Blessed, then, are those who have loved eternal life, for they will not falter. So there is a struggle going on in the toil and hidden sweat of the heart against the thought that stifles you, in order not to allow its arrow to wound your heart, and it will require an effort on your part to heal it, unless your sins are ever before you.[7] If you hear that some evil was done against you by someone, hold up your good will in order not to return the evil in your heart, neither blaming, judging, criticizing, nor even delivering him to the words of others; then you will think to yourself, 'No evil was done against me'. If you have the fear of Gehenna inside you, then you will triumph over the evils that want you to render evil against your neighbor, for it will say to you, 'Wretched person, pray for your own sins and God will support you at all times without revealing them, whereas you angrily cast your neighbor into the mouths of

5. Mt 6:12.
6. In fact, Mt. 6:14.
7. Cf. Ps 51:3.

others. Therefore, it is clear that your sins are not removed, since no forgiveness has touched you.' So, if your heart is softened and you guard yourself from evil, you will have mercy from God, but if your evil heart is hardened toward your neighbor, you have not yet become mindful of God.

Forgive me. I[8] am in every way impoverished and humbled by sins, and by writing these things am ashamed within my heart, for unless a person reaches the natural state of the Son of God, all of his efforts are in vain. A farmer who sows his seed expects to make a manifold return, but if the wind destroys it, he is completely saddened in his heart about the damage to the crops and the toils that he rendered to the earth. When the Apostle Peter was crucified in Rome, he requested to be hung head down, thereby revealing the mystery of the unnatural condition that dominates everyone, for he was saying that each person who is baptized must crucify the wicked conditions contrary to nature which possessed Adam and drove him from his glory to an evil rebuke and eternal shame. Therefore, it is necessary for the intellect to struggle courageously, to hate everything that is seen by people, and to become their enemy to the end with a very bitter hatred. These are the principal evils that dominated all the sons of Adam—gain, honor, repose, pride in what is abandoned, beautification of the body in order to render it healthy and shapely, and the seeking of good clothes. These things feed the sensual pleasure which the dragon placed in Eve's mouth. We, too, know that we are children of Adam from the evil thoughts which have made us enemies of God. Blessed, then, is the one who has been crucified, who has died, been buried, and arisen in newness, when he sees himself in the natural condition of Jesus, following his holy footprints which were made when he was incarnated for the sake of his holy saints. Therefore, it is to God that belong humility, baseness, poverty, detachment, forgiveness, peace, enduring reproach, not caring for the body, not fearing the conspiracies of evil people, and—the greatest of these—knowing everything before it occurs, and tolerating people with calmness.

8. It is not clear whether this is being said by Abba Isaiah or his disciple Peter.

So, one who has reached these and eliminated the condition that is contrary to nature, shows that he is truly from Christ, and is the son of God and brother of Jesus, for to him is due glory and worship to the ages of ages. Amen.

19

On Passions[1]

I TOO, LIKE TO SAY WITH THE PROPHET ISAIAH, '*I have been patient like a woman in labor, until I dry <the passions> up and destroy them*'.[2] If, then, you see that the source of the Holy Spirit is dwelling within you, this is the sign that they have been dried up and destroyed. As our Savior said, '*The kingdom of God is neither here nor there, but within you*',[3] for there are some people who talk about the things of the kingdom, but do not accomplish them, and there are others who accomplish the works of the kingdom, but neither with vigilance nor with knowledge. Those in whom the Savior's words, 'The kingdom of heaven is within you' have taken effect, are few, rare, and difficult to find. To these the Holy Spirit of God has come, and in them the words of the Evangelist John, '*To those who believed in His name, He gave power to become children of God, for they were born not of blood, or of the will of the flesh, or of the will of man, but of God*',[4] have been fulfilled.

These are the ones who have been rid of the sorrow that possessed Eve, namely, '*In grief you will bring forth children*'.[5] They are the ones who have been rid of the bitter decision issued against Adam, that

1. On passions, see Athanasius of Alexandria, *Against the heathen* 1:3–5, SCh 18; Gregory of Nyssa, *On the creation of man* 18; Dorotheus, *Instruction* 11:113–23; and Symeon the New Theologian, *Catecheses* 5, 7, and 10. See also *Discourses* 2 and 28.
2. Is 42:14.
3. Lk 17:21.
4. Jn 1:12, 13.
5. Gn 3:16.

'*Cursed is the earth because of your works*'.[6] They are the ones who have seized the joy received by Mary, that '*The Spirit of God will come upon you, and the power of the Most High will overshadow you*',[7] for just as grief possessed Eve and her descendants until now, joy also seized Mary and her descendants to this day. This is why, therefore, since we were once the children of Eve <and know her curse that came upon us through our dishonorable thoughts>, so we, too, must know that we are born of God through the confession of the Holy Spirit, as well as through the sufferings of Christ, if these are truly in our body, for it is written by the apostle, '*Test yourselves to see whether Christ is in you; unless, indeed, you fail to meet the test*'.[8] Therefore, when we wore the image of the earthly flesh,[9] we knew that we were his children, through the dishonorable matter of his thoughts that dwell in us, namely the passions. However, those who have put on the image of the heavenly nature,[10] know that they are his children through the Holy Spirit which lives in them, for Isaiah cried out, saying, '*In fear of you, Lord, we conceived, experienced the pangs of labor, and gave birth.* We gave birth to the spirit of salvation on the earth'.[11] Again, it is written in Ecclesiastes, 'Like bones in the womb of a woman in labor, such is the way of the Spirit',[12] for just as the Holy Virgin conceived him in flesh, so also those who have received the grace of the Holy Spirit, conceive him in their heart, according to the apostolic word, '*Christ may dwell in the inner person within your hearts through faith, as you are being rooted and grounded in love, in order that you may be able to present yourselves with all the saints*'.[13] Again, '*But we have this treasure in clay jars, so that it may be made clear that this extraordinary power belongs to God, and does not come from us*'.[14]

If, then, you have attained these words, '*being transformed into the*

6. Gn 3:17.
7. Lk 1:35.
8. 2 Co 13:5.
9. Cf. 1 Co 15:49.
10. Cf. 1 Co 15:49.
11. Is 26:18.
12. Cf. Qo 11:5.
13. Ep 3:16–18.
14. 2 Co 4:7.

same image from one degree of glory to another',[15] and the words of the apostle, '*Let the peace of Christ rule in your hearts*'[16] have been fulfilled in you; if Christ Jesus is in your intellect, and you have attained these words, '*The light of God's knowledge has shone out of darkness in your hearts*',[17] and the saying, '*Be dressed for action and have your lamps lit; be like those who are waiting for their master to return from the wedding banquet*'[18] is fulfilled in you, so that your mouth may not be sealed, having no defense among the saints; if you know that your vessel contains oil, like the wise virgins, in order to enter the bridal chamber and not be left outside;[19] if you have perceived that your spirit, your soul, and your body have been blamelessly united, and will rise spotless in the day of our Lord Jesus Christ, and you have become beyond reproof and condemnation in your conscience; if you have become an infant, according to the Savior's words, '*Let the little children come to me; for it is to such as these that the kingdom of heaven belongs*',[20] then you have truly become his bride, and his Holy Spirit has inherited you, even while you are still in the body. If, however, this is not the case, expect sorrow and bitter sighing, because shame and reproach will bring you before the saints. Know this, just as a young woman arises each morning and deals with no other concern before she beautifies herself for her lover, often using a mirror in case any spot appears on her face and she is not pleasing to her lover, the saints also show great care, day and night, to examine their actions and thoughts to find out if they are under the yoke of God and the Holy Spirit or not.

Therefore, brother, struggle hard, with pain of heart and body, as well as with knowledge, to acquire that eternal joy, for those who are deemed worthy of it are few, having acquired *the sword of the Spirit*,[21] and liberated their soul and senses from every defilement of the passions,[22] as the apostle said.

15. 2 Co 3:18.
16. Col 3:15.
17. 2 Co 13:5; 4:6.
18. Lk 12:35–36.
19. Cf. Mt 25:1–13.
20. Mt 25:1–13; 19:14.
21. Ep 6:17.
22. Cf. 2 Co 7:1.

God is powerful enough, however, to assist us in our weakness, in order that we be made worthy to arrive there with his saints. Amen.

20

On Humility

WHAT IS HUMILITY? HUMILITY IS CONSIDERING oneself to be sinful[1] and not doing any good before God. The work of humility consists of being silent, not measuring oneself in anything, not loving strife, submission, looking downward, holding death before one's eyes, guarding oneself from falsehood, not holding vain conversations, not contradicting one's superior, not wishing to impose one's opinion, enduring insult, hating repose, subjecting oneself to ascetic discipline, being vigilant to cut off one's own will, and not irritating anyone.

Therefore, brother, take care to accomplish these <precepts> with precision, in order that your soul may not become a dwelling place of every passion, and be vigilant in each one of these, so that you do not end your life fruitlessly, to the ages. Amen.

1. Cf. John Damascene, *Sacred Parallels* PG 96:370.

21

On Repentance

SOMEONE[1] ASKED ABBA ISAIAH, 'What is repentance[2] and what does "to flee from sin"[3] mean?'

He replied, 'There are two ways: one of life and one of death.[4] The person who walks along one does not progress along the other. The person who walks along both is not yet reckoned for the kingdom, or for punishment. When such a person is dead, his judgment is in the hands of God, who also has mercy. Whoever wishes to enter the kingdom keeps watch over his actions because the kingdom puts an end to every sin. The enemies sow[5] but their thoughts do not grow. If, through the Spirit, a person contemplates the loving kindness of the Godhead,[6] the arrows of the enemy penetrate him.[7] He is, in effect, putting on the armor of the virtues,[8] which guards against the enemy, taking care not to allow him to be troubled. It frees him in order that, in his contemplation, he may

1. Note that the questioner is not necessarily Abba Peter but could be an unknown person.

2. On *metanoia*, repentance, see Basil, *Long Rules* Prologue, 6, and 55, and *Short Rules* 3–6, 8, 10–13, 17, 57, 177, 287–88, and 295; Cassian, *Conference* 20; Mark the Monk, *On repentance* PG 65:965–84; John Climacus, *Ladder* 5; Symeon the New Theologian, *Catecheses* 4–5, 23, 28, 30, and 32. See also *Discourse* 25.

3. On fleeing from sin, see Basil, *Long Rules* 5–6, 8, and 32, and *An Ascetical Discourse and Exhortation on the Renunciation of the World*; Cassian, *Conference* 3; Pseudo-Macarius, *Homily* 5; John Climacus, *Ladder* 1.

4. Cf. also *Didache* 1.1; *Letter of Barnabas* 18–20. Cf. Jr 21:8.

5. Cf. Mt 13:39.

6. Cf. 1 P 2:3.

7. Ep 6:16.

8. Cf. Ep 6:11.

see, know, and distinguish between the two ways, fleeing from one and embracing the other.'

'If a person knows the glory of God, he also knows the ferocity of the enemy. If a person knows the kingdom, he also knows Gehenna. If a person knows love, he also knows hatred. If a person knows the wrath of passion, he also knows the hatred of the world. If a person knows purity, he also knows the stench of impurity. If a person knows the fruit of the virtues, he also knows the fruit of evil. The one rejoices together with the angels[9] because of his works. The other knows that the demons rejoice because he has carried out their work.'

'If you do not flee from the enemies, you will not recognize their ferocity. How will you recognize the love of money unless you renounce[10] <it> and live in great poverty for the sake of God? How will you recognize the bitterness of envy unless you acquire gentleness? How will you recognize the disturbance of anger unless you acquire forbearance in everything? How will you recognize arrogance unless you acquire humility? How will you recognize the stench of evil unless you know loving-kindness? How will you recognize the disgrace of scandal unless you know yourself to be inferior? How will you know the rudeness of laughter unless you know compunction? How will you know the disturbance of despondency unless you order, perceive, and contemplate the light of God?'[11]

'All malice is the evil produce of enmity. All the virtues have only one mother, which is called the fear of God.[12] Those who acquire such fear in purity produce the virtues and cut off the branches of evil,[13] as I said. Therefore, acquire fear of God, beloved, passing all your time in tranquility, for the fear of God is the mother of virtues. If a person has not overcome these vices, he does not yet belong in the heavenly kingdom. He must gradually struggle until he has removed each of the passions mentioned.'

9. Cf. Lk 15:7.
10. On renunciation see *Discourse* 15.
11. Cf. 1 P 2:9; 1 Jn 1:5–7.
12. Cf. Pr 1:7.
13. On the branches of evil see *Discourse* 29.

'Here is the sign for the person who is anxious to know whether his struggle is successful or not: as long as the left[14] practices its own works, sin is not yet dead, neither are the virtues of the right concealed with him. It is written, "Present yourselves as slaves for obedience. You are slaves of the one you obey, either of sin, which leads to death, or of obedience, which leads to righteousness.[15] *Do you not perceive that Jesus Christ is in you? Unless you are counterfeit*".[16] James also says, "*If a person thinks himself to be religious but does not control his tongue, his piety is barren*".[17] The Holy Spirit teaches us all this. We learn to refrain from sin and to guard against it.'

'Repentance is to turn away from all sin because there is not only one sin. This is why the Old Person is called "sin".[18] As the apostle says, "*Do you not know that all the people in the stadium run but only one person receives the prize?*"[19] Who is this, then, other than the one who stands firm in the battle? It is also written, "The person who struggles exercises self-control".[20] Let us take care then, brothers. What is this care if not throwing ourselves before the goodness of our Lord Jesus Christ when we slip in his eyes?[21] He has power to stop the evil violence of our enemies; we are merely flesh and blood.'

Again, someone asked, 'What does it mean "to be quiet in the cell"?'[22]

He replied, 'To be quiet in the cell is to prostrate oneself before God; to do his powerful works and to resist every evil thought which comes from the enemy. All this is what is meant by "to flee from the world".'

Yet again, someone asked, 'But what is meant by "the world"?'

14. Cf. Mt 25:33.
15. Cf. Rm 6:16.
16. 2 Co 13:5.
17. Jm 1:26.
18. Cf. Rm 6:6.
19. 1 Co 9:24.
20. Cf. 1 Co 9:25.
21. Cf. Ps 55:22; 1 P 5:7.
22. On monastic silence, see Basil, *Long Rules* 13, 32, and 45, and *Short Rules* 47, 173, and 208; John Climacus, *Ladder* Step 11; Antiochus the Monk, *Homilies* 16, PG 89:1476ff, and 22, 1501ff; and Symeon the New Theologian, *Catechesis* 12.

He replied, 'The world is where sin is trained, unnatural acts are carried out, the will of the flesh is accomplished,[23] the body, and not the soul, is cared for, and where you think you will remain to boast in all this.'

'What I say, however, is not of my own authority but comes from the apostle John who says, "*Do not love the world or worldly things.*[24] *If anyone loves the world, the Father's love is not in him because everything in the world—carnal desire, lust of the eyes, vainglory of life—is not the Father's way of love but the world's. The world and worldly love are passing away but whoever is carrying out his will remains unto the ages of ages. Children, let nobody lead you astray. Whoever acts righteously is righteous, as the Father is righteous, but the person who commits sin belongs to the Devil. From the beginning the Devil has sinned.*[25] *The world's friendship is God's enmity*".[26] The apostle Peter, in order to make his children strangers to the world's sin, also says, "*I exhort you brothers, as strangers and foreigners, to abstain from carnal desires which wage war against the soul*".[27] Our beloved Lord Jesus, knowing that the world of sin disturbs, strengthens his own, until he has abandoned sin, with the words, "*The world's ruler is coming and in me he finds nothing of his*".[28] Again, Jesus says, "*The world is in the hand of the evil one*".[29] Yet again, regarding his own, he says, '*Of the world*'.[30] From which world has he withdrawn, unless from all training of sin?'

'The one who wishes to become a disciple of Jesus flees from the passions but only in order to remove them. He is not able to leave the dwelling place of God, nor to see the loving-kindness of his Godhead, unless he turns away from sin. Jesus, himself, says, "*The eye is the lamp of the body. When your eye is healthy your whole body shines but when your eye is bad your whole body is in darkness*".'[31]

'Watch, therefore, for unless the intellect is restored from evil to

23. Cf. Ep 2:3.
24. 1 Jn 2:15–17.
25. 1 Jn 3:7–8.
26. Jm 4:4.
27. 1 P 2:11.
28. Jn 14:30.
29. 1 Jn 5:19.
30. Jn 15:19.
31. Lk 11:34.

health, a person is not able to perceive the light of the Godhead. The darkness builds a high wall for the spirit and turns the soul into a desert. It is written in the gospel, "*No one having a lamp hides it under a measure but places it on the lampstand in order that those who are entering may see the light*".[32] It is said that the measure of this world is injustice. Inasmuch as the Spirit is against nature, the light of the Godhead cannot be contained inside the intellect, but in becoming a lamp, the light of the Godhead is in the intellect. The sin is thrown out and the sinner has peace. The intellect is taught through these commands. The Godhead himself announces, "*I say to the people who are listening: love your enemies, do good to those who hate you, bless those who curse you, pray for those who insult and pursue you*".[33] He says this to those who flee from the world, abandoning all that belongs to this age, preparing to follow their Savior and becoming lovers of a mature love, "*Get up, let us go hence*".[34] Where, then, does he take them when he says to them, "*Get up, let us go hence*"? He alone, then, takes their spirit out of the activities of this age and gives it rest in his kingdom. Because of this, he says to them, "*I am the vine you are the branches. Remain in me and I will remain in you. As the branch cannot bear fruit of its own accord unless it remains in the vine so you also cannot, unless you remain in me*".'[35]

'He says these words to those who have departed from the world because the Spirit is in them, dwelling in their hearts, "*I will not leave you orphans; I am coming to you*".[36] Therefore, if someone loves God and wishes to dwell in him, and not be left as an orphan, he takes care, first of all, to observe that Jesus protects him and dwells in him because *he is not far from us*[37] nor among us. There are only passions, nothing else, within us.'

'Therefore, brother, if you say that you have renounced the world but you find yourself doing worldly things you have not renounced it but are deceiving yourself. He has given to those who have truly

32. Lk 8:16.
33. Lk 6:27–28.
34. Jn 14:31.
35. Jn 15:5, 4.
36. Jn 14:18.
37. Ac 17:27.

renounced the world this sign, "The person loving his soul will utterly destroy it but the person who destroys it on account of me I will save".[38] How, then, does a person leave the world? Only through removing his all carnal desires. Again, he says, "*Who does not carry his cross and follow me cannot be said to be my disciple*".[39] Which cross, then, does he tell us to carry? Only to be always alert in the intellect, to hold it firm in the virtues and to descend from the cross, that is to say, to abstain in self-control from the passions until the intellect removes them and finally stands invincible.'[40]

'He has given a sign to those who have woken saying, "*In very truth I tell you, unless a grain of wheat, falling to the ground, dies it remains alone but if it dies it bears much fruit*".[41] In consoling those who, like the grain, have withered, he says, "*The person who serves me will be honored by my Father and where I am my servant will also be*".'[42]

'How, then, does he serve Jesus except by detesting the world, giving rest to his passions and perfecting his commandments. He keeps his perfect ones with him, saying, "*We have all left and you have not followed*". What will he do? Jesus shows them what he will be for them, saying, "*You, having followed me into the new world, when the Son of Man sits on the throne of his glory, you, yourselves, will also sit on twelve thrones, judging the twelve tribes of Israel. Everyone who has left brothers, sisters, father, mother, wife, fields, or houses on account of my name will receive in abundance and will inherit eternal life*".'[43]

'Our beloved Lord Jesus, knowing that unless a person is free from all anxiety,[44] his intellect is unable to ascend the cross, ordered him, therefore, to cut off all that attracted him or oppressed his intellect and to descend from the cross. This person, therefore, says to the One who comes, 'I will follow you, Lord, but first let me take

38. Cf. Mt 10:39.
39. Lk 14:27.
40. On spiritual warfare, see Pseudo-Macarius, *Homily* 21; Diadochus, *On spiritual knowledge*; Dorotheus of Gaza, *Instruction* 13:138–48; Symeon the New Theologian, *Catecheses* 3 and 6.
41. Jn 12:24.
42. Jn 12:26.
43. Mt 19:27–29.
44. Cf. 1 Co 7:32.

my leave from those in my house'.[45] Our beloved Jesus, knowing that, unless the person then kept a watch on his heart, he would be inclined again toward them and to what they were accomplishing in preventing him from his act of righteousness in going, says, '*No one, I say, who puts his hand to the plough and looks back is fit for the heavenly kingdom*'.[46] He also says, with sadness, '*If a person comes to me and does not hate his father, or mother, or wife, or children, or brothers, or sisters, in addition to his soul, he cannot be my disciple*'.[47] He says all this to teach us that the person who wishes to enter into his kingdom, unless he plans beforehand to hate in himself all that attracts his heart toward the world, will not be able to enter as he desires.'

'He warns us not to put our confidence in faith alone without works, saying, "*Entering, the king looked at the people who were reclining and saw there a man not wearing a wedding garment. He threw him into the outer darkness*".[48] They enter because they bear the name Christians, but are thrown outside because they do not do works. The apostle, knowing that a person is not able to love the things of God and the things of the world, wrote to his own Timothy, "*No soldier is involved with the affairs of life in order to please the person who enlisted him*".[49] Moreover, if anyone wrestles lawfully he is crowned.[50] To strengthen him in the hope that his labors were not in vain, he also said to him, "*The hardworking farmer ought to be first in partaking of his fruits*".[51] Writing to others, he also said, "*The unmarried individual cares for the Lord's things but the married one cares for the world's things*".[52] The one who listens, takes heed of the terrible voice which says, "*Throw him into the outer darkness where there is wailing and gnashing of teeth*".'[53]

'Let us do, then, what will enable us to put on the garment of virtues, brothers, in order that we might not be thrown outside

45. Lk 9:61.
46. Lk 9:62.
47. Lk 14:26.
48. Mt 12:11, 13.
49. 2 Tm 2:4.
50. Cf. 2 Tm 2:5.
51. 2 Tm 2:6.
52. 1 Co 7:32–33.
53. Mt 22:13.

because on that day there will be no preference in his eyes.[54] On account of this, the apostle says to his own, '*The people who do these things cannot enter the kingdom of God*'.[55] That is why the apostle, seeing that those who merit to be raised up from dead passions, no longer having an opponent, points out to them the fruit of the Spirit: '*Love, joy, peace, long-suffering, kindness, goodness, faithfulness, meekness, self-control. Against such things I say there is no law*'.[56]

'Our beloved Lord Jesus, pointing out to us that the work must be manifested on that day, says, "*Many seek in order to enter and are not able to do so because the master of the house has risen and has shut the door. He will then say to those who knock, I do not know you*".[57] We are not able to say that God ignores something, when he hears, 'Lord, Lord, open it for us',[58] because he says to them, "*I do not know you*". He shows us again the fate of those who possess the faith without having works, and say, "Lord, Lord".'

'God purifies those who bear good fruit in order that he will carry more. Again, showing us that he does not love those who carry out their carnal desires, he prays, "*I pray, not concerning the world, but concerning those whom you have given me, because they are yours.*[59] *I take them up from the world, because the world loves its own,*[60] *saying, Father guard them from the Evil One because they are not of the world*".'[61]

'Let us examine ourselves, therefore, brothers. Are we of the world, or not? If we are not of the world, he guards us from the evil one. For he says, "*But I pray, not only concerning these but also those who believe in me through their word, that all may be one as we are one*",[62] and again, "*Where I am, may they also be, with me*".'[63]

54. Cf. Rm 2:11.
55. Ga 5:21; cf. 1 Co 15:50.
56. Ga 5:22–23.
57. Lk 13:24–25.
58. Lk 13:25.
59. Jn 17:9.
60. Jn 15:19.
61. Jn 17:15.
62. Jn 17:20–21.
63. Jn 17:24.

'See now, therefore, with how great a love he has loved us. We the ones who have fought in this world and hate the carnal desires of our heart because we reign with him in eternity.[64] The apostle John, contemplating that great glory, says, "*We know that when he is made manifest we will be like him*",[65] that is to say, if we keep his commandments and do, before him, that which pleases him in his eyes.'

John also says, '*Do not wonder, beloved, if the world hates you. We know that we have been removed from death into life because we love our brothers*'.[66] Again, '*Everyone not doing righteousness or loving his brother does not belong to God*'.[67] Elsewhere, John says, '*The one doing righteousness has been created by God. The one committing sin belongs to the devil*'.[68] Also, '*The one created by God does not sin because His seed remains in him. He is not able to sin because he has been created by God*'.[69]

Let us do, then, what we can, brothers, with the encouragement of these witnesses.[70] His kindness, with which we are pitied, empowers us to remove the burdens of this impure world.[71] Do not be silent! Our enemy pursues us at all times, seeking to capture our souls,[72] but our Lord Jesus is with us, rebuking him through his holy words,[73] if we observe them, for how can one make an obstacle to hinder the enemy except with the words which God has said against him? They oppose and crush him without anyone's knowledge.

'The apostle Peter educates and shows us the saving works of humanity, saying, "*Supplement your faith with virtue and virtue with knowledge, knowledge with self-control, self-control with steadfastness, steadfastness with godliness, godliness with brotherly love, and brotherly love with love. We, possessing these things are kept from being ineffective or unfruitful*

64. Cf. Rv 22:5.
65. 1 Jn 3:2.
66. 1 Jn 3:13–14.
67. 1 Jn 3:10.
68. Cf. 1 Jn 2:29.
69. 1 Jn 3:9.
70. Cf. Heb 12:1.
71. Cf. 2 P 1:4.
72. Cf. 1 P 5:8.
73. Cf. Mk 9:25.

in recognizing our Lord Jesus Christ. The person who lacks these things is shortsighted and blind, forgetting that he has been cleansed of his past sins".'[74]

'John the Baptist also says, "*Produce fruit worthy of repentance. Even now the axe is laid at the root of the trees; every barren tree is being cut down and thrown into the fire*".'[75]

'Our Lord Jesus says, "*The tree is known by its fruit*".[76] *Do people gather grapes from thorns, or figs from thistles?*'[77] Again, '*Not everyone saying, "Lord, Lord" to me will enter the heavenly kingdom but the ones doing the will of the Father, who is in the heavens*'.[78]

'Elsewhere, James says, "*Faith without works is dead. The demons believe this and shudder*",[79] for just as the spirit is dead when it is apart from the body, faith, when it is apart from works, is dead.'

'The apostle, instructing his infants that faith requires works, strongly advocates, "*It is not suitable for you, his holy ones, to name fornication and uncleanness. It is more fitting for you to give thanks, knowing that every fornicator, unclean or greedy man who is an idolater has no inheritance in the kingdom of God. Let no one deceive you with empty words. Because of these things the wrath of God is coming on the sons of disobedience. Do not associate with them for you were once darkness but now you are light in the Lord. Walk as children of light for the fruit of the spirit is in all goodness and righteousness and truth.*[80] *Let every bitterness, and anger, and wrath, and noise be removed from you along with all evil*".[81] He also says, "*Be my imitators as I am Christ's*",[82] and, "*For as many as are baptized into Christ, put on Christ*".[83]

'Let us examine ourselves, therefore, brothers. Have we put on Christ, or not? Christ, is recognized through purity because he is pure and lives in the pure. How, then, do we become pure

74. 2 P 1:5–9.
75. Mt 3:8, 10; Lk 3:8, 9.
76. Mt 12:33.
77. Mt 7:16.
78. Mt 7:21.
79. Jm 2:17, 19, 20, 26.
80. Ep 5:3, 5–9.
81. Ep 4:31.
82. 1 Co 11:1.
83. Ga 3:27.

except by no longer committing the evil which we have already committed? Such is the goodness of God that, in the same hour that a person turns away from his sins, he receives him with joy, without imputing him about his former sins. It is written in the gospel concerning the younger son who ended by squandering his share among the pigs caring for them with their food and satiating himself with their scraps. Later, as he repented, he understood that he had made no satisfaction through his sins, except by work. The more one commits, the more one burns. At this moment, therefore, he repents without delay and returns to his father's house in humility, abandoning all his carnal desires, for, in effect, he believes that his father is merciful and that he does not impute him for his action. That is why his father immediately arranges that the robe of purity and security of adoption be given to him.[84]

'Our Lord Jesus Christ tells us this so that, if we turn to him, he will first of all leave us the food of the swine and then he will receive us because we are pure. He says this in order that despondency be taken away from the soul when we ask, When will God hear me? He knows the moment when the one who asks is worthy of receiving justice and then he will immediately forgive him.'[85]

'So let us turn with a whole heart and be encouraged in our prayer[86] and he will be swift to listen to us because he says, "*Ask and it will be given to you, seek and you will find, knock and it will be opened to you*".[87] If, therefore, brothers, we ask, or seek, or knock, we know that it is necessary to seek, or ask him because, coming to his friend in the middle of the night, he will enfold him, saying, "Lend me three loaves because one of my friends has arrived from his journey". To the one who stands knocking, it will be given.'

'Let us, therefore, throw laziness far away from us, brothers, and let us prepare ourselves for a similar boldness. If God sees our steadfastness, he will give us what we ask because he is merciful[88] and wills the conversion of humanity, as it is written, "*Truly I tell*

84. Cf. Lk 15:11–32.
85. Cf. Lk 18:7.
86. Cf. Lk 18:1.
87. Mt 7:7; Lk 11:9.
88. Cf. Ps 86:15.

you that there will be joy in heaven over one repenting sinner".[89] In this way, brothers, we will enjoy such an abundance of his mercy.

'Let us work with a whole heart while we are still in our bodies because our life span is brief. If we struggle, we will inherit eternal and ineffable joy, but if we turn back, we will become like the young man who asked the Lord Jesus how he could be saved.[90] He replied, "*Sell everything you have and give to the poor.*[91] Take your cross and follow me".[92] He pointed out to him that the inclination to lament is to be saved. Hearing these things, he became exceedingly sad and went away.[93] He learned that work is not to give his things to the poor but to carry the cross. To distribute to the poor is not the only virtue; a person accomplishes it by carrying the cross. He engenders love and without the cross there is no love.'

There is no charity in presuming to have a virtue or a perfection of the virtues. The apostle says, '*If I speak in the languages of men and angels, or give away all my possessions and deliver my body to be burned but do not have love, I am a noisy gong or a clanging cymbal. Love suffers long, is kind, not jealous, is not proud, or arrogant or rude. It does not seek its own things, is not provoked. It does not resent evil.*'[94]

'The person who wishes, then, to walk in the way of love is free from the care of anyone, good or bad. The eager desire of God dwells in his heart. This desire engenders hostility in him to conform to nature. Anger sets him against everything coming from the enemy. The law of God, then, finds pasture in him and through fear love manifests itself in him and, finally, this person says, like the apostle, "*I am ready, not only to be bound, but also to die in the name of our Lord Jesus Christ*".[95] Blessed is the soul who attains such love; it has become unsurpassable.'

'We have left the world, brothers, and we know where we are because the Lord Jesus is merciful and he will give rest to each

89. Lk 15:7.
90. Cf. Mt 19:16–21.
91. Mt 19:21.
92. Cf. Mt 16:24.
93. Cf. Mt 19:22.
94. 1 Co 13:1, 3–5.
95. Ac 21:13.

one, according to his actions; the least according to his paucity, as it is written: According to my Father, there are many rooms.[96] If, therefore, the kingdom is for one, each one finds his place and his work in it.'

'Let us, therefore, struggle accordingly, brothers, against laziness[97] and tear out the shroud of darkness from ourselves, that is to say, oblivion and we will see the light of repentance.'

'Let us have the example of Martha and Mary before us, that is to say, mortification and mourning before the Savior. This is why he raised Lazarus, whose spirit was bound up by the many strips of cloth of one's own desires. He had pity and restored him to life but the others remain bound. He untied and released Lazarus. Then the zeal of Mary and Martha was shown. Lazarus found the others free from anxiety, reclining at table with Jesus. While Martha carries out her duty with diligence and joy, Mary carries the alabaster jar of myrrh and anoints the Lord's feet.'[98]

'Let us struggle, then, brothers according to our power and God will assist us, according to the abundance of his mercy. If we have not guarded our hearts, as our fathers did, and do all we can to guard our body from sin, as God desires, we believe that, when the time of famine assails us, he will have pity and treat us as his holy ones. There is one glory of the sun, and another of the moon, and star differs from star in glory[99] but is in a holy and secure foundation. Their glory and honor belong to him, both now and until the ages of ages. Amen.'

96. Cf. Jn 14:2.
97. Cf. John Climacus, *Ladder* Step 4.
98. Cf. Jn 11 and 12:1–3.
99. Cf. 1 Co 15:41.

22

On the Conduct of the New Person[1]

MY DEAR BROTHERS, THE JEW is known by three works: circumcision, Passover, and Sabbath. It is written in Genesis, '*The child who is eight days old, the one who is born in the house and he who is bought with money will be circumcised by you. The one who is not circumcised will be utterly destroyed from its family because he has broken my covenant*'.[2] Abraham was the first to be circumcised.[3] This signified that the left[4] was no longer alive in him. Such a figure was given to the patriarchs as an example. The New Person was made manifest in the Lord Jesus' holy body. The Old Person is the one who concealed his penis, was circumcised, and buried. The apostle says, '*In him you were circumcised with a circumcision not made with the hand of man but by putting off the body of flesh in the circumcision of Christ. You were buried with him in baptism; you were also raised up in him through faith in the working of God*',[5] and '*It was necessary to put off your old nature which belonged to your old life. The Old Person is corrupted through deceitful lusts. You are renewed by the transformation of your thought and put on the New Person, created in the likeness of God, in righteousness, holiness and truth*',[6] and again, '*You die to sin and live to righteousness*'.[7]

1. The discourse is based on Ep 4:22–24.
2. Gn 17:12–14.
3. Cf. Gn 17:24.
4. Cf. Pr 4:27; Mt 25:33.
5. Col 2:11–12.
6. Ep 4:22–24.
7. 1 P 2:24.

That is all concerning circumcision. The one who does not have that is neither circumcised, nor Jew, because he violated the Covenant which the Lord Jesus established through his own sacred blood.[8]

There is also much to say about the holy Passover: first, circumcision; second, the Passover; third, the Sabbath. Moses said, '*This is the Law regarding the Passover. No stranger nor slave bought with money will partake of it, but every circumcised slave bought with money will eat it. The man who is not circumcised will not eat it. In one house it will be eaten, girding your loins, your sandals on your feet and your staff in your hand.*'[9] It is not possible to eat the Passover meal unless it has been '*cooked in the fire*'[10] and is accompanied by '*unleavened bread and bitter herbs*'.[11]

Moses did not say, 'Have your girdle round your loins', in case someone said that he talked about the waist, but '*girding your loins*'.

Regarding purity, Moses also said 'Free from all passions', which depend on impure carnal business.

He talks about sandals because of the readiness[12] to flee from every sting which injures the conscience and prevents the intellect from seeing its contemplation in purity.

The staff symbolizes the courageous hope of journeying without fear on the way and entering the promised land. All this is remembered on the Sabbath.

The blood symbolizes our Lord Jesus Christ's blood[13] when he returns in his Parousia and takes back the children of Israel, his inheritance. They appear ready and anointed. His sign will be clearly visible on their souls.

Regarding the sprig of hyssop, this symbolizes mortification because Moses says, '*Eat this with bitter herbs*'.

Examine yourselves, therefore, brother. Are you circumcised?

8. Cf. Lk 22:20.
9. Ex 12:43–48.
10. Ex 12:8.
11. Ex 12:8.
12. Cf. Ep 6:15.
13. Cf. Heb 9:12.

Have you anointed the lintels of your house with the blood of the spotless Lamb?[14] Have you turned away from all worldly thought? Are you prepared to walk fearlessly and enter the Promised Land?

There is also much to say about the Sabbath. It also belongs to those who have been deemed worthy of true circumcision who have eaten the holy Passover meal, who have been delivered from the Egyptians, who have seen all those who have drowned in the Red Sea,[15] and who have celebrated the Sabbath after their bitter slavery.[16]

God says to Moses, '*Work on six days. The seventh day is the Sabbath rest of the Lord*'.[17]

Now our Lord Jesus Christ himself will celebrate the true Sabbath. He has taught his own that it is necessary to celebrate it, ascending the cross on the day of preparation. He made all his own preparation, that is to say, the injuries which he suffered for us, before ascending the cross. Nailed there himself, he will support them without removing, or loosening himself from the wood. He only had enough breath to cry, '*I thirst*',[18] so that they brought him a sponge of vinegar. After tasting it, he cried, '*It is accomplished*',[19] and someone lifted his motionless body down.[20]

Now, the Lord Jesus celebrated the Sabbath in truth. He rested on the seventh day. He consecrated it. He, himself, rested from all his work,[21] through which he had annulled human passion,[22] as the apostle says, 'Enter into his rest. He rests from all his labors as God did from his.'[23]

This is the true Sabbath.[24] The person who does not celebrate it is not Jewish, for as Jeremiah, weeping over the people, said, '*Carry*

14. Cf. Ex 12:7.
15. Cf. Ex 15:19.
16. Cf. Heb 4:9.
17. Ex 20:9–10.
18. Jn 19:28.
19. Jn 19:30.
20. Cf. Jn 19:40.
21. Gn 2:2; Ex 20:11.
22. Cf. Rm 6:6.
23. Heb 4:10.
24. Cf. Pseudo-Macarius, *Homily* 35.

no burdens on the Sabbath. Do not go out through the gates of Jerusalem, carrying burdens on the Sabbath'.[25]

What a miserable wretch I am, sinning against the holy commandments! I, who carry heavy burdens on the Sabbath! In carrying, I have died with him[26] and have celebrated the Sabbath with him.

What is this heavy burden that I carry, this sin that I bring to fulfillment? The hostile burden is anger, jealousy, hatred, vainglory, gossip, to prick, to provoke, arrogance, self-centeredness, to bustle about, to quarrel, to love oneself, and envy. I carry all that in my soul.

As for the body, its burden is greed, vanity, sensual delight, lust, passion, and a loose heart.

All these and similar burdens the Lord Jesus wiped out in the body of saints and put to death in his holy body. As the apostle said, '*Through the cross he kills the enemy within him*'.[27] The Law and the commandments were all brought to naught on the holy Sabbath.[28]

And so, how can the person who carries these heavy burdens and works on the Sabbath say, 'I am a true Jew'? Such a person deceives himself.[29] He is only insisting that he is a Jew by name and will not, therefore, receive anything from the Lord Jesus because he disowns him because of his actions.[30] He has brought back to life that which he has killed and refreshes that which he has buried. He is clearly not a true Jew but an imposter who is not circumcised and has not celebrated the Sabbath.

Therefore, when the Lord Jesus comes in his glory,[31] he will enable the children of Israel to enter into his eternal kingdom, all those whom he has gathered from all the nations, all who are circumcised for him. As the apostle says, '*Hardness has come on part of Israel until all the nations have entered*'[32] and '*Peace and mercy to all*

25. Jr 17:2.
26. Cf. 2 Tm 2:11.
27. Ep 2:16; Cf. Ep 2:14–15.
28. Cf. Heb 4:9.
29. Cf. 1 Jn 1:8.
30. Cf. Tt 1:16.
31. On eschatology see *Discourse* 16.
32. Rm 11:25.

the people, and God's Israel, who follow this rule'.[33] Therefore, you see that God's Israelites are the people who have circumcision of the heart, those who keep the Sabbath and wipe out sin. He also says, '*He is not a true Jew who is only outwardly Jewish, nor is circumcision an outward show. The true Jew, however, is inwardly Jewish and circumcision is a spiritual, not a literal, matter of the heart.*'[34]

Let us, therefore, be attentive ourselves, brothers. Are we as attentive when we work hard and lose ourselves in our labor by our negligence, unaware that our enemy is in us, flattering and gnawing away at us every day, not allowing our eyes to contemplate anything of light and divinity?

Examine yourself, wretched one, who has been baptized into Christ and his death.[35] What sort of death is it that he died? If you follow his footsteps,[36] show me your way of life. He is sinless and presents himself to you in everything. He has walked in poverty. He did not make a place to rest his head.[37] You, however, do not joyfully endure being a stranger. He endured insults but you cannot bear any injury. He has not returned evil for evil, you cannot resist returning evil. He was not angry when he suffered. You, on the other hand, are irritated when you do suffer. He was not distressed when someone insulted him, but you become agitated, even when someone is not insulting you. He humbled himself, comforting those who sinned against him. You injure with words even those who love you. He joyfully tolerated afflictions but you are disturbed by the least new unpleasantness. He, he was with those who had fallen but you, you are arrogant to those who expiate you. He was handed over for those who had sinned against him, in order to ransom them. You are incapable of giving anything, even for those who love you.

See what he has given you. What do you give him in return? Know him through his works and you through yours. *If you have died with him*,[38] who commits these sins?

33. Ga 6:16.
34. Rm 2:28–29.
35. Cf. Rm 6:3.
36. Cf. 1 P 2:21.
37. Cf. Mt 8:20.
38. 2 Tm 2:11.

Beloved, let us be attentive, as it is necessary, to his holy commandments. Let us remove our will and we will see the light of the commandments.

If we love the person who holds us in high esteem, what more can we do than the heathen?[39] Do you pray for benefactors? *Even tax-collectors do as much*![40] If you take delight with the one who praises you, the Jew already does this. What more, therefore, are you doing? *You, who are dead to sin and alive in Christ Jesus*?[41] If you only love the person whom you obey, what more can you do than the sinner? The sinner does as much. If you hate the one who makes you suffer, disobeys and annoys you, you are like the heathen. Instead, it is necessary to pray in order to receive forgiveness. If you have become annoyed with the person who insults you, the tax collector does this too.

Examine yourself, therefore, you who have been baptized in Jesus' name, if these are his works by which he is made manifest. How will you appear and be crowned on the day of his glory, if you do not have the crown of victory over the passions? Your king has already overcome them, presenting himself to you as a model in his glory, for he, *the King of kings and Lord of lords*,[42] will appear in his great glory, in the sight of every nation, bearing marks of the one who suffered for us. You, however, intend to appear without having any of his sufferings in your body. He will say, '*I do not know you*',[43] but you intend to see all the saints who have died for his name, bearing his mark,[44] but you will not and will be ashamed to appear before them.

Search for the way of the saints and you will discover that they have endured evil but have not returned it.[45] Their blood cries out, '*Avenge us against those who live on earth*',[46] but I, who love rest, what will I have to say on that day, seeing prophets and apostles,

39. Cf. Mt 5:46.
40. Mt 5:47.
41. Rm 6:11.
42. Rv 19:16.
43. Mt 25:12.
44. Cf. Rv 7:3.
45. Cf. Rm 12:17.
46. Rv 6:10.

martyrs and all the other saints who have endured punishment, without returning evil or being angry. They persuaded those who were angry that it was not any human will but the injustice of the devil which compelled their persecutors to treat them so cruelly. The saints were not annoyed with those who sent them to death or stoning,[47] to burning or drowning. They prayed for them, in order that they would receive forgiveness, knowing the one who forced them to do these things.

Examine yourself, then, dear brother. What more can you do? Take notice of this thought. What do you have in the eyes of God? You cannot do anything to conceal it in that hour.[48] The one who speaks will not pay attention to the human will. When the Resurrection comes, each person will be raised so they may account for their behavior, which they have worn like a garment, whether righteous or sinful. His conduct will be known and his place will be determined.

Blessed are those who have fought and deprived the one who dragged them toward Gehenna, putting on that which pulled them toward the kingdom. The apostle says, '*We know that if this earthly tent is destroyed that we have a house which is made by God, eternal and heavenly. It is not a building made by human hands.*'

The length of our life is nothing.[49] We deceive ourselves each day until we reach that hour in which we groan with everlasting tears.

Let us not relax our heart but do our utmost with care and vigilance, imploring the loving-kindness of God at all times to help us. Do not let us grow angry with those who involuntarily utter foolish thoughts. Being imperfect, they serve as instruments of the enemy. They become estranged from God until they are thrown out and flee from the stadium.

Have care in everything, beloved, in behaving with humility, suffering injury,[50] with patience, bearing insults and use every hour

47. Cf. Heb 11:37.
48. Cf. Lk 12:2.
49. Ps 39:5; Jm 4:14.
50. On suffering see Origen, *Commentary on Matthew* 10:18; Basil, *Quod Deus non est auctor malorum* PG 31:329–353; John Chysostom, *Ad Stagirium a daemone*

to renounce your will because holding on to it loses all the virtues. The person whose thoughts are clearly righteous removes his will in gentleness, fearing discord like a dragon who overturns the entire building, shrouding the soul until it no longer sees the light of the virtues.

Take care, therefore, of this confounded passion which mixes itself with the virtues until they are completely destroyed. Our Lord Jesus did not ascend the cross before driving out Judas from the midst of his disciples. If a person does not remove this vile passion, he is unable to progress toward God because of all the evil which follows him. Do not be proud in tolerating it, however. God hates all rivalry and arrogance which dwells in the soul and persuades everything in the heart to come to God. According to all the Scriptures, this is deceit.

Therefore, to judge yourself, behave with humility before everything else. Secondly, consciously renounce your will. Purity consists of praying to God. Do not allow yourself to rest but rather to weep. Do not judge others but show charity. Long-suffering consists in not thinking anything against your neighbor. The heart which loves God does not allow you to bother yourself with things which do not concern you. Poverty requires an innocent heart. To master one's understanding leads to peace, to endure needs gentleness, to show mercy is to have compassion. In order to do all this, it is necessary to remove your will, to have harmony among your virtues, and to put the untroubled intellect at the head.

In the final reckoning, I do not read in any of the Scriptures that God has any will for us other than we humble ourselves in all things before our neighbor, we remove all our own will, plead without ceasing for his assistance, and guard our eyes against the sleep of oblivion[51] and the error of captivity. Human nature is prone to evil and mutability. From God comes care, the power to guard oneself, to shelter that which protects our poverty, conversion which brings us back to him, grace to thank him, and protection which guards

---

vexatum PG 47:423–94, and *Quod nemo laeditur*; Maximus the Confessor, *Ad Thalassium, quaestio* 61 PG 90:625–41.

51. Palladius, *Lausiac History* 10.

us from the hand of our enemies. To him belongs honor and glory unto the ages. Amen.

All this, however, gives rise to contention which cruelly overthrows the soul, gossip, curiosity, adulation, license, duplicity, and arrogance. The virtues in the soul of the person who has all this are barren. If, after all this, the soul does not sweat over each virtue, it cannot expect to attain the rest of the Son of God.[52]

Do not, therefore, be careless of your life, brothers and your intellect will not seize the opportunity each day to sin or withhold you from good, before receiving the rest of the Son of God, which consists of humility in everything, innocence, no hatred for anyone and no consent to anything which does not come from God, but holding your sins before you and dying to all evil.[53] In his mercy, he comes to help us in our weakness. *God is not a liar.*[54]

52. Cf. Ps 95:10–11, and Mt 11:29.
53. Cf. Rm 6:2.
54. Cf. Ti 1:2.

23

On Perfection

One of the fathers said, 'Unless a person acquires faith in God, the continual desire for him, innocence, not returning evil for evil,[1] mortification, humility, purity, brotherly love, renunciation, gentleness, long-suffering, endlessly imploring with a troubled heart, true love—that is, not looking back to the one who follows[2]—concern for spiritual success, placing no confidence in his own good works or service,[3] and seeking God's aid against the one who appears each day, he cannot be saved. The enemies, O people, are not silent on your behalf.

Therefore, do not be careless or negligent. Pay attention to the conscience. Do not put confidence in one simply because you have attained one thing worthy of God. See yourself in the land of your enemies.[4] Mortification seizes the products of indifference and the compunction of perception heals the enemies' wounds from within. Perfect love of God, according to his will, resists the invisible wars because the hidden victory of purity is ready to receive the rest of the Son of God.[5] Shining purity guards the virtues.

If this is the product of knowledge, it is also the thing which guards. To find the action of thanksgiving at the moment of temptation causes a person to turn away from the things which arise.

1. Cf. Rm 12:17.
2. Cf. Ph 3:13.
3. Palladius, *Lausiac History* 20.
4. Cf. Ba 3:10.
5. Cf. Mt 11:29.

Not to believe that your labor is pleasing to God prepares one for his help in guarding you. The person who sees his heart seeking God,[6] in reverence and according to the truth, is not able to think that he pleases God because conscience disciplines him about such unnatural things. That person is a stranger to freedom, for as there is punishment, there is also an accuser. In as much as there is an accusation, there is no freedom.

If you see others as you pray, no evil one accuses you.[7] Then you are truly free and you have entered into God's holy rest,[8] according to his will.

If you see that the good fruit has grown stronger and that the charnel of the enemy is no longer choking it,[9] and that the enemy has resisted because it is no longer confident of its cunning, then you are no longer struggling against your understanding. If the cloud has enveloped the tent,[10] then *the sun does not burn you by day nor the moon by night.*[11]If you have found everything in readiness for the tent, and you keep it according to the will of God, then the victory comes to you from God. All the rest from now on will overshadow the tent[12] because it is his will and he will walk in front of it and prepare, beforehand, his place of rest, for unless he appoints a place for it as he wills, you will not be able to rest, as it says in the Scriptures.

Danger is great for the other person, until he knows himself and learns, with certainty, that there is nothing in him which comes from those who devote themselves to provocation through making the golden calf,[13] the symbol of unnatural things.

Therefore, we need to fear God's goodness which governs us and remember that which pricks us and allows holy humility to dominate our hearts at every hour, through the mercy of God.

Do not neglect all that which prepares these things and guards

6. OGtI 18 and 19.
7. Cf. Evagrius, *On prayer* 21:26, PG 79:1171.
8. Cf. Ps 95:11; Mt 11:29.
9. Cf. Mt 13:7, 25.
10. Cf. Ex 40:34; Nm 9:15.
11. Ps 121:6.
12. Cf. Ex 40:35.
13. Cf. Ex 32:4–10.

them, preserving the intellect until the end, in which we unceasingly know our sins. To put our confidence in ourselves is evil slavery.

To continue to judge our neighbor, to blame a brother, to despise him in the heart, to criticize him whenever possible, to angrily teach him a lesson, or to speak ill of him in front of somebody produces a stranger to mercy, which the saints have obtained, and glorious virtues. Such actions destroy the work accomplished by people and wipe out their good fruits.

If someone says, 'I weep over my sins', but commits another, he is foolish. If he says, 'I weep over my sins', but keeps another, he is deceiving himself.[14] The person who searches for quietness, but does not take care to remove the passions, is blind to the holy building of the virtues. The one who ignores his sins but is anxious to correct another is lazy in his requests of the heart and his exhortations to God.

This is a description of the brave person: the person who struggles against his former sins and implores to be completely pardoned, pleading for the power not to consent again in his heart, actions, and senses to sin. Unless the memory of his sins does not unceasingly rule his heart and he does not turn back to all that which is in the world, until there is no subjugation, he cannot contain his sins and he contains those already committed, apostatizing from being created by God in case he has judged him. Blessed is the person, therefore, who has been counted truly worthy of these things, neither through hypocrisy, nor satiety of malice.

This is the work of those who truly mourn in their intellect and senses for yielding to visible things: not to judge a neighbor. If your sins satisfy you, they render you a stranger to those neighbors of yours. To return evil for evil is to be far away from mourning. Not to take a worldly thing as a model through vainglory is for the spirit to be far away from mourning. To grieve that your opinion has not been taken as a model is to be far away from mourning. To want to do your will is to be far away from mourning. To carry out your will, whether good or bad, is to be far away from mourning. All this is completely shameful and base. That some people will know

14. Cf. 1 Jn 1:8.

about an affair which does not concern them is shameful and makes a person behave improperly, in evil captivity, which prevents him from knowing his sins.

If someone injures you and you are in some pain, true mourning is not found there. If, in a business affair, someone cheats you so that you suffer, fear of God is not found there. If someone has spoken a word to you which you do not remember but by which you are troubled, it is not there. If someone glorifies you and you accept their praise, it is not there. If someone insults you and you are saddened, it is not there. If you surround yourself with the illustrious of the world, desiring their friendship, it is not there. If, in a discussion, someone is in disagreement with you and you wish to keep your point, it is not there. If someone pours contempt on your words and causes you distress, it is not there. All this shows that the Old Person[15] is living and that he prevails because there is nobody there to fight him and that he is not truly mourning.

It requires spiritual eyes for the one who works according to God to know that he is an enemy of God.[16] If you keep the commandment of God and do all your work in the knowledge that it is being done because of God, if you are persuaded that you are not able to please God to the measure of his glory, and if you put your sins before your eyes, you will find yourself resisting the one who wishes to overturn you because of the thought that you are justified.

If you preserve the building constructed by mourning, then you will be aware that you know yourself. You will know where you dwell and that you do not put your confidence in your heart because you have obtained the victory. Moreover, if such a person has not appeared for judgment, has not heard the sentence and does not know where he will dwell, he cannot have faith because fear is pleasing to God.

According to God, grief, which gnaws at the heart, can be returned to the senses and vigilantly resists, keeping the faculties of the intellect sound. Because the person is insufficiently able to have confidence in himself, he does not cease from needing to work. Blessed are those who do not count on their work, as if it

15. Cf. Ep 4:22; Col 3:9.
16. Cf. Jm 4:4.

pleased the Lord, and are aware of meeting God. Because they do not depend on their work, they perceive his glory. They do not anticipate doing God's will, according to his wish, but recognize their weakness. They content themselves with their necessary grief, which they pour over themselves. They do not worry themselves about being created by God, by whom they are about to be judged.

Victory is for the person who works, bringing everything to perfection in God.[17] When he becomes perfect, according to his will, that is to say, when his name is written in the Book of the Living,[18] when those who dwell in heaven testify that he has escaped from the princes of the Left,[19] he will be remembered by those heavenly inhabitants.

Until that time there is war,[20] and humanity is in fear and trembling,[21] victor or vanquished today, he is vanquished or victor tomorrow,[22] because the struggle seizes the heart, but the active person ignores the war because he has received the prize and no longer has anxiety for the fate of the three distinct things which have arrived to make peace between them, thanks to God. According to the apostle,[23] these three things are the soul, the body, and the spirit. He says at one point in his epistle that when these three have become one, through the operation of the Holy Spirit, they cannot be separated again, For Christ died, is risen and no longer dies. *Death no longer rules over him.*[24] His death has become our salvation, because through his death sin has died, once for all,[25] and his resurrection is life[26] for all those who firmly believe in him and who have cured their own passions, in order that they live in God and produce the fruit of justice.[27]

17. Cf. Heb 13:21.
18. Cf. Rv 21:27.
19. Cf. Mt 25:33.
20. OGtI 18.
21. Cf. Ph 2:12.
22. Cf. Pseudo-Macarius, *Homily* 3.
23. Evagrius, *Tractatus ad Eulogium* 5–6 PG 79:1101. Cf. Mt 5:9 and 1 Th 5:23.
24. Rm 6:9.
25. Cf. Rm 6:10.
26. Cf. 1 P 1:3.
27. Cf. Ph 1:11.

Do not, therefore, fear death as if you were being assailed by the enemies during the watch, or sleep, because the wretched person is in the stadium, he lacks courage and, looking from afar, does not have confidence in his works. The senseless person, however, who falls every day seems vanquished because there is no struggle in the stadium.[28] That is why our Lord, sending his disciples to preach, says, '*Do not greet anyone on the road.*[29] Greet them in the house and *if there is a son of peace, remain there with him and your peace will rest there*'.[30] Again, Elisaie, sending Giezi, says to him, '*If you meet a person, do not greet him*[31] nor receive a blessing from him'. He knows that he did not render his life to the little infant nor was able to revive him. When the man of God entered, he saw the infant stretched out on the bed, closed the door on the infant and himself, led the struggle with each of the senses and knowingly, lay on the bed, close to the infant, descended and rose seven times and, according to the will of God, perceived the infant's senses as he opened his eyes.[32]

What have we to say, therefore, the wretched ones, preferring the glory of this world to the love of God, the ones who do not know how to fight, but are eager to enter into rest and do not know the long-suffering of God? He leaves the chaff with the good fruit and does not send someone to gather the chaff if the good fruit does not reach maturity.[33] Giezi ran along the road but did not arrive in time to revive the little infant, preferring the glory of people to the glory of God.

Blessed are the eyes which do not dare to know shame, looking steadily toward God. Blessed are the people who care about prudently healing their bruises, knowing their sins and praying for forgiveness, but misfortune to those who lose their opportunity, believing themselves to be sinless, trampling their conscience underfoot, wishing that it had not pricked them, nor recognizing their need.

28. Cf. 1 Co 9:24.
29. Lk 10:4.
30. Lk 10:6.
31. 2 Ch 4:29.
32. Cf. Ch 4:32-35.
33. Cf Mt 13:24–30.

Just as the farmer is left in vain with all the seed that he has scattered if it has not reached maturity, he is troubled because it has not ripened. In the same way, a person, if he knows every mystery and all knowledge[34] and does some wonders and cures,[35] if he suffers a number of ills and wears only his undergarments, is still under the power of fear because he has enemies who continue to track him down and plot against him, until he listens to this word, '*Love never falls but believes all, hopes all, endures all*'.[36]

How much trouble the Way of God is! Even as he says, '*Straight is the gate and narrow is the way which leads to life and few are those who find it*'.[37] We, the idle lovers of the passions, have it for a rest because we cannot carry the yoke as he says, '*Carry my yoke and learn from me because I am gentle, and lowly of heart and you will find rest for your souls. My yoke is easy and my burden is light*.'[38]

Who is the wise person, according to God? The one who struggles with all his power for mortification, in all work and flight, in meditation and vigilance, worrying that he will not find himself to be accounted worthy but calls on the name of God?

The passions at work in us, the Master, the Lord Jesus, came to put to death. He does not lead us according to the will of the flesh[39] but according to the Spirit and we make manifest all the will of the Father. In his command to his disciples, he says, '*We are unworthy slaves. We have done only what was our duty*.'[40] He says that to people who labor and guard their work, knowing those who rob and steal it.

If someone sees a dangerous animal, he flees in fear, whether it is a serpent, or snake, or scorpion, or any venomous animal. The shameless and wretched soul remains immobile before the things which would kill it, neither fleeing, nor creeping away, but taking pleasure in them, persuading the heart to obey. That is why the soul loses its opportunity and is barren and fruitless.

34. Cf. 1 Co 13:2.
35. Cf. Mt 7:22.
36. 1 Co 13:7–8.
37. Mt 7:14.
38. Mt 11:29–30.
39. Cf. Ga 5:16.
40. Lk 17:10.

24

On Tranquillity

On the way of virtues is the fallen, enmity, change, variation, excess, measure, distribution, discouragement, joy, heartache, gloom, peace of heart, progress, and violence. That is the journey you must undergo, until you attain rest.

But tranquillity is far from all that. Tranquillity lacks nothing because it dwells in God and God in it.[1] It no longer knows enmity, nor fall, nor unbelief, nor the effort to guard oneself, nor fear of the passions, nor any desire, nor pain caused through enmity. Its glories are great and innumerable.

As long as a person has fear of some passion, he is far from tranquillity. As long as a person has a heartfelt accusation against another, he is a stranger to tranquillity. The Lord Jesus took such a body and taught his own such love, to practice in joy.

With a view to all that, the ignorant think that they have arrived at tranquillity,[2] although the passions are still alive in their soul, and their body is not completely purified. They are wandering from their duty. God forgive me!

1. Cf. Jn 15:4.
2. Cf. Palladius, *Lausiac History*, 'Prologue'.

25

To Abba Peter, His Disciple

In informing me, 'I wish to do penance to God for my sins, if the Lord sets me free from the bitter care which I have of the world'; you do well to say, 'If I am set free from the work of this age'. It is not possible for the intellect to care for two things. As the Lord said, '*You cannot serve God and Mammon*'.[1] Mammon represents all the work of this world and unless a person renounces this, he cannot serve God. The service of God means not having anything extraneous in our intellect while praying to him, no sensual pleasure as we bless him, no malice while living fearlessly before him, no hatred while exalting him, no evil jealousy hindering us as we converse with him and no sensual pleasure in our limbs when calling him to mind, for all these things are full of darkness; they are a wall which imprisons our wretched soul, and it cannot worship God with purity whilst these remain in it. They impede its ascent in the air[2] and prevent it from meeting God. They hinder it from blessing him in secret,[3] offering prayers to him with sweetness of heart, and receiving his illumination. Because of this, the intellect is always shrouded in darkness and cannot progress toward God because it does not try to remove these thoughts by means of spiritual knowledge. There are two things that imprison the soul. The external one cares for bodily rest in this world but the internal one considers which of the passions

1. Mt 6:24.
2. Cf. 1 Th 4:17.
3. Cf. Mt 5:5.

hinder the virtues. The soul, however, does not see the interior one regarding the passions unless it is freed from the exterior one. This is why the Lord says, 'Whoever does not renounce all his wishes cannot be my disciple'.[4] The exterior one arises from the will but the interior one from outward behavior. Our Lord Jesus, knowing that the will dominates both, commanded its removal. The intellect, as much as the soul, regards the exterior one through mortification while the interior passions direct their energies against purity. If, however, the soul hears the word of Jesus, it removes all its own will, hates all the work of this age, raises the intellect and stands, until it is not thrown off course by its desires, unceasingly keeping watch over and guarding the soul, in case it returns to the things which were left behind and ill-treat it.

The soul is like a degenerate young woman living with her husband. Whenever her husband goes away, she neglects her housework but, when her husband returns home, she immediately becomes full of fear. She leaves what she was doing and busies herself according to her husband's wish whilst he busies himself on his return to all the necessary business of his house. In the same way, if the intellect is raised, it takes care of the soul and unceasingly guards it until it produces and nourishes its infants. From the time that both become a single heart,[5] the soul is submissive to the intellect and obeys it. As it is written by the apostle, '*The husband is the head of the woman*'[6] and again, '*The husband ought not to cover his head since he is the image and glory of God but the woman is the glory of man because the man was not made from the woman but the woman out of the man. Moreover, man was not created for woman but woman was created for man; that is why the woman needs to have on her head a sign of subjection because of the angels. But in the Lord's eyes there is no woman without man, nor man without woman, because, in the same way that the woman is taken from the man, the man is born through the woman and both come from God*'.[7] This word is for those who have been counted worthy of becoming one with the

4. Cf. Lk 14:33, 26.
5. Cf. Ac 4:32.
6. 1 Co 11:3.
7. 1 Co 11:7–12.

Lord and are no longer separated from him. Those who praise God in all purity, those who bless God with a holy heart, those whom God illumines[8] are all true worshipers whom God looks for.[9] Those are the ones of whom he says, '*I will live in them and I will walk among them*'.[10] He also says, '*If two work well together in everything, all that they will ask in my name will be given to them*'.[11] They therefore wish that their will be purified of visible matter, like one who is concealed in the soul, and from all that is hidden in the soul, and all that is wiped away in their body through his Incarnation. As God has said, '*Abide in me and I in you*'.[12] See, brother, God therefore wants us to live in him by our conduct and he will live in us through the purity according to our power.

But someone said, 'I live in you through Baptism but I cannot lead this life'. Listen, well beloved, it is certain that everyone who receives Baptism receives it for the wiping out of sin. As the apostle says, '*Through baptism we have been buried with him in death for wiping sin out of the body in order that we are no longer enslaved to sin*'[13] It is impossible for Christ and sin to live together. '*If, therefore, Christ lives in you, sin is dead and the spirit lives to the cause of justice*'.[14] As the apostle says, '*The woman is bound by law to her husband for as long as he lives but if her husband dies, she is legally released from her husband. It is, therefore, in living with her husband that she will be called adulterous if she sleeps with another man. But if her husband dies, she is freed by the law and is not adulterous if she sleeps with another man*'.[15] Also, the person who wishes to know that Christ lives in him will recognize Christ through his thoughts. If sin seduces his heart, God no longer lives in him and his Spirit does not find its rest in him. Therefore, of necessity, God lives in a person if he accomplishes works, and that person lives in God if his soul is free. As the apostle says, '*The person who is joined to a prostitute becomes a single body and*

8. Cf. Ep 1:18.
9. Cf. Jn 4:23.
10. 2 Co 6:16.
11. Mt 18:19.
12. Jn 15:4.
13. Rm 6:4, 6.
14. Rm 8:10.
15. Rm 7:2–3.

the one who is united with the Lord becomes a single spirit'.[16] In effect, all that is contrary to nature is called prostitution. If, therefore, the soul is freed and cleared of those things which impede its ascent in the air,[17] then it lives in God and participates in his Spirit according to the word, '*The person who is united with the Lord becomes a single spirit*'. It teaches him how to pray.[18] He unceasingly adores God, is united with him and lives in him, conducting himself and constantly giving rest to him, revealing his honors and ineffable graces to the Lord. It revives him through baptism[19] and the inspiration of his Spirit,[20] as it is written, '*The person who is born of God does not sin and the evil one does not touch him because he is born of God*',[21] as it is written by the evangelist, 'Unless you repent and become like little children, you will not be able to enter the kingdom of heaven',[22] and again, 'Become like little children newly-born, desiring spiritual milk, without deceit, in order to increase in him'.[23] What, then, is the work of the little infant? If someone hits the little infant, he cries, but he rejoices with those who rejoice with him.[24] If someone injures him, he does not become angry, and when someone praises him, he does not become boastful. If someone honors another more than him, he is not jealous.[25] If someone takes his business, he does not become troubled.[26] If someone leaves him a little something in an inheritance, he ignores it. He does not enter into judgment with anybody. He does not quarrel over his belongings. He hates no one.[27] If he is poor, he is not sad. If he is rich, he is not conceited. If he sees a woman, he does not desire her. Neither pleasure nor anxiety tyrannizes him. He judges no one nor lords it over anybody. He envies no one. He does not become arrogant if someone ignores

16. 1 Co 6:16–17.
17. Cf. 1 Th 4:17.
18. Cf. Rm 8:26.
19. Cf. Jn 3:5.
20. Pseudo-Macarius, *Homily* 30. Cf. Jn 20:22.
21. 1 Jn 5:18.
22. Mt 18:3.
23. Cf. 1 P 2:2.
24. Cf. Rm 12:15.
25. Cf. 1 Co 13:4.
26. Cf. Lk 6:30.
27. Cf. 1 Jn 4:20.

him.[28] He does not mock his neighbor because of his expression.[29] He does not bear enmity toward anyone. He does not hide. He does not look for this world's honor. He does not seek to accumulate wealth. He does not like to command. He is not self-important. He is not quarrelsome. He does not teach under the influence of the passions. He does not harass anyone. If anyone deprives him of something, he is not saddened. He does not hang onto his own will. He has no fear of hunger, or criminals, or wild beasts,[30] or war.[31] If he survives one persecution, he is not worried. Such is the one of whom our Lord Jesus said, '*Unless you repent and become like little children, you will not enter into the kingdom of God*'.[32] But when the little infant grows into a child and malice begins to live in him,[33] the apostle brings him back, saying, '*We are no longer to be infants thrown about and carried into all kinds of doctrine, the treachery of men and their trickery. We are to live in truth and charity. Let us grow fully into him.*'[34] Again he said, '*I have given you milk to drink like small infants and not solid nourishment because you were not ready. Even now you are not ready.*'[35] He also said, 'For a long time, until he becomes master of everything, the infant does not differ in anyway from a slave *but is submissive to guardians and to stewards until the date set by the father. In this way, when we were little infants, we, too, were enslaved to the elements of the world.*'[36] Again, 'Flee from youthful lust'.[37] He therefore teaches us to leave infancy in saying, '*Brothers, do not behave as infants in making judgment but be innocent of evil, and show yourselves as mature men for judgment*'.[38] What, then, is the work of these infants if not this, according to the apostle Peter, 'Like newborn infants, reject all evil and all deceit, hypocrisy, envy, and every sort of malice'.[39]

28. Cf. 1 Co 13:4.
29. *Sayings*, Theodore of Pherme 28.
30. Cf. Jb 5:21–22.
31. Cf. Lk 21:9.
32. Mt 18:3.
33. Cf. Rm 7:17, 20.
34. Ep 4:14–15.
35. 1 Co 3:2.
36. Ga 4:1–3.
37. 2 Tm 2:22.
38. 1 Co 14:20.
39. Cf. 1 P 2:1–2.

Again, brother, you know what is meant by the word said by our Lord Jesus, '*Truly, truly I tell you, unless you repent and become like little children you will not enter into the kingdom of Heaven*'.[40] This saying is fearsome because our Lord pronounced it with the oath, '*Truly, truly I tell you*'. This is because he, himself, is the Amen. This is why the apostle says, '*Since there is no other who is greater than he, he swears according to himself. Yes, certainly, blessing you I will bless you.*'[41] Let us, therefore, understand the saying precisely. Let us busy ourselves with this word at all times, in fear and trembling,[42] every time the enemy arouses us with an arrow against a neighbor, when someone blesses, or insults, or slanders us, or when our neighbor quarrels with us, not wishing to obey us, or when an impure anger torments us, threatening to arouse in us a bad memory of something our neighbor did to us, with the intention of overshadowing our soul with wrath and hatred. If, therefore, one of these things touches upon our soul let us hasten to recall our Lord's word that he swore with an oath, '*Truly, truly I tell you, unless you repent and become like little children you will not enter into the kingdom of Heaven*'. Who, wisely desiring to save his soul, is not afraid when hearing this word? Who will not reject from his heart all blame that he addresses to his neighbor? Who, fearing to be sent into Gehenna, will not reject all hatred from his heart, in order to be accepted into the kingdom? For our Lord Jesus' saying, '*Unless you repent and become like little children you will not enter into the kingdom of heaven*', is telling. This word, '*Unless you repent and become like little children you will not enter into the kingdom of heaven*', is burdensome for those who love the world, for those who do not know the gift of the Holy Spirit, because when it came it would bring them forgiveness of all evil and teach them[43] those things which would be theirs: sweetness instead of anger, peace instead of enmity, humility instead of discord, charity instead of hatred, patience instead of faintheartedness. Such are those who are worthy of rebirth.[44]

40. Mt 18:3.
41. Heb 6:13–14.
42. Cf. Ph 2:12.
43. Cf. Jn 14:26.
44. Cf. Jn 3:3–5.

Let us hasten, therefore, to remove from our heart that which has been listed for us by the great apostle, to abandon it in order to arrive at the measure of the child. Those who have taken heed and have removed it from their souls have also attained holy charity and perfection, for the Savior, after having breathed on their faces, saying, '*Receive the Holy Spirit*',[45] appeared to them by the Sea of Galilee and asked, 'Children, have you anything to eat?',[46] reminding them it is through the inspiration of the Holy Spirit that they have become little children again, and not through the flesh.[47] It is again written, 'Here am I with the children God has given me. Since the children share flesh and blood in common, God, too, shared in them and in the end broke the power of the one who had death at his command, that is to say the devil, so that he might free them'.[48] Whose flesh and blood is it that has come, sharing in common, if not those who have abandoned every adversity and attained the measure of holy infancy, those who have become perfect? As the apostle says, '*Until we have all attained unity with the faith of the Son of God, to the mature man, to the measure of the full stature of Christ*'.[49] Again, 'Grow fully, being built up in love'.[50] It is to these that the apostle John writes when he says, '*I write to you little infants because you have known the Father; I write to you fathers because you have known the one who has been since the beginning; I have written to you young people because you have overcome the evil one*'.[51] Know that these who have *become little children regarding malice*[52] are the ones who have become fighters against the enemy because they have deprived him of his armor, which is malice; that those who have become fathers attaining the measure of perfection are the ones who have trusted in revelations and mysteries until they arrive at wisdom, unity, bounty, kindness, sweetness and purity. These things

45. Jn 20:22.
46. Cf. Jn 21:5.
47. Cf. Rm 9:8.
48. Is 8:18; Heb 2:13–15.
49. Ep 4:13.
50. Cf. Ep 4:16.
51. 1 Jn 2:12–13.
52. 1 Co 14:20.

pertain to sweetness and those are the ones who glorify Christ in their bodies.[53]

Let us, therefore, well-beloved brother, according to the great famine which has come to earth,[54] without being discouraged by anything but unceasingly implore God's kindness not to be led astray by the trickery of the enemy and evil one who unpityingly creates evil and impudently perseveres saying, 'If it is not today, it will be tomorrow; I will not release you until I have you in my power'. As for us, let us therefore persevere, saying, as Saint David says, 'Watch, O Lord my God, and answer me, illumine my eyes with fear that I may not sleep the sleep of death lest my enemy says, "I have overthrown him" and my persecutors delight in my weakness'.[55] If they assail us, let us cry out, 'Who is like you, O God? Do not fall asleep, or be inactive, God! These are your enemies who, hating you, have made an evil plot against your people. They lift up their heads and growl, "Let us leave no trace of Israel!" ' Having progressed in the Holy Spirit, he says, '*My God, make them like a wheel; like chaff blown by the wind! Fill their faces with shame until they know that you alone are Lord!*'[56] Here, those who fight for their faith strengthen their heart against the enemies and, having fought against them, build their foundation on the Holy Father who is Christ,[57] saying with a firm heart, '*They have swarmed around me like bees* around a beam of light. They have burned *like a fire among thorns but in the name of the Lord I have repelled them.*'[58]

If we see the enemies surrounding us with their deceit, which is to say despondency, and they release our soul with delight because we cannot contain our anger against our neighbor if he troubles against his duty, or if they overcome our eyes in order to attract them to carnal lust, or if they want to bring us to enjoy the pleasant taste of nourishment, or if they bring the neighbor's word to us like poison, or if they make us supplant another, or if they bring

53. Cf. 1 Co 6:20.
54. Cf. Lk 15:14.
55. Cf. Ps 13:3–4.
56. Ps 83:14, 17.
57. Cf. 1 Co 10:4.
58. Ps 118:12.

us to make differences between brothers saying, 'One is good and another is bad', if these things surround us, we are not discouraged but believe, like David, with a firm heart saying, '*Lord, defender of my life, if an army is arranged in battle against me, my heart will not be afraid. If war raises itself up against me, I myself will hope in that. I have asked one thing only of the Lord and I seek it; that I may live in the house of the Lord all the days of my life in order to contemplate his sweetness and visit his holy temple, for he has sheltered me and see, now, he has lifted up my head over my enemies.*'[59] There is that which makes those who have raised their intellect between the dead that the apostle calls night when he says, '*We are not of the night, or of darkness*'.[60] Taking again those who were not themselves worried, he says, '*Those who sleep sleep at night, and those who become drunk are intoxicated at night*'[61] Yet again, 'The day of the Lord comes like a thief and they cannot escape because they are in the night'.[62] He says to those who arouse their intellect between the passions who are night, '*Let us put on the armor of faith and love and the helmet of the hope of salvation*'.[63]

Let us, therefore, do everything with the intellect aroused face-to-face with dead works, attentive at all times to our soul in order that it makes nothing outstanding of those things which conform to nature, for it is naturally versatile. As the prophet Isaiah says, '*The Lord is gracious to you. Humbled and deeply distressed, you have not been consoled*'.[64] The soul resembles fire: it burns if someone neglects it and when someone stokes the fire; the fire purifies it as long as it is in the fire. Like the fire, no one is able to hold it because it is aflame. So it is with the soul. As long as it dwells with God and converses with him, it becomes a fire which burns all its enemies, those who heat it up to a time of carefree attitude and purification, like fire in its novelty. It no longer finds pleasure in worldly things but it finds its rest in the nature of one who has been rendered worthy because it was his in the beginning. But if it leaves its own nature, it dies,

59. Ps 27:1, 3–6.
60. 1 Th 5:5.
61. 1 Th 5:7.
62. Cf. 1 Th 5:2.
63. 1 Th 5:8.
64. Is 54:10–11.

in the same way that animals die if someone drowns them in water, for they have a terrestrial nature, or fish, if someone places them on dry ground, for they have an aquatic nature. Yet again, birds are comfortable when they are in the air but when they land they are afraid of being captured.[65] Such is the perfect soul that dwells in its nature;[66] if it leaves its nature it also dies. In the same way those who have been judged worthy and have obtained these gifts perceive the world as their prison and do not wish to mix there lest they die, and this soul cannot love the world, even if it desires it. It remembers where it found itself in the beginning, dwelling in God, before this world made it return barren to him. In the same way, when the king's enemy has entered a town, the courageous ones are afraid of taking him in hand and soon, urged on by his malevolence, he overturns the king's statues and abolishes his laws. He replaces these with other, severe laws, erects his own statue and finally obliges all the people to worship it. But if the citizens secretly warn the legitimate king saying, 'Come and help us', he arrives, full of anger, with his army to this new one. The inhabitants joyfully welcome him. He enters, causes his enemy to perish, brings down the statue erected by oppression, and abolishes his laws. The city rejoices and the legitimate king reestablishes his own statue and laws, he is installed in the city, strengthens its fortifications in such a way that no one can again seize it and teaches those who live there to fight every enemy fearlessly. The same thing happens in the soul. After holy Baptism, the enemy dominates it afresh, humbles it by every shameful act of trickery, overturns the king's statue and establishes his own laws, causes it to be occupied all of the time, persuades it to commit impiety without scruple and makes of it what he will. But finally, through the kindness of the holy and great king Jesus, is sent repentance[67] and the soul rejoices. Repentance welcomes him, and Christ, the great king, enters, causing his enemy to perish, wiping out his statue and his impious laws, and brings freedom back. Christ erects his holy statue, gives the soul holy laws, and teaches all the

65. *Sayings*, Antony 10.
66. Pseudo-Macarius, *Homily* 15.
67. Cf. Rm 2:4.

soul's faculties to fight. From this time Christ takes his rest in this soul because it has become his own. All this takes place due to God.

It is therefore impossible for the soul to enter into the rest of the Son of God if it does not bear the heavenly king's likeness. In the same way, no new business receives or is given a coin that does not carry the likeness of the earthly king that no expert can judge, and that the king does not introduce into his treasury. In the same way, if the soul does not bear the likeness of the great king Jesus,[68] the angels do not rejoice with it but reject it asking, 'How do you come to be here without bearing my likeness?'[69] The mark of his likeness is love, as he himself says, '*By this all will know that you are my disciples, if you have love for one another*'.[70] But it is impossible that Christ's love can be with us if the soul is divided, seeking God and loving worldly things. In the same way that a bird cannot fly with only one wing, the soul is not able to progress toward God if it is bound to some worldly thing.[71] In the same way that a boat which lacks part of its rigging cannot be sailed, the soul is not able to rise above the streams of passions if it lacks one of the virtues. In the same way that sailors cannot set sail if they wear fine clothes, neither sleeves, nor sandals, for unless these parts of the body are uncovered they cannot sail, it is impossible for the soul to rise above the wind's waves against malice if it is not found stripped of worldly things. Again, in the same way that a soldier who leaves to fight the king's enemies cannot hold their head if he lacks a piece of his armor, it is not possible for a monk to resist the passions if he lacks one of the virtues. Also in the same way, if the enemies wish to enter into a fortified city which has part of its fortifications in ruins, they bring their attention toward the breech in order to enter there, because the guardians are at the gates, they cannot resist the enemies if the ramparts, having been thrown to the ground and not having been built up; it is impossible for the monk to lead an ascetic life, to resist the enemies, when he is under the influence of a passion and he cannot attain to the measure of perfection.

68. Pseudo-Macarius, *Homily* 5 and 30.
69. Cf. Mt 22:12.
70. Jn 13:35.
71. Pseudo-Macarius, *Homily* 32.

It is not I who says these things but Holy Scripture, for it is written in Genesis, 'And God said to Noah, I have seen you alone and perfect in this generation'.[72] Again, he says to Abraham, 'Be blameless in my presence and I will make an everlasting covenant with you'.[73] Also, Isaac, blessing his son, Jacob, says to him, 'May my God strengthen you in order that you may fulfill all his will'.[74] It is also written in Numbers, '*Anyone who makes a vow is to abstain from drinking wine, wine vinegar, grape juice and all that comes from the vine*'.[75] Yet again in Deuteronomy it says, '*If you leave in order to fight your enemies, guard yourself from every evil word until your enemy is given into your hands.*[76] *Of these seven people you will not release anyone who breathes, for fear that they will bring you to sin against me.*'[77] Also, for us to learn not to be discouraged, we say, 'How will we wipe out those who are so numerous?'[78] He says, 'You cannot wipe them out in a single year for fear that the earth will become barren and the wild beasts will multiply, but you will gradually increase and multiply and God will enlarge your borders'.[79] He will give them this commandment to remember, 'Take guard not to make an alliance with the Canaanites that I am going to wipe out before you'.[80] When Joshua, son of Naue was encircling and destroying Jericho, God said, 'You are destined to be cursed with all that it contains'.[81] And having wished to fight Gai, Israel took fruit before their eyes and was not able to beat the enemy because Achar had desired to take some of the anathematized things. Joshua, prostrating himself on the ground cried before God, 'Israel has turned its back on its enemies. What shall I do?'[82] The leader of the Lord's army replied, 'Because anathema is in you, Israel, you will not be able to resist your enemies'.[83] He no longer went

72. Cf. Gn 7:1.
73. Cf. Gn 17:1, 2, 7.
74. Cf. Gn 27:27–28.
75. Nm 6:2–4.
76. Dt 23:9.
77. Ex 23:33.
78. Cf. Dt 7:17.
79. Cf. Dt 7:22.
80. Cf. Dt 7:2.
81. Cf. Jos 6:17.
82. Cf. Jos 7:8.
83. Cf. Jos 7:13.

out in order to fight until he had removed Achar. We see that God withdrew the monarchy from Saul because he took to Amalec[84] that which was anathematized.[85] Because Jonathan had plunged his spear in a honeycomb[86] and had carried it to his mouth, God did not forgive Israel that day. Ecclesiastes also teaches us that one very small passion wipes out the power of the virtues, 'Dead flies spoil a dish of oil'[87] Ezekiel says again, '*The day when the righteous person wanders from the way of righteousness*, I will put affliction before his face and *I will not remember his righteousness*'.[88] The apostle also says, '*A little yeast leavens all the dough*'.[89] Ananaias and his wife Sapphira who came, bringing some of the proceeds from the sale of the field and laid these at the apostles' feet[90] died because of this mean action. James also says, '*The person who keeps all the law but slips on a single point, will become guilty of everything*'.[91] But to give us strength to turn back to him, God says in the book of Ezekiel, '*When the sinner turns away from all his iniquity and practices righteousness and justice I will no longer remember his sins but he will live* because I do not desire the death of a sinner but *that he repents and lives*'. '*Turn and repent, why should you die, house of Israel?*'[92] Jeremiah also says, 'Turn to me, house of Israel, and I will be gracious to you', says the Almighty Lord'.[93] Again, the Lord says, '*Shall the person who falls not rise? Shall the person who has turned away not repent? Why have my people turned insolently away? Why have they strengthened themselves in their resolution? Do they not wish to return to me? Return to me and I will return to you*.'[94] The Lord Jesus also says, '*If you pardon others their misdeeds, your heavenly Father will forgive you also; but if you do not pardon, your Father will no longer forgive you*'.[95] And the Apostle says, 'If one of you slips, *you,*

84. Cf. 1 K 15:9.
85. Cf. 1 K 15:15.
86. Cf. 1 K 14:27.
87. Cf. Qo 10:1.
88. Ez 18:24.
89. Ga 5:9.
90. Cf. Ac 5:1–10.
91. Jm 2:10.
92. Ez 18:21–23, 30–31.
93. Cf. Jr 3:22.
94. Jr 8:4–5.
95. Mt 6:14–15.

the spiritual ones, should restore him in a spirit of gentleness'.[96] James, too, says, '*Brothers, if someone wanders far from the way of truth, and another brings him back, he should know that the one who brought back a sinner from his wandering saves his soul from death and covers a multitude of sins*'.[97]

Here are all the scriptural accounts which encourage us to examine ourselves for fear that in accomplishing our work we may be spiteful to our neighbor, or fear that we remain angry with him by not pardoning him and by doing this our efforts are lost. For these reasons our Lord Jesus Christ does not help us at the time when our enemies torment us, for he himself blamed those who behaved in this way saying, '*Wicked slave, I forgave you all this sin because you implored me; should you, yourself, also not have pity for your companion?' And in his wrath he delivers him to the torturers until he has paid his debt.* 'That is enough', he says, 'my *heavenly Father will act if you do not pardon your neighbor with all your heart*'.[98] Examine yourself, therefore, brother, in observing your heart every day. What is found there before God? Blame of a neighbor, hatred, injury, jealousy or pride? You say, however, 'I cannot see that there; how exasperating!' If such poison is carried in your heart, remember the word of the Lord Jesus who says, 'It is enough. Your heavenly Father will act toward you if each does not pardon his neighbor with all his heart'.[99] But the person who fears to go into Gehenna will reject all malice from his heart, in order that this baneful sentence does not fall upon him. Watch your heart, therefore, brother, as your enemies do, for they are cunning in their malice. May your heart be persuaded by this saying, 'It is impossible for a person to do well when he does wrong, similarly, one cannot wish to do evil under a good pretext'. That is why our Savior has taught us to be aware, saying, '*The gate is narrow and the way which leads to life is close and there are few who find it, but broad and large is the gate which leads to perdition and there are many who walk there. Guard yourself, then, against false prophets who come*

96. Ga 6:1.
97. Jm 5:19.
98. Mt 18:32–35.
99. Cf. Mt 18:35.

disguised in sheep's clothing to you; beneath are ravaging wolves. You will recognize them by their fruits'.[100] What, therefore, are their fruits, if not all that which is contrary to nature, with which they overwhelm us, making our heart consent to them? But those who love God with all their heart are not persuaded by false prophets to consent to each of their works, as the apostle says, '*Who will separate us from the love of Christ? Tribulation, distress, persecution, hunger, nakedness, dangers, the two-edged sword? For I am sure that neither death, nor life, nor angels, nor principalities, nor present, nor things to come, nor any other creature can separate us from the love of Christ'*.[101]

Do you see, my brother, that nothing worldly can separate those who love God with all their heart from his love. Therefore, guard yourself, for fear that something distressful, or money, or house, or pleasure, or hatred, or injury, or someone who talks your praises, or all the venom of the serpent[102] who breathes in our heart will turn you away from the love of God. Therefore, do not trouble yourself but let us, rather, try hard to fix our eyes on the bronze serpent which Moses made according to God's command. He places it, then, on the wood at the top of the mountain in order that anyone bitten by a serpent could look at it and immediately recover.[103] Our Lord Jesus resembled the bronze serpent because Adam, hearing the serpent, that is the enemy, became the enemy of God.[104] Our Lord Jesus Christ, however, was made the perfect person in every respect except sin.[105] He is similar to Adam for our sake and, therefore, the bronze serpent, because Christ resembled the one who became an enemy of God except that he did not have a single evil thought, nor the venom of malice. He did not crawl, or wheeze, or have the enemy's breath. Our Lord Jesus took this figure in order that, extinguishing the venom that Adam had eaten from the serpent's mouth, He brought back nature, which had become contrary to nature, to conform to nature. He said to Moses, '*What is this thing*

100. Mt 7:14, 13, 15–16.
101. Rm 8:35, 38–39.
102. Cf. Rv 12:9.
103. Cf. Nm 21:8–9.
104. Cf. Gn 3.
105. Cf. Heb 4:15.

in your hand?'[106] He replied, 'A rod'. God said, 'Throw it to the ground'. He threw it onto the ground and it became a serpent, and Moses fled before it, but God told him, 'Stretch out your hand and grasp hold of its tail'. He took it and it became a rod in his hand. God said to him, 'Take the rod which was turned into a serpent and strike the egyptian river in front of Pharaoh and its water will become blood'.[107] Again, 'Take the rod which became a serpent and strike the Red Sea and it will become dry land'.[108] Yet again, 'Take the rod which you have in your hand with which you struck the sea. You will strike the rock and it will give you its water'.[109] See, the person who walks in the steps of our Lord Jesus Christ, after having been an enemy and a serpent, was changed by a rod and none of the enemies were able to resist him. *This is a great mystery.*[110] If the serpent injects its venom into us, let us try hard to fix our eyes on the one who ascended the cross, for the one who did that did it for us and bore it without flinching, without being angry with those who maltreated him, without responding with a harsh word, but remaining motionless like the bronze serpent. If, therefore, we look at the cross and walk in his footsteps, we are healed from the bites of the invisible serpent. Power and help belong to him, to the one who said, '*In the same way that Moses raised the serpent in the desert, so must the Son of Man be lifted up in order that everyone who believes in him* will not perish but *receive eternal life*'.[111] Walk, then, in his footsteps in order to be healed by him. We will not be healed unless we believe that he is powerful, for the bronze serpent did not come by itself to treat those who were bitten in the desert but the one who was bitten by the serpent looked at it in faith and was healed.[112] Also, there were many who were bitten by serpents for they did not believe in the word of God as the apostle says, '*We must not put God to the test as some of them did and were destroyed by the serpents*'.[113] Know, brother,

106. Ex 4:2–5.
107. Cf. Ex 7:15, 17.
108. Cf. Ex 14:16.
109. Cf. Ex 17:5–6; Nm 20:8.
110. Ep 5:32.
111. Jn 3:14.
112. Cf. Nm 21:9.
113. 1 Co 10:9.

there are also serpents in the soul today that come to tempt Jesus. What is meant, therefore, by 'the temptation of Jesus' if not to ask him about his commandments, then not to do them as it is written, '*One of the lawyers said, in order to test him, "Master, what is the greatest* and most important *commandment in the Law?" Jesus replied, "You must love the Lord your God with all your heart and with all your soul, and your neighbor as yourself. On these two commandments rest all of the Law and the Prophets.*" '[114] You see, people are called tempters if they ask without doing, for they have no desire to believe that the bronze serpent can save them from the venom of the invisible serpent. Therefore, control your heart and do not say, persuaded by despondency, 'How can I guard the virtues then if I am a sinful person?', for when the person leaves his sinful ways and turns to God, his repentance gives him new birth as the apostle says, '*In the same way that we have carried the worldly image, we will also carry the heavenly image*'.[115] You see, God has given us transformation through repentance; through it, we become completely new. Whilst the little infant is in his mother's bosom, she guards him at all times from every evil. When he cries, she offers him her breast. Gradually, she gives him breath with all her strength, making him fear, drinking his milk with fear, in order that his heart does not become full of self-importance. When he cries, however, she is moved to pity him, for he is born through her entrails. She consoles him, embraces him and comforts him again when he takes her breast. If a person is greedy for gold, or silver, or precious stones, or every earthly object, he looks at them but then is in the bosom of his mother. He scorns everything in order to take the breast.[116] His father does not scold him if he does not work, or if he does not go to war against his enemies since he is small and weak. He has healthy feet but he cannot stand up. He has hands but he cannot hold weapons. His mother treats him with condescension until, gradually, he grows. When he has grown a little and wishes to fight with another who throws him to the ground, his father is not angry with him, knowing that he is only a child. When he becomes

114. Mt 22:35–40.
115. 1 Co 15:49.
116. Pseudo-Macarius, *Homily* 45.

a man, his zeal shows itself.[117] If he is hostile to his father's enemies, he confides in him his interests because he is his son; but if, after all the trouble his parents have taken with him, he turns into a big nuisance, if he hates his parents, if he betrays his race and joins his enemies, they deprive him of their benevolence and chase him from their home, not leaving an inheritance for him.

As for us, brother, may we ourselves therefore be careful in order to rest in the shelter of repentance and let us receive the milk of God's holy breast for it will nourish us. Also, let us spurn all that which is seen, so that his milk may be tasty in our mouth. Let us carry the yoke of his teaching in order that it may take care of us. If we fight against our enemies and they overpower us, small though we are, let us mourn before the yoke for it prays to our Father to avenge us against those who maltreat us. Let us remove all the will of our heart and may we love to live amongst strangers, so that, like Abraham,[118] it might save us. Let us, like Jacob, subject ourselves to Rebekah's hands in order to receive our Father's blessing.[119] Let us, like Moses, hate the will of our heart, and our Father will guard us with his protection and shelter us against those who wish to kill it, like one free from every sensual pleasure.[120] Let us not, like Esau, spurn fear, which detests us. Let us, like Joseph, guard its purity so that it exalts us in our enemies' ground, that it may be a good shelter for us, as it was for Naue's son Joshua: 'This was a child', it was said, 'who did not leave the Tent'.[121] Let us not leave room in our heart for despondency, for fear that it will disinherit us of the Promised Land.[122] Let us love humility in everything, and let us, like Kaleb,[123] do all in our power to enter the land flowing with milk and honey. Let us not, like Achar,[124] covet anything that leads to distress, lest we be wiped out. Let us, like Rahab, love our conscience that brings us at all times to compunction so that it saves

117. Cf. Heb 6:11.
118. Cf. Gn 12:1ff.; Heb 11:9.
119. Cf. Gn 27:6–10.
120. Cf. Ex 2–3.
121. Ex 33:11.
122. Cf. Nm 13:31.
123. Cf. Nm 14:24.
124. Cf. Jos 7.

us in the hour of temptation. Let us not, like the sons of Eli,[125] love greed for some dish at all, for fear it will kill us. Let us, like Samuel, guard against all injustice that does not reproach our conscience when it commits evil against its neighbor.[126] Let us not, like Saul,[127] love to have malicious jealousy against others lest it rejects us. Let us not, like David,[128] love to render evil against our neighbor in order that it keeps us from the evil one. Let us not, like Absalon,[129] love boastfulness and vainglory lest it banishes us from the face of our Father, but let us, like Salomon,[130] love humility and modesty so that it makes us avengers of our Father's enemies. Let us, like Elias the Thesbite,[131] love renunciation in everything, mortifying our members of every work of death to receive a courageous heart against our enemies. Do not, like Achaab,[132] let us be friends of the will and full of concupiscence lest it wipes us out. Let us, like Nabouthe the Jezraelite,[133] fight until death in order not to lose his holy inheritance. Let us be obedient to our fathers in everything, removing our every will, to be submissive to them so that their blessing rests upon us, as it did with Elisaie.[134] Do not, like Giezi,[135] let us be greedy for human respect, or untruthful for fear that it curses us. Let us, like the Soumanite woman,[136] love faithfulness in everything, more than ourselves, in order that it blesses us. Let us not, like Achiab and Sedekias, fried in the fire by the Babylonian king,[137] have a culpable love of shameful things lest it wipes us out before it. Let us, like Susannah, hate sin until death because of our souls so that it comes to our assistance, in the day of necessity. Let us not desire various dishes for fear that it leaves us like those

125. Cf. 1 K 2:12–17.
126. Cf. 1 K 12:3.
127. Cf. 1 K 18:9.
128. Cf. 2 K 16:11.
129. Cf. 2 K 14:25.
130. Cf. 1 Ch 2:5,.
131. Cf. 1 Ch 17.
132. Cf. 1 Ch 21:21.
133. Cf. 1 Ch 20:3.
134. Cf. 2 Ch 2:15.
135. Cf. 2 Ch 5:20–27.
136. Cf. 2 Ch 4:8–10.
137. Cf. Jr 36:21–23.

who received their nourishment at the table of Nebuchadnezer. Let us, like the companions of Azarius,[138] love mortification in everything so that it rejoices with us. Do not let us be deceitful, like the Babylonians who murmured against the faithful.[139] Let us, like Daniel,[140] carry out our service without obeying the laziness of our bodies, for it prefers to die soon than to omit the offices which it observes every day, for God is powerful. He saves those who love him and who destroy the evil ones with the test, for the faith that the just had in God renders the wildcats as a flock of sheep.[141] Blessed is God for repentance, that he blesses those who love this and subject the nape of the neck to the yoke of the will of repentance until he is reborn from on high in the will of God.

Therefore, my brother, a person has great need of discernment, which removes all carnal lust, and an attentive vigilance in all his ways to avoid going astray and falling into the hands of the enemies of repentance, for there are many who surround and wish to separate him from it. The so-called pretension of justice cuts his throat, to judge the sinners the chase, to scorn the negligent ones stop. It is described in Proverbs, '*All her ways are straight: she does not lazily eat her bread; she makes clothes and lined over-clothes for her husband. She is like a ship, trading from afar, and in this way she procures her livelihood*'.[142] Let us understand that she is like the merchant who loads the boat not only with merchandise but all that he knows will make a profit.[143] If he sees someone who has suffered a loss, he does not envy him but he soon envies those who have become rich and have withdrawn into their home. He avoids all harmful work and borrows everything that can be returned until he has made a purchase. He is constrained to buy any necessary new stock which he can return and asks those who are not jealous but have become rich and have withdrawn into their house, 'How will I sell this? How will I buy that?' Such is the soul that wishes to meet God without

138. Cf. Dn 1.
139. Cf. Dn 3:12.
140. Cf. Dn 6:11.
141. Cf. Is 11:6.
142. Pr 31:27, 22, 14.
143. Pseudo-Macarius, *Homily* 33.

reproach. A single piece of work does not satisfy God but the soul is busy with all advantageous work. If, on the other hand, it learns that some work is harmful, the soul avoids it, lest it is harmed itself. Then, as for you, my brother, you negotiate with Jesus. Take care, for negotiation with this king has removed all harmful work! These are the things that are removed: the glory of humanity, pride, self-justification, disdain, irritating words, love of luxury, vainglory, and love of distraction. All that is unfavorable for the negotiators of Jesus and it is impossible for them to please him when they have all that in their possession. Examine what you yourself possess, then, brother. Does your intellect watch your faculties, to discern which are fruitful for God and which consent to sin? Your eyes, are they possessed for pleasure? Your tongue, is it defeated for ardor?[144] Do you see that your heart is agreeably flattered by honor received by humanity? Your ears, do they rejoice from gossip? All that is disadvantageous for the intellect, as it is written in Leviticus, 'He said to Aaron, "Do not offer on my altar an animal which has a defect for it will not die" '.[145] Aaron is a symbol of the intellect. Because enmity mixes its malice with the so-called pretension of justice, he prescribes to first examine the offering lest it will not die. Death is out of sight and it is accorded to those who wish to soil their faculties. Such are the words of those who love Jesus, hoping in him and having him for the holy bridegroom. Their soul becomes a bride, clothed with every virtue and possessing his holy reflection according to the word of the apostle, '*And we, with unveiled face, beholding*, as if in a mirror, *the glory of the Lord, are transformed in this same image of glory*, in glory, as by the Spirit of the Lord'.[146] '*For now we see in a mirror, in an obscured way, but then we will see him face to face*'.[147] Also, those who have become his brides in purity look at themselves as in a mirror, in case there is, by chance, a stain in their image which displeases their bridegroom, for he searches the pure, spotless souls of virgins as it is written of Rebecca, '*The virgin was very beautiful.*

144. Evagrius, *Chapters on Prayer* 1.
145. Cf. Lv 22:20.
146. 2 Co 3:18.
147. 1 Co 13:12.

She did not recognize any man'.[148] The prophet also says, '*The virgins will be brought to the king in his room*; his children will be brought to you'.[149] The word, '*They will be brought*', foreshadows his holy Incarnation. 'His children', signifies being united with him, because rebirth through holy baptism has renewed all that has grown old, repentance purifies them and in sanctifying the virgins they have forgotten all dilapidation and cannot remember it any longer, as he says to them, '*Listen, my daughter, see and lend an ear, forget your people, your father's house, the king has desired your beauty*'.[150] All their followers admire it on account of purity. He has given repentance that unites a body with him and they say, '*Who is it who shows, all white, supported on his brother?*'.[151]

Let us, therefore, do everything possible, with tears, gradually struggling until the conduct of the Old Person is stripped away. We watch every distressful act until our love comes to us. We remove the earthly image and erect his holy statue in our heart until we become worthy of him, pure and spotless, as the apostle says, '*In the same way that we have carried the terrestrial image, let us also carry the heavenly one*'.[152] The Apostle knows that repentance can restore us again to a sinless new creature. Because of that, he tells us to abandon the conduct of the one who disobeyed the commandment in order to exercise the conduct of our Lord Jesus Christ, that is to say, the holy commandments of the one who has mercy. He has endured human slavery to introduce him into the hidden paradise, to accord him every holy virtue. He has enabled him to eat from the tree of life, that is to say, from purity that has appeared in him. He has calmed the Cherubims and the flamboyant sword that they waved to guard the way to the tree of life. This is knowledge of his holy words, which places peace in the intellect of the believers, guarding them without ceasing and closing their ears to every malicious word of the serpent. It calls them back to the bitter slavery of their former life, for they do not return there, their endless work returns graces

148. Gn 24:16.
149. Ps 45:14.
150. Ps 45:10–11.
151. Sg 8:5.
152. 1 Co 15:49.

to the one who has bought them with the price of his blood. He has untied the bond of their slavery on the cross[153] and has made them his brothers and friends.[154] He, through grace, has poured his spirit on them. 'Calm your hearts', he said, '*I am going to my Father and your Father, my God and your God*';[155] and again, '*I wish, Father, that where I am, the others, also, will be, with me, for I have loved them as you have loved me*'.[156] He again shows us that he is not speaking of everyone but of those who have abandoned their wills and followed his holy will, and have removed from themselves all complicity with the world, for he says, 'I have taken them out of the world; that is why the world hates them, because they no longer belong to it'.[157] You see, those have been judged worthy of becoming his brides and live in unity with him as the apostle says, '*This is why a man will leave his father and mother to be joined to his wife, and the pair will become one body. This is a great mystery. I refer,* in saying that, *to Christ and his church*'.[158] He says again, 'Pagans are admitted to the same inheritance, as *members of the same body, recipients of the same promise in Christ Jesus, through the Gospel*'.[159] You see, his Holy Spirit lives in those who have not been judged worthy to become one body with him and is concerned with them as it is written, '*It is not you who is speaking but your Father's Spirit talking in you*'.[160] The apostle also says, '*God has revealed this to us through the Spirit; for the Spirit searches all,* to the depths of God,[161] for *we have,* he says, *the mind of Christ*'.[162] Can *the mind of Christ,* then, conceive sin? Understand in your heart then, brother, this mystery: each creature on the earth is born in unity with the members of the same creation and not of a different creation. There are livestock, wild beasts, reptiles and birds. That is why God created all things before Adam, in order for him to see that they bear

153. Cf. Col 2:14.
154. Cf. Jn 15:14, 15.
155. Jn 20:17.
156. Jn 17:24, 23.
157. Cf. Jn 15:19.
158. Ep 5:31–32.
159. Ep 3:6.
160. Mt 10:20.
161. 1 Co 2:10.
162. 1 Co 2:16.

a resemblance to him, and, therefore, he found that they did not share a resemblance to him.[163] Then, God, taking one of his ribs, made woman, then made her take her husband. It is a great mystery for those who have become brides. They share, through rebirth, his essence and belong to his holy body as the apostle says, '*We, though many, are a single body in Christ, and are members, one of another*'.[164] Again, '*We are members of his body, of his flesh and blood*'.[165] Look, Christ wishes us to be like him in everything, in the same way that Eve is Adam's issue and resembles him in everything. Consequently, if we share something of the unreasonableness of animals, or of the greed of wild beasts—we deprive them of the others—the instability of birds, or the venom of reptiles, such souls cannot be virgins for him for their conduct is not his. Look, brother, how he wishes a person to resemble him, healthy from everything that is contrary to nature, to be worthy of becoming a bride for him. The soul recognizes his thoughts about conduct, for if it practices works, the Holy Spirit lives in it, because the works cause the soul to be reborn. It is impossible that God's Spirit does not live in this soul, as the Lord says, '*If you love me, keep my commandments, and I will pray the Father, and he will send* the Paraclete, *the Spirit of truth*, to you'.[166] The apostle also says, '*Do you not realize—unless, perhaps you are found wanting—that Christ lives in you?*'.[167] Look, unless a person acquires the conduct of Jesus, he is not put to the test, nor does he become a virgin, close to him. All the virgins prepared their lamps, but those who did not have works were thrown out from the door.[168] The net tossed into the sea catches every species of fish but only accepts the good ones and leads them into the kingdom.[169] The tares grow with the wheat but when harvest comes, they are separated and thrown into the fire.[170] The branches grow on the vine but those that do not

163. Cf. Gn 2:19, 21.
164. Rm 12:5.
165. Ep 5:30.
166. Jn 14:15–17.
167. 2 Co 13:5.
168. Cf. Mt 25:1, 12.
169. Cf. Mt 13:47–48.
170. Cf. Mt 13:25–30.

bear fruit are thrown onto the fire.[171] The ewes eat with the goats, but God does not bring both in, the goats are thrown out.[172] The sower sows his seed but is delighted only with that which pushes through good soil.[173] He gives his money without dissimulation but delights only with the one who gives back double.[174] All were called to the wedding but he threw the one who did not have clothes for the wedding into eternal darkness.[175] These words are addressed to us, for all may say 'We believe' but he will throw out those who have not behaved according to his divinity as it says, '*Many are called but few are chosen*'.[176]

Let us examine ourselves, brothers, and consider our own behavior before the we meet with him. Do not let us pay attention to those who fulfill the carnal desires of their heart in order that we do not lose but find such great wealth in the hour of need. Let us struggle to acquire it and scorn like an enemy that which we had to abandon. Let us, therefore, watch those who accomplished all the work in the care of perishable things. They have left them and have gone away, causing them to have inherited Gehenna, because they have not wished to follow the Lord's footsteps in order to be worthy of becoming his brides. Let us struggle, therefore, in tears before God, with a full heart, with secret groans, lest we fall into the same shame as them, for there is mist over the sea and numerous boats have become lost. Saved by others, people do not say, 'We will be swallowed up like them!' but strengthen one another in order not to be discouraged and implore God to help them. In truth, the mist grows thicker over the earth! Let us strip, then, and shout, lest we perish, for if there is a storm at sea, you find sailors and all aboard encouraging the captain. The one who is not found stripped of everything which belongs to distress cannot escape from this turbulent sea, for Moses could not sing to the Lord without having first crossed the Sea and seen the death of those who wished

171. Cf. Jn 15:6.
172. Cf. Mt 25:32–46.
173. Cf. Mt 13:3–9.
174. Cf. Mt 25:14, 23.
175. Cf. Mt 22:11–13.
176. Mt 22:14.

to bring back his people in slavery into Egypt. Just as he brought them across they became free and he said, '*Let us sing to the Lord for he is magnificently clothed in glory. He has thrown horse and rider into the sea*'.[177] If, therefore, the intellect saves the faculties of the soul[178] and the desires of the flesh and makes them cross the sea, the pillar of his divinity will separate the soul from carnal desires. Then, if God sees that the arrogance of the passions hurls itself on the soul, wishing to retain its faculties in sin, and if the intellect unceasingly keeps itself in secret with God, he sends it his assistance and wipes out everything with a single blow as it is written, '*God said to Moses, "Why are you calling me? Prepare to arrange the children of Israel. As for yourself, take the rod which you are holding in your hand and strike it on the water of the sea and it will separate."*'[179] God will faithfully give his hand again to Moses today in order to save Israel from the hands of the Egyptians, who are the carnal desires which satisfy us, so that we may also be worthy of singing a new song: '*Sing to the Lord for he is magnificently clothed in glory*'.[180] How, therefore, can we say, '*For he is magnificently clothed in glory*' and then give in to our enemies, following our will, and return into Egypt, coveting that which is eaten when we serve Pharaoh and we constrain Aaron, 'Let us make gods to lead us into Egypt'.[181] Through despondency we demean ourselves to disparage spiritual food but almighty God makes Moses go down the mountain toward us until he robs the calf by which we become enemies of God. God is powerful. He procured for us repentance in order that we may return to him. He gave to Moses the power of prayer for us, saying, '*If you pardon them their sins, pardon them, if not erase me from the Book of Life*'.[182] He gave to Joshua in his time the power to wipe out the seven races for whom the Promised Land had matured by their envious malice, until Israel received their inheritance and lived there without being an object of envy for the ages of ages. Amen.

177. Ex 15:1.
178. OGtI 19.
179. Ex 14:15–16.
180. Ex 15:1.
181. Cf. Ex 32:1.
182. Ex 32:31–32.

From him comes power, assistance, protection, wisdom and safeguard. He is in us, our Lord Jesus Christ, for the glory and honor of God the Father and of the Holy Spirit before the ages, now and unto the ages of ages. Amen.

If you read this, brother, do everything possible to follow it yourself, in order that the Lord will protect you in the hour of temptation. Amen.

26

Recorded by Isaiah's Disciple, Abba Peter, who had Heard it Spoken by his Master

My father said, 'Act maturely! Amend that which needs correcting. The pure pray to God. Their anguish and fear of God remit their sins. The person who has the evil of vengeance in his heart provides fruitless service. Do not wish that someone would seek your counsel or a word about the present time. Do not fall down before the person who does ask you. Listen unceasingly to those who talk with you and implore God to give you knowledge of whom you ought to listen. Do your utmost not to say one thing with your mouth whilst knowing another in your heart.'

He also said, 'Fortify yourself with this word: work, poverty, being a stranger, stability and silence engender humility, and humility remits sins, but if anyone does not obey this, his renunciation is in vain. Do all you can to become detached in order that you may become free to mourn. Take as much care as you cannot to question matters of faith which the fathers have taught you.'

I visited <Abba Isaiah> again when he was ill and found him very tired. Seeing me saddened, he said, 'What sorrow is this that is composed of the prospect of rest? Fear of this dark hour, when I am thrown before the face of God, oppresses me. No one will hear me. No one will have rest as a prospect.'

He also said, 'All these drive the soul away from the memory of God: anger, faintheartedness, and the wish to teach empty words. Patience and gentleness, on the other hand, lead to love.'

He also said, 'Throw yourself in knowledge before God[1] and humbly obey the commandments concerning love. Love leads to freedom from sin.'

Again, he said, 'The solitary needs to examine himself at all times. Has he escaped to be with those who have withdrawn into the air? Is he free from those in order that he may live again? Having submitted to their slavery once, is he now free? There is work to do in order that mercy may come.'

Yet again, he said, 'The person who bears an accusation in their heart is far from the forgiveness of God'.

I asked him for a word and he replied, 'If you wish to follow our Lord Jesus Christ, keep his word. If you wish to crucify the Old Person with him, you must remove those things that force you to descend from the cross. Prepare your heart to bear the contempt of the evil ones. They will humiliate you in order to rule your heart. Impose silence so that you do not judge someone whom you know in your heart.'

He also said, 'The fear of coming before God must be the very breathing of the solitary. If sin continues to seduce his heart, he does not yet have any fear and is far away from mercy.'

Again, he said, 'The thing which tires us is activity in the mouth, and iniquity and malice in the heart'.

Yet again, he said, 'If a person does not struggle until death to give back his body which he takes until the beloved Jesus comes, he will not arrive with joy, neither will he be delivered from bitter slavery'.

He said, 'Mercy, mercy, mercy. Where has the soul arrived? In what purity it was created! Under what domination it finds itself! To what vainglory it approaches!'

He also said, 'I beg you, do not let go of your heart while you are in your body.[2] Just as the farmer cannot put his confidence in

1. Cf. Ps 55:22.
2. OGtI 15.

the seed which grows in his field because he does not know what will happen to it until he has locked it in his loft, a person is unable to release his heart while he still has breath in his nostrils.[3] The person who sows his seed, expecting good fruit, works with hope, but he is more fearful when the seed comes to maturity and prays to God for the outcome. In the same way, the person who ignores the passions in his body until his last breath is unable to control his heart while he lives. It is always necessary to grow toward God in order to obtain his help and mercy.'

I asked him, 'Abba, what is humility and where is its origin?'

He replied, 'It is found in obedience, in humbly and happily removing one's will, in purity, in bearing insults, in accepting your neighbor's word without grieving. All this is humility'.

He also said, 'Blessed are those who acquire the New Person before meeting Christ. As the apostle says, '*Flesh and blood are not able to inherit the kingdom of God*'.[4]

Again he said, '*There is so much jealousy and discord among you. Is this because you are in the flesh and conduct yourselves in human fashion?*'[5]

Yet again, he said, 'If we have so much to suffer from our enemies, it is because we do not know our own sins well enough. We ignore that which causes us to mourn. If mourning was revealed to us, it would reveal our sins to us and if it enabled us to truly see our sins, we would be ashamed to look prostitutes in the face because they are to be more respected than us. They commit their sins with effrontery because they do not know God.'

Yet again, he said, 'The person who carries blame in himself and repudiates his will for his neighbor on account of God does not allow the enemy to put him amongst themselves because he is a hard worker. If he has a high intellect and wishes to bear himself before the feet of the Lord Jesus[6] in knowledge, he applies himself to removing his will. He does not wish to be separated from his beloved Lord. The person who maintains his will is not even at peace with

3. Cf. Jb 27:3.
4. 1 Co 15:50.
5. 1 Co 3:3.
6. Cf. Jn 11:32.

the faithful because impatience, anger, and irritation against others pursue his heart in which he believes to possess knowledge.'

Again, he said, 'The person who unceasingly watches his sins does not have the words to speak with another'.

He also said, 'Hate all worldly things which render you an enemy of God.[7] Just as a person who has an enemy fights him, we ought to fight our body to prevent it from resting.'

Again, he said, 'The person who works and loves God must pay attention to each of his thoughts in order to deliberate their subject and discern whether they are carnal or not. As long as the thoughts are contrary to nature, having some influence on one of the parts of his body, he is not yet considered a virgin.'

I asked him what was meant by the evangelist's prayer, '*May your name be sanctified*'.[8]

He replied, 'That is a matter for the perfect ones. It is impossible for the name of God to be sanctified in us who are dominated by the passions'.

He also said, 'Our ancient fathers have said that retreat is flight from the body and meditation of death,[9] but it is dangerous to leave someone alone if he has not opposed the sins which surround his soul by his works, or does not have repentance in his heart for those things which he has done since the time of his disobedience, while he believes that God has forgiven his sins and says to his enemy, "I will not put trust in any of my works when I appear before the tribunal. I do not have any pretension of justice and I mistake those who overturn the complete edification of the soul since my heart is conniving with them".'

He said again, 'A person is in great need of humility and must throw himself before the loving-kindness of God[10] in order to know the thieves' hiding places and their means of escape'.

He also spoke about peace with one's neighbor.[11] 'God no longer

7. Cf. Jm 4:4.
8. Mt 6:9.
9. Evagrius, *Praktikos* 33.
10. Cf. Ps 55:22; 1 P 5:7.
11. Cf. Mk 9:50; Rm 12:18.

lives wherever there is no peace, but the person who sees his sins also sees peace. Humility, not the one who forgives sins, lives there. David, when he sinned with the wife of Uriah, found no sacrifice to offer God.[12] That is why he said, "*The agreeable sacrifice to God is a contrite spirit and a bruised and humble heart*".'[13]

Again, he said, 'Impatience and the reality of reprimand troubles the intellect to the point of not allowing a person to see the light of God'.[14]

Yet again, he said, 'Do your utmost to escape from the three passions—gain, honor and rest—that overturn the soul. When they become the soul's mistresses they impede its progress.'

He also said, 'If he comes in spirit to judge your neighbor when you are sitting in your cell, consider how more numerous your own sins are than your neighbor's. If you believe that you are doing righteous things, do not think that these will please God. Each one of the body's vigorous limbs takes care of the weaker members in order to correct and look after it, but the cruel person who busies himself, asking, "What have I to do with the weak?", does not belong to the body of Christ because the strong sympathize with the weak until the latter heals and says in his heart, "I am never weak". The person who has acquired humility takes the blame of his neighbor upon himself saying, "It is I who have fallen", but the person who mistakenly thinks in his heart that he is wise and has never injured anyone and has the fear of God is preoccupied with his virtues in case any one of them dies.'

Again, he said, 'If you are sitting in your cell as you finish your office to God in silence and your heart yields to something ungodly which you consider is a thought rather than a sin, say to yourself, "If these are thoughts, not sin, then my office offered in silence is not sincere". If you say, however, "God receives the office of my heart which I have offered silently", then your heart has given into evil in the silence and your thoughts will be counted as a sin before God.'

12. Cf. 2 S 11:27.
13. Ps 51:17.
14. Cf. 1 P 2:9; 1 Jn 1:5–7.

I asked him for a word and he replied, 'The person who does not find assistance in the time of war cannot believe in peace'.

He also spoke about teaching. 'It is necessary for fear not to correspond to that which you teach. In so much as you are incorrect in that, you are unable to teach.'

He also spoke about communion. 'Woe is me! Woe is me! What sort of Communion will I have with God[15] if I commune with his enemies? I commune, therefore, for my condemnation[16] and embarrassment.'

I asked what is meant by 'fear of God'.

He answered, 'The person who puts his trust in something ungodly does not have fear of God'.

I also asked him what is 'a servant of God'.

He replied, 'If a person is a slave of the passions, he is not yet reckoned as a servant of God. He is, rather, a servant of the one who dominates him. As long as a person is in servitude, he cannot teach the one dominated by the same passion. It is shameful for a person to teach before he himself is delivered from the thing about which he is teaching. How can he pray to God for another person if he himself is still dominated? As long as he is in bitter servitude he is neither friend, nor son, nor servant of God. How can he pray for another? Instead, it is necessary for that person to implore God unceasingly to deliver him from the thing to which he is enslaved. Then he will see his shame and lament in seeing himself unworthy of the familiarity of being a son, lacking the purity which God desires of him.'

He also said, 'Woe is me! Woe is me! I have not struggled to purify myself in order to receive mercy. Woe is me! Woe is me! I have not struggled to win the war against my enemies in order to rule with Christ. How can a leper approach a king? Woe is me! Woe is me! I carry his name, Lord, then I serve his enemies. Woe is me! Woe is me! I eat what horrifies my God and because of that he does not heal me.'

15. Cf. 1 Jn 1:6.
16. Cf. 1 Co 11:29.

I visited him when he was ill and found him to be very tired. Perceiving the sadness my heart had because of his suffering, he said to me, 'In such illness I sadly approach death. I can remember this bitter hour. This is why bodily health is useless. The enemy of God finds vigor in this. A tree which is watered every day is not dried out but may not produce fruit.'

He also said, 'It is necessary for a person to have a courageous and big heart and be concerned with keeping the Lord's commandments'.

Again, he said, 'Woe is me! Woe is me! I have before me accusers whom I know and others I ignore and cannot deny! Woe is me! Woe is me! How will I be able to recognize my Lord and his saints? My enemies have not released a single healthy member before God.'

I asked him what is necessary for a person who lives in retreat.

He replied, 'The solitary needs three things: unceasing fear, incessant prayer, and never to relax his heart'.

Yet again, he said, 'The person who lives in retreat needs to guard himself against hearing any word which is useless to him because it will make him lose his work. Just as a pregnant woman who holds someone on his guard drives out that which has been sown in her, anyone coming into her house announces a new illness, or strikes a foot, how long must she be treated before being able to conceive again? She aborts and dies in great heartache because she has given herself pain and has not seen the infant, and her husband is saddened.'

He also spoke about Abba Serapion. An old man asked him, 'For the sake of love, tell me what you yourself see'. He replied, 'I am like a person on a journey who looks out and makes signs to passers-by not to approach him'.

The old man, who had put the question to him, said, 'I see myself as if I had raised a rampart,[17]reinforced with bolts of iron, in order that if someone knocks and I do not recognize who it is, or know where he comes from, or what he wants, I do not open for him until he goes.'

17. Palladius, *Lausiac History* 18 and 36.

He also said, 'If someone searches for the Lord with a heart full of sorrow, he listens to his condition, asks with knowledge and becomes anxious with heartache, that he is not attached to a worldly thing but fearfully takes care of his soul to present it without reproach[18] to God's tribunal in the full measure of his strength.'

18. Cf. Ph 1:10.

27

In which he says, 'Attend Diligently'

ATTEND DILIGENTLY, FIRMLY BELIEVING that our Lord Jesus Christ, who is God, possesses glory and ineffable majesty. He has made himself a model for us who follow in his steps,[1] profoundly and deeply humbling himself and taking the nature of a slave.[2] He showed that he did not attach importance to shame and endured many offensive ignominies, as it is written, '*Like a sheep, he was led to slaughter. Like a silent lamb, not opening his mouth, he was brought before the one who sheared him. In his abasement, justice was denied him*'.[3] He suffered death for us, bearing many offences, in order that we, too, because of his commandments, may willingly suffer for our sins if someone, justly or unjustly, injures or defames us until we die. May we allow ourselves to be led like sheep to the slaughter. Like a speechless animal, may we not protest, accepting if you are afraid, or rejecting if you are unafraid, with great humility.

Attend diligently in order that, whether standing, or sitting, or whatever you are doing, you possess great fear and terror before God. Have neither exaltation nor pride, but live always in gentleness and contemplation. Have no anger, or distress, or agitation, knowing that God watches your every movement.

Attend diligently, knowing that it is written, '*When you have done everything that is commanded, say, 'We are unworthy slaves. We have*

1. Cf. 1 P 2:2.
2. Phm 2:7.
3. Is 53:7–8; Ac 8:32.

only done our duty'.[4] Whatever work you do, according to God, do not complete it as if you were owed wages but in all humility, like a truly unnecessary slave, who owes much and gives little.[5] Consider, you increase your sins each day through negligence, as it says, '*Whoever knows what is right to do and fails to do it commits a sin*'.[6] Above everything else, you fail to obey the commandments of God. Always work with the eye of your intellect. You may unceasingly groan and be sad. Pray to God, on account of the multitude of your sins, that he will pardon you because of his great pity, love of humanity, and mercy.

Attend diligently in order that in every thought, or word, or action which comes to your will you do not, in any way, search for rest but if it is the will of God, bring it to perfect completion.[7] If this appears to involve hard work endure it because *this commandment of the Lord is eternal life*.[8]

Attend diligently, believing that the insults and disgraces received on behalf of the Lord are great, beneficial, and salutary for your soul. Bear them willingly, without anger, always saying, 'I deserve to suffer and endure for the Savior. By tribulations and insults I imitate the passion of my God.'[9] Every time you remember those who have grieved you, pray for them with all your soul and in truth. Never utter a word against those who have obtained great benefits for you, but if someone praises or honors you, trouble yourself and pray that you may be spared this burden.[10] In this way, on every occasion that brings you glory and superiority, no matter how small, pray fervently with all your soul to God so that he will remove from you everything of this kind. Think, 'I am unworthy' and always scrupulously examine the ways and works of the most humble people. Conduct yourself in mourning and great humility,

4. Lk 17:10.
5. Cf. Mt 18:24–25.
6. Jm 4:17.
7. On God's will, see Origen, *De oratione* 26 PG 11:500ff.; Basil, *Short Rules* 42; John Chrysostom, *Concerning the statutes* 18:3ff, PG 49:185.
8. Jn 12:50.
9. Cf. Ep 5:1; 1 P 4:13.
10. Cf. Heb 12:1.

like the dead and buried of this world, the last of all, and the greatest sinner. These things are of the greatest profit for your soul.

Attend diligently, having a horror and perfect hatred, equal to a great death, or the loss of your soul and eternal punishment, of all love of command and glory, all desire for the glories, honors and praise of people, and the thought that you are something, someone. Remove, also, all lust, shame, and every sensual delight, no matter how small. Consider what is unnecessary. Do not touch the body of another person. If it is not necessary, do not ask anyone, 'Where is it?' Do not eat outside the appointed hour, no matter how little. By guarding and assuring yourself in small matters, you will not succumb in serious things, nor gradually fall by scorning little things.

Attend diligently, knowing that the Lord, *although he was rich, became poor for our sake*[11] and died. In dying for us, he bought us with his own blood[12] *in order that we, also, may consider living no longer for ourselves but for the Lord*,[13] being his perfect slave in everything, living always in front of him, like a very gentle animal who does not answer back but is submissive to his master, dead to human passions, all lust,[14] not having a will or desire of his own but aspiring only to do the work of God. In this way, we no longer believe ourselves to be free, nor detained by any power, but serving God and being submissive to his will.

Attend diligently, truly behaving, with your whole soul, like the last[15] and most sinful of all Christians. Have an unceasingly mournful soul, humbled and groaning. Always keep silent, considering yourself to be unworthy and ignorant, and only speaking when absolutely necessary.

Attend diligently, always remembering to have before your eyes eternal fire[16] and punishments. In this way, consider yourself as one of the living amidst those who are condemned and tortured. Since this is a time of repentance, adopt continual mourning in order

11. 2 Co 8:9.
12. Cf. Rm 3:25.
13. 2 Co 5:15.
14. Cf. 1 P 2:11.
15. Cf. Mk 9:35.
16. Cf. Mt 18:89.

to escape these great and fearful punishments and much sorrow and shame. Seeking the will of God, fulfill it with the sorrows and exhaustion of body and soul because of your sins. Apply yourself to manual work, fasts and many other humiliations in truly being the last *of all* and the *slave of all.*[17] In your soul, remember unresting lamentation and grinding teeth[18] as you meditate on the scriptures. During brief periods of meditation utter groaning and fervent prayer, in order that demons do not find an opportunity to slip into the heart of your perverse thoughts.[19]

Attend diligently, knowing that our Lord is dead and risen for us and has bought us through his blood.[20] In this way, *we might no longer live for ourselves but for the Lord, who died and was raised*[21] for us. Firmly believe that you are always in front of him and, as he scrutinizes your heart, that your conscience has left your body to appear unceasingly before him.

Attend diligently in order that, always being ready to obey the will of God, whether for death or life,[22] you do not eagerly introduce such tribulation but, through faith, await those great and formidable temptations, trials, tortures, and a fearful death which come to you.

Attend diligently in order that, considering you are before God, you do not speak, or visit a person, eat, or drink, sleep, or do even the slightest thing, without his will. In everything that you decide to do, search first of all for what is according to God, recognize the reason for the action and then act in a way that is acceptable in the eyes of God. In this way, confess your deep affection and freedom for God in every action.

Attend diligently in order that you always behave like a slave who, with fear, trembling,[23] and great humility, is near his Lord and follows him, without going away from him, always ready to obey his will.[24] Behave yourself also, whether sitting or standing, alone

17. Mk 10:44.
18. Cf. Mt 8:12.
19. Cf. Mt 13:39.
20. Cf. Rm 3:25, 5:8; 1 Co 6:20, 7:23.
21. 2 Co 15:15.
22. Cf. Ph 1:20.
23. Cf. Ph 2:12.
24. Cf. Ps 123:2; Mt 8:9.

or with others, so that you are always like this when you come, with fear and trembling, into the presence of God. Wish that your intellect be completely purified of evil thoughts and all reproach, have much humility, and be completely silent, because you know that God watches you. Do not, by any means, take the liberty of raising your head because of your sins.

Attend diligently in order that, if someone distresses you in an unimportant matter, you plan, in sadness or anger, to conceal yourself and say nothing.[25] When prayer has calmed your heart then, alone, implore your brother. If it is necessary for you to reprimand your brother, but you perceive yourself to be angry and deeply distressed, say absolutely nothing to him, in order not to increase your sorrow. When you see that you and he are together, and that you are calm and mild, then talk to him, not accusingly but warning him in all humility. Always restrain from any speech when you are angry, firmly believing that you are under the eyes of God who examines your heart. Hold fast and tremble, as if you always saw his glory and ineffable majesty, knowing that you are, by comparison, only dust and ashes,[26] putrefaction and worm.[27]

Attend diligently, waiting each day for whatever ordeal comes, whether death, tribulations, or great dangers. Endure each one willingly, without troubling yourself, with the thought that *it is necessary to endure many tribulations in order to enter the heavenly kingdom.*[28]

Attend diligently in order that in every situation that arises, whether word, or work, or thought, you do not in any way search your own will, or rest, but examine carefully in order to see what is the will of God and fulfill it with perfection, even if it appears to consist of hard work. Bear and truly carry it out because of the heavenly kingdom, believing with all your heart that it is more useful for you than all human caution because *his commandment is eternal life*[29] and those who look for it will not diminish in good things.[30]

25. Cf. Ep 5:4.
26. Si 17:32.
27. Ps 22:6.
28. Dorotheus, *Letter* 2. See also, Ac 14:22.
29. Jn 12:50.
30. Cf. Ps 34:10.

Attend diligently, being always before God in everything. Do not hope for anything of any person but, with faith, from him alone. If you need something, pray to God that this will be given to you, as soon as you require it, according to his will. Always give thanks to God for what you may find because he is the one who has given it to you. If something upsets you, do not put any hope in another person, nor sadden yourself, nor grumble against anyone but endure it willingly, thinking I am worthy to receive tribulations because of my sins, if God wills to have pity on me, he is able. If you think in this way, he himself, will fulfill all your needs.

Attend diligently in order to try and find, as hard as you can, every opportunity to humble yourself in every thought, word and deed. Debase yourself like dung[31] and conduct yourself every single way with low esteem, like dust and *ashes*.[32] Reckon yourself to be *the last* and most sinful *of all*[33] Christians, saying, 'In comparison with every Christian, I am merely dust and *ashes*. All my righteousness is like a woman's cloth at the time of her period[34] and if I do not receive mercy through God's great pity and grace, I am worthy of eternal punishment. *If God wills to enter into judgment with me*,[35] I cannot bear it because I am full of ignominy.' In this way always keep your soul in mourning and wait for death every day. Fervently and unceasingly implore God to correct your soul through his great mercy. He will have pity on you, in order that you feel overcome with sorrow. Never rejoice nor smile but always *turn your laughter into mourning and your joy into sorrow*.[36] Always walk with a somber attitude because your soul has had more than enough of mockery.[37] These things will greatly profit your soul and lead to salvation.

Attend diligently in order that you never accept anything unless you have been persuaded that God has sent this, like a just desert, to you. Receive it, then, with great peace, but separate and reject

31. Cf. Si 22:2.
32. Si 17:32.
33. Mk 9:35.
34. Cf. Is 64:6.
35. Jb 9:3.
36. Jm 4:9.
37. Cf. Ps 38:7.

whatever you see to be provided through injustice, struggle, deceit or duplicity, saying, '*It is better to share something small with the fear of God*[38] than to have much as a fruit of injustice'.

Attend diligently and force yourself to practice silence. God will enable you to struggle and discipline yourself in not speaking even the slightest word, unless it is necessary, nor to ask, 'Where is this?', or, 'What is that?' If you need to speak, first of all ask yourself if this need is well founded. If, according to God, it is better to speak than to keep silent, open your mouth with Godly fear and trembling, lowering your head and speaking with fear and in a low voice. If you meet someone, out of charity say little and soon become quiet. If someone asks you something, only listen if it is necessary and do not say more in answering.

Attend diligently in order that, just as you abstain from all carnal desire, you also abstain from *lust of the eyes*,[39] ears, mouth, and touch. Make sure that your eyes always pay attention to you and your hard work. Do not look at anyone, unless you perceive that the need is well founded. Never look unless absolutely necessary at a woman or man's handsome face. Do not allow your ears to hear anything concerning another, nor listen to unprofitable conversation. See to it that you fall silent, never talking without necessity.

If you read this, beloved, do your utmost to apply it to yourself in order that God protects you in the hour of temptation. Amen.

38. Pr 15:16.
39. 1 Jn 2:16.

28

The Branches of Malice[1]

To talk about the branches of malice, it is necessary for a person to know that it is a passion which separates him from God. We implore God's kindness for each of them, in order that his assistance may help us and give us power so that we may be capable of being stripped, for they are wounds in the soul, separating us from God. The person who is stripped of them is happy for he will be a spiritual lamb, received on the altar of God.[2] He will listen to the Lord's joyful voice saying, '*Well done, good and faithful servant! You have been faithful in some things, I will establish you over much. Enter in the joy of your Lord!*',[3] but those who wish to fulfill their carnal lust[4] and refuse to be treated by the holy remedy of repentance, in order to become pure, will find themselves naked in the hour of need, without the robe of the virtues,[5] and they will be thrown into the outer darkness,[6] where the devil is,[7] dressed in the robe of the passions which are fornication, covetousness, avarice, gossip, anger, envy, vainglory, and pride. Those are the branches, and there are many others which are like them.

1. On different kinds of evil thoughts, see Evagrius, *Praktikos* 6–14.
2. Cf. Rm 12:1.
3. Mt 25: 21, 23.
4. Cf. Ep 2:3.
5. Cf. Lk 15:22; Rv 6:11.
6. Cf. Mt 8:12 and 22:11–13.
7. Cf. Mt 25:41.

What is meant by fornication? It is intemperance, which is the taste of the body's finery, distraction, laziness, the talk of the fool, and shameless peeping.

What is meant by avarice?[8] That is when you do not believe in the promises of God, you love comfort, you desire worldly glory,[9] you love to lack pity, you love vainglory, you do not take account of others, you lack conscience, and you pay no attention to the judgment of God.

What is meant by gossip? The ignorance of the glory of God,[10] jealousy toward your neighbor because he does not take account of you, calumny, envy, regard of humans, and false witness.

What is meant by anger?[11] The desire to take advantage of your will, discord, false knowledge,[12] the desire to teach, love of worldly goods, cowardice, lassitude, impatience and commercial transactions.

What is meant by envy? Hatred against your neighbor, refusal to accept blame, laziness, refusal to see that the neighbor glories in God, love of useful friends, and the desire to interfere in worldly affairs.

What is meant by vainglory? Love of the perishable life, mortification by drinking to make known your name, love of the glory of people rather than of God, ignorance of that which saddens your heart, making your actions evident in order to be glorified by people, not to see the glory of God and satisfying your heart with bodily passions.

What is meant by pride? To be scandalized by someone of whom you hold little account, lack of submission toward your neighbor, vainglory because you say, 'I have no need of anybody', confidence in your own ability, and the desire to be known.

All that, the shrewd one works in the wretched soul in order to separate it from God. These are the heavy burdens[13] which Adam

8. On avarice, see *Sayings* Isaiah 9.
9. Cf. 1 Jn 2:16.
10. On calumny, see *Sayings* Isaiah 10.
11. On anger, see *Sayings* Isaiah 11.
12. Cf. 1 Tm 6:20.
13. Cf. Jr 17:24.

carried when he ate the fruit of the tree.[14] It was there also when he said, '*He has taken our weakness and has borne our ills*'.[15] These are the curses which were heaped upon Adam. This is what our Lord Jesus Christ killed upon the cross.[16] These are the old skins into which no new wine is poured.[17] These are the foxes which destroy the vineyard.[18] These are the strips of cloth which bound Lazarus.[19] These are the demons which Christ sent into the herd of pigs.[20] It is the Old person that the apostle orders to be skinned.[21] It is *flesh and blood* which *cannot inherit the kingdom of God*.[22] It is that of which He also said, '*If you live according to the flesh, you will die*'.[23] These are the wounds which the thieves inflicted on the one who was traveling down from Jerusalem to Jericho.[24] It is the chaff which the earth produced for Adam until he was thrown out of paradise.[25] It is Cain's offering, hated by God when he came to mix the unnatural things with the natural and, because it was not accepted by God, led him to kill Abel.[26] It is the part which Esau preferred until he lost his birthright for common food.[27] It is the Egyptian killed by Moses who became the Pharaoh's enemy and ran away into the Midian, until he received freedom from God and returned to face Pharaoh, until he had saved his brothers.[28] It is the Egyptians' leaven of which God said to Moses, 'Do not take with you leaven from the territory of the Egyptians and for seven days you will eat unleavened bread and on the eighth day there will be a feast for the Lord God',[29] in order that the soul becomes free from the seven passions. It was a

14. Cf. Gn 3:6–7.
15. Mt 8:17; cf. Is 53:4.
16. Cf. Ep 2:16.
17. Cf. Mt 9:17.
18. Cf. Jg 15:4–5.
19. Cf. Jn 11:44.
20. Cf. Mt 8:31:32.
21. Cf. Col 3:9; Ep 4:22.
22. 1 Co 15:50.
23. Rm 8:13.
24. Cf. Lk 10:30.
25. Cf. Gn 3:18.
26. Cf. Gn 4:3–8.
27. Cf. Gn 25:29–34.
28. Cf. Ex 2:11–15.
29. Cf. Ex 13:7.

feast for the Lord God in being healthy and neither bad nor old and being familiar with God. These are the false prophets who opposed Eliae.[30] If he had not wiped them out, the rain from the sky would not have come onto the earth. These are the lions which took hold of the lost sheep.[31] These are the thorns of which Isaiah said, '*I will attend it so that it produces grapes and it produced grapes*'.[32] It is the vine of which Jeremiah cried, '*How has the true vine turned in bitterness?*'[33]

Christ's burden is light; it is purity, the absence of anger, kindness, gentleness, the joy of the spirit, continence of the passions, love toward all, discernment, holiness, steadfast faith, patience in tribulations, comes to be regarded like a stranger in the world, and desires to leave its body and to meet Christ. These are the light burdens which Christ prescribes us to carry.

This is the way along which those saints have endured many labors before arriving. This is that which no person can acquire unless he strips away the Old Person,[34] frees it, and acquires love. Love renders it immaterial to all. It is therefore impossible for love to live in us, in order that we may love some worldly thing, as it is written, *You cannot share both the tables of God and of the devils.*[35] Isaiah also says, '*Who will tell us that the fire burns, who will describe the eternal place for us? Is it not the one who walks in injustice, who talks with frankness, who hates iniquity and injustice, who shakes hands in order not to accept presents, who stops his ears lest he hears bloodthirsty judgment and shuts his eyes in order not to see injustice?*'[36] *That person will live in a high, rocky cavern; he will be assured of receiving bread and water.*[37]

Consider the honor accorded by God to those who fight in this short space of time and strip away worldly burdens in bearing their tribulations. You see how God's help comes to assist those who remove their wills and cause all of the passions to disappear far from them, because they have followed the will of God. On the

30. 1 K 18:40–45.
31. Cf. 1 S 17:34; Jr 27:17.
32. Is 5:4.
33. Jr 2:21.
34. Cf. Col 13:9; Ep 4:22.
35. 1 Co 10:21.
36. Is 33:14.
37. Is 33:16.

other hand, those who maintain their wills and search to fulfill them begin well in the spirit but, as they cannot resist their enemies from making them find and accomplish their wills, end in the flesh. They struggle in search of adventure and in vain.[38] That is why the prophet Jeremiah answered saying, '*Confounded are those who do the Lord's works without care*'.[39] You see, God does not give his aid to those who desire at the same time to serve both God and the passions. He leaves them to their own wills and frees the hands of those who hate them, and in the place of honor, where the people wait, it is disgrace for those who fail them, for not having resisted their enemies until God brings them help and humiliates their enemies. After all the writings, we are not fulfilled by God without labor, fatigue, and pain.

As it is written in the Gospel, '*Many will say to me concerning that, "Lord, Lord, have we not prophesied in your name and carried out many miracles?" And he will answer them, "I do not recognize you!"*',[40] because they carried out work but did not guard it. We stay well withdrawn in the cell but our interior being[41] turns in impurities. We observe our offices but captivity serves to remove them from us. We observe fasts but calumny serves to lose them from us. We give bread to the destitute but hatred and contempt toward our brother causes us to lose it. We meditate on the words of God but frivolous entreaties cause us to lose them. We prepare the table before our brother on account of God but avarice and envy causes us to lose merit for this. All that happens to us because we do not keep the will of God. That is why he says to them, 'I do not recognize you',[42] because they have not fought with knowledge but they have struck the air,[43] for they have not seen a crown for their heads. He tells them, 'I do not recognize you, because you have not carried my mark. Go far away from me'.[44]

38. Ga 3:3.
39. Cf. Pseudo-Macarius, *Homily* 19. See also, Jr 31:10.
40. Mt 7:22–23.
41. Cf. 2 Co 4:16.
42. Cf. Mt 7:23.
43. Cf. 1 Co 9:26.
44. Cf. Mt 7:23.

Let us, therefore, do all we can, brothers, to fulfill our work and to pray to God to send us his fear and to be our guardian. He will guard all their works for them, for fear that in leaving our body we may not be found naked of virtues and fall to the serpent's power, for the enemy is full of deceit. He is envious and cruel. His aspect is odious. He is unpitying in his maliciousness, for he is the help of those who desire the world. Observe all the saints. They were stripped of worldly things and in this way have left to fight the enemy. When the Lord is brought down before them he has been a runaway to their eyes. When Daniel left to fight with God, the Lord did not find anything in Daniel which belonged to him, for the lions sniffed him[45] and did not find in him the scent of the one who had been eaten in disobedience. Job suffered the struggle after first being freed from worldly things and proved that the one who spoke highly—'I have covered that which is below the sky: here I am!'—was a runaway and he was held, following bound before God, like a sparrow in the hand of a little infant.[46]

Let us implore, then, the kindness of God in the application of the heart, the tears, and mortification. We are subject to every person because of the Lord.[47] We humble ourselves before our brothers, considering that they are more lucid than us, *not rendering to anyone evil for evil*,[48] not having any malicious thought against anyone in our heart, but not having all that in a single heart, without saying about good worldly things, 'This is mine'.[49] Each day we measure our spirit's progress, keeping it from impure thoughts, refusing to satisfy the body[50] in order to prevent it from waiting for the satisfaction of its passions from us, until it is ruled by the soul and that this one is submissive to the spirit[51] and becomes a pure and spotless bride,[52] who calls to her bridegroom, 'My brother descends in his garden

45. Cf. Dn 6:18.
46. Cf. Jb 40:24.
47. Cf. 1 P 2:3.
48. Rm 12:17.
49. Cf. Ac 4:23.
50. Cf. Col 2:23.
51. Cf. 1 Th 5:23.
52. Cf. 2 Co 11:2.

and eats the fruit of its trees'.[53] Therefore, let us struggle, brothers, in order that, having obtained such an assurance before him, we hear him, we hear him say, '*There, where I am, I wish that those also may be with me, because I have loved them as you, Father, have loved me; you in me and me in them*'.[54]

To the Holy Trinity, consubstantial and coeternal, is our power to have mercy, until we will find rest with his saints on the day of judgment. To him be glory and power in the ages of ages. Amen.

53. Cf. Sg 4:16 and 5:1.
54. Jn 17:24, 23.

29

Lamentations

WOE TO US, THE VOLUPTUOUS and ephemeral ones who, because of a passing and iniquitous carnal desire, will not see the glory of the Lord!

Woe to us, because *the corruptible ones do not inherit incorruptibility*[1] and, despising incorruptibility, impetuously attach ourselves to corruptibility!

Woe to us whose bodies, fed by our carnal sins, are destined to be decomposed as we approach and dwell in rot and who fear neither the fire, which unceasingly tortures us, nor the worm, which never rests![2]

Woe to us, for good Christians greet and embrace our impure bodies; we are *white sepulchers*,[3] stinking of mortal sin!

Woe to us who, by greed and through feebleness, accumulate semen in us and are aroused by carnal actions of an iniquitous manner!

Woe to us who prepare ourselves to be a den for demons instead of a receptacle for God!

Woe to us who are full of benevolence when somebody flatters us but lack this virtue when someone irritates us!

Woe to us who do not discern the corruptibility of incorruptibility and scorn the terrible divine justice!

1. 1 Co 15:50.
2. Cf. Is 66:24.
3. Mt 23:27.

Woe to us who are freed for good actions but are full of zeal for and attention to malice!

Woe to us who are destined for eternal light but have prepared our bodies for eternal darkness!

Woe to us for whom the Son of Man has come, who, consubstantial with God the Father was born for us, but has nowhere among us to rest his head, while foxes, evil and deceptive spirits, dig a hole in us for their lairs![4]

Woe to us, for while those who have an upright heart present to the Judge their immaculate souls and holy and spotless bodies, we, who have soiled souls and impure bodies, wait for the sentence of eternal punishment!

Woe to us who are full of covetousness for excesses and every kind of impurity, yet seek the same honor as the holy ones!

Woe to us, for although we are condemned and charged for many sins, live among holy ones and innocents as if we were holy and innocent!

Woe to us for, although we are entirely reprehensible, we bring back and correct those who greatly surpass us!

Woe to us for, although we have a beam in our eye, we angrily blame our brothers who have sinned lightly, as if we were irreproachable![5]

Woe to us who complain to others of heavy and insupportable burdens but refuse to touch theirs ourselves, claiming to have a weaker body![6]

Woe to us who do not thank God for all he has given us and, forgetful of misfortune, pain, and past ordeals, do not show ourselves worthy before the loving-kindness of God's help and present grace!

Woe to us who love that which is worse and, because of that, painfully support that which is good!

Woe to us who care for bodily needs under the pretext that we have exhausted our bodies through many ascetic practices, when we

4. Cf. Mt 8:20.
5. Cf. Mt 7:3–5.
6. Cf. Mt 23:4.

have to do penance under sackcloth and ash, with bread and water in tears and groans!

Woe to us who abandon divine monastic observance and have the temerity to teach others the practice of virtue!

Woe to us who forgetting our past sins, have neither anxiety nor tears for those that we are about to commit!

Woe to us who, after having begun well through the help and grace of God, have now become full of lust![7]

Woe to us who are so plunged into impure thoughts that we ask ourselves if we have really committed such sins, as if we have not been paying attention!

Woe to us who, as we eat and drink, do not reflect on the war that our gluttony comes to wage in us!

Woe to us, for at the moment when demons arouse impure memories in us, they find us well prepared to accord our thoughts to them!

Woe to us who do not know how we have great blessings through the worth of our immortal soul but hold our flesh in higher esteem to it, although it is inferior to it, because of carnal delights!

Woe to us, for piety restricts us in word and habit!

Woe to us who, leaving prayerful meditation and divine reading, waste our days in distraction and gossip!

Woe to us, for our hearts are so hardened that often, when we seek compunction and tears, we do not find them because of the excess of our careless attitude and indolence!

Woe to us for, although God has said, 'The soul which has sinned has died',[8] we never care that it is always sinning!

Woe to us who by greed and feebleness excite our bodies to incline to sin, in impure desires and malicious thoughts, regarding these as the arrows of the evil one entering our hearts, which through bodily contact become like roving stallions, and for which we do not heed eternal punishment or fear for our spiritual worth!

Woe to the voluntary degeneration of our soul, for it separates its own free will from heavenly glory and, by the malicious covetous-

7. Cf. Ga 3:3.
8. Ez 18:4.

ness of ephemeral things, associates with impure demons through its ill-disciplined flesh!

Woe to us who, mistakenly disowning ourselves, are assailed by domestic passions!

Woe to us who groan so much when distressed by sicknesses and bodily pain, but are insensitive to the injuries and pains that attack the soul!

Woe to us, for the soul's authority is in complete servitude to the flesh, like the best command to the worst, and the will of neither is to serve God their creator!

Woe to us, for evil and impure thoughts are rejuvenating our sins, and we do not discern when God withdraws himself and impure spirits arrive!

Woe to us who, in our madness and lack of reason, demand the praise due to the holy ones and do not crave their works or way of life!

Woe to us who, in obeying the commandments of God, have neither fear of slavery, nor the zeal or good disposition of mercenaries, nor the love of children!

Woe to us who do not refuse any word or action to please people but completely neglect the righteous ones!

Woe to us who, through shame, sin in front of people yet have no regard for eternal shame!

Woe to us who do not recognize that we are born of poor and obscure parents but, having made profession of love for God, poverty and humility, are ambitious to be likened to riches and greatness!

Woe to us who practice abstinence in the world, for the sake of poverty, yet, now that we are called through vocation, take great care to satisfy our stomach and give rest to our flesh!

Woe to us, for while *the angels encamp around those who fear God*[9] and the demons around those who do not fear him but break his commandments, we arrange ourselves in the demons' camp!

Woe to us, for our eyes stay dry here below but we will withstand the torrent of tears, burning and bitter in the fire, lamentation and unceasing suffering!

9. Ps 34:7.

Woe to us who are anxious to please for the riches and powers that we encounter, but divert the poor who approach us in supplication, like unfortunate ones!

Woe to us who do not act according to our duty toward all people but determine our actions according to what pleases us best!

Woe to us who define, judge, and condemn the person who is righteous and whom we hold to be far from the practice of good!

Woe to us who, carefully cleaning the ground of brambles, thistles, and fruit harming plants, do not carefully clear our souls through fear of God of evil and impure thoughts which harm the holy virtues!

Woe to us who, although having to leave the earth where we live, consecrate much time to worrying about earthly and ephemeral matters, over which we have no control when we come to the moment of our inevitable departure from here below!

Woe to us who, in giving account of every action of our earthly life, of every vain word, every malicious and impure thought, and the slightest preoccupation to the terrible judge, are not fearful about our souls, as if we had to pass all our life in a carefree manner!

Woe to us impetuous ones, who are not only certain of the cause of impiety and iniquities that we have committed, but also of the cause of our contempt and incredulity concerning the promises of God!

Woe to us who, like mad things, take pleasure in corruption and have the chance of participating in incorruptibility through a life conformed to the Gospel, are held back through love of earthly things associated with corruption and strangers to eternal incorruption!

Woe to us who have preferred confounded corruption to incorruption!

Woe to us who are able to overcome every sensual delight but through complaisance with ourselves have preferred to be vanquished by our passions!

Woe to us who are not worn down by experience and discernment in our words, thoughts and actions but who, like beasts lacking reason, follow that which is more agreeable and attractive to us!

Woe to us, for when Almighty God manifests himself to us in

order to wipe out the works of the devil we are still attached to them![10]

Woe to us who blush and fear to sin before people, yet neither tremble nor fear when we commit impiety and sin under the eyes of those who see hidden things!

Woe to us who do not season our word with divine salt[11] but unceasingly utter useless and disrespectful words toward our neighbor!

Woe to us whose conversations with people are full of flattery, lies, and hypocrisy but do not fear to be condemned by them!

Woe to us, for sleep and lethargy allow the demon to deprive our hearts of compunction!

Woe to us who have renounced the world but surpass the worldly in vice!

Woe to us, for when we have great need of being taught and instructed we correct the trifles of others!

Woe to us if the Lord put us to the test on earth and saw us arrive for judgment without the thing that we knew corrected us!

Woe to us who do not consider what is in our stomach and for that are overcome by carnal pleasure and pride!

Woe to us, for while we unceasingly soil our souls with impure thoughts, we wish to be taken for holy ones and honored with their titles!

Woe to us who, entirely preoccupied with vain things, forget the struggle against the devil!

Woe to us who insolently sin here below, for there we will be received through the inextinguishable fire of Gehenna, outer darkness, the worm which knows no rest, tears, and grinding of teeth[12] and eternal shame before all creation, both superior and inferior!

Woe to our soul, stripped of discernment and impenitent, for until the resurrection of the dead it will lament, groan, and will not know what to do in its sinful body with tears and grinding of teeth

10. Cf. 1 Jn 3:8.
11. Cf. Col 4:6.
12. Cf. Is 66:24; Mt 25:30.

because of the very painful torture and bitter and grievous eternal fire!

Woe to us who through egotism do not love God or our neighbor and this is why we have fallen prey to all the passions, dissolute desires, and diabolic pride!

Woe to us, where fear and love of God are not preponderant and this is why we are so far from Christ who loves us!

Woe to us, for when many opportunities are given to us for repentance, we wait until someone snatches us like the barren fig tree which wore out the earth![13]

Woe to us who, in our passing exile love confounded pleasures without calling to mind the delights of paradise but scorn even the heavenly kingdom!

Woe to us who through our hardness, like the foolish virgins who do not buy the oil which lights the lamps here below, lack generosity toward our neighbor![14]

Woe to us who address prayers night and day to God saying, 'Lord, Lord',[15] yet do not carry out what he ordained for us!

Woe to the writer of these lamentations! I am prey to everything I write and have not the slightest sigh of regret!

Woe to the one who is distressed by others and deprives himself of doing anything for them!

Woe to us who do not feel any shame when our conscience reproaches us, accusing and unceasingly testifying against us, nor fear of God's judgment, in spite of the chastisements we have incurred because of our actions!

Woe to us who, despite the stench of our actions, rejoice in the praise of people!

Woe to us, for dream, distraction and forgetfulness remove the fear of God from our hearts!

Woe to us, for our zeal for ephemeral things renders our intelligence barren and obtuse!

Woe to us, for God's patience supports us without making us

13. Cf. Lk 13:7.
14. Cf. Mt 25:8–9.
15. Mt 7:21.

perish because of our actions, and we do not hurry ourselves to always profit from improving!

Woe to us who now do not remember our sins, but who, once our soul is deprived of the body, then see with a sad and very bitter repentance all that we have committed in words, thoughts, and deeds, written and engraved on our intellect's memory!

Woe to us who—despite the affirmation of the apostle, '*The one who eats the bread and drinks the cup of our Lord unworthily eats and drinks his own condemnation, because he does not discern the Lord's body*'[16]—full of impurities, approach the fearful and formidable mysteries of God, according ourselves forgiveness of that which we have committed in nocturnal imaginings and impure thoughts. For how many bodily injuries and infirmities of his soul does he not reveal before passing to eternal punishment and immense shame, this one who approaches God without pure thoughts, spotless eyes, a chaste body, and surges of the soul and of the body which soils it!

Woe to me who writes this in bitterly weeping but has not begun the work of repentance!

Woe to me who says the truth but does not follow it well!

Woe to me who praises good but does wrong!

Woe to those who sin in sensual delight, because a bitter end and eternal shame await them!

Woe to those who grow sad without profit, for they have deprived themselves of the sadness that is useful for repentance!

Woe to those who insult and have a fiery nature, for they separate themselves from blessed charity!

Woe to the envious and jealous, because they render themselves strangers and enemies to the kindness and charity of God!

Woe to those who seek to please people, for they are not able to please God!

Woe to those who make exception to people, for they separate themselves from the truth of God!

Woe to the proud, because the prize of the devil's renegade belongs to them!

16. 1 Co 11:27, 29.

Woe to those who do not fear the Lord, for, because of this, they will be entangled in more numerous sins, and be beaten here and below!

Woe to us, who cannot bear the stings and bites of fleas, nits, lice, moths, mosquitoes and bees, and do not receive any help or refuge against the great mouth of the dragon which chews and swallows us as if we were reduced by being boiled, and injects us with his deadly venom!

Woe to us, because the devil wears us out in pleasures, injuries, constraints, and in every type of deception which are of this world, and we do not wish to cease from our pains!

Woe to us for, while apostasy bears it for numerous years and increasingly rejects orthodox faith, we do not cry, we do not have a troubled heart, and we do not refrain from our daily passions, but we pile sin upon sin in order to receive both bitter and eternal punishments in Gehenna for our evil work and incredulity!

Woe to us, before the writing of these lamentations, for, when we arrive at the end of the world and repentance and tears for the faults of our youth are far from us, we find we have added greater and more serious misdemeanors and more intolerable sins during our old age!

Woe to us who are not ashamed of the entirely intolerable sufferings and different ills of our bodies, but still strengthen ourselves with sins and nourish our soiled and sinful bodies with contempt and with much overindulgence and carelessness!

Woe to us who have to pass through a fire whose rage is more than the currents of the sea, *in order that each one* of us *receives whatever he deserves whilst he was in the body either good or bad*![17]

Woe to us who do not think about this hidden and spiritual blaze, nor of bitter mourning, or grinding of teeth in the other world.[18] God will remove his light from the flame and the impious and sinners will share the burning and darkness of the fire!

Woe to me, wretched soul, for *I am tested by sadness and unceasing*

17. 2 Co 5:10.
18. Cf. Mt 25:30.

grief in my heart.[19] Weeping for myself, I will say that malice has changed my conscience, corruptibility has overcome incorruptibility, lying has concealed truth, death has carried life away, perishable and ephemeral worldly things have replaced incorruptible and lasting heavenly things, that which is abominable and worthy of hatred has seemed more sweet and appealing to me than the true love of Christ and his holiness. Error, having banished truth from my soul, has chased away joy for sadness. I have chosen shame and dishonor instead of confidence and praise. I have preferred bitterness to sweetness. I have loved the earth and its dust more than heaven and its kingdom. The darkness of the enemy, which hates all good things, has heart and has wiped away the light of knowledge from my intellect!

Woe to me, woe to me! What are the traps of the devil that have ensnared me, have overturned me and have caused me to stumble from so great a height? I have been completely broken and my sweat has run from me in vain. Who will not lament for me, who will not shed bitter tears on my behalf, who has been crushed by useless sorrow, and who has been shipwrecked near to port? *Have pity on me, have pity on me, have pity on me, O friends!*[20] Do not hesitate to pray to my good and forbearing Lord Christ, so that, touched with compassion, he will dissipate from my intellect the horrifying darkness which produces the devil, the enemy of good, and I will see in what mire I am set, and what will be able to lift me, for I am afraid, I do not wish to have all hope removed from me in the little rest which I have left to me! There is no suffering greater than mine, no wound comparable to mine, no grief like that in heart, for *my iniquities flowed over my head,*[21] *my injuries have not been inflicted by the sword, and my deaths are not caused through combat*[22] but by the inflamed darts which the enemy has driven into me[23] and I have blinded my

19. Rm 9:2.
20. Jb 19:21.
21. Ps 38:4.
22. Is 22:2.
23. Cf. Ps 38:2.

inner self. I blunder into the unfathomable abyss,[24] *the fear that I feared has come to me*,[25] and *the shade of death has recovered me*![26]

Woe to my soul, look at the present ephemeral things that will pass away with bitterness and grief, and see the horrifying future. Consider, O soul, what good and hopeful things you have fallen away from, and which punishments you will soon receive in an inheritance which is without success or consolation! Having that light above your head extinguished, follow those in front of you, advance, prostrate yourself, pray and intercede to the giver of immortal light in order that he may withdraw you from the devouring flame and somber darkness, for it behooves him to pardon sins and accord goodness to us who are unworthy of pity. To him belongs glory and power unto the ages of ages. Amen.

24. Cf. Ps 69:2.
25. Jb 3:25.
26. Ps 44:19.

Bibliography

PRIMARY SOURCES: Select

Abba Isaiah. *Abbé Isaïe, Recueil ascétique—Introduction et traduction française par les moines de Solesmes*. Collection Spiritualité Orientale no. 7. Abbaye de Bellefontaine, 1985.

———. *Asceticon*. Edited by Victor Arras. CSCO 458–59/Scriptores Aethiopici 77–78. Lourain, 1984.

———. Edited by S. Schoinas. Augoustinos [Monachos]. Τοῦ ὁσίου πατρὸς ἡμῶν ἀββᾶ Ἠσαίου Λόγοι κθ. Jerusalem, 1911; Volos, 1962r.

———. *Les cinq recensions de 1'Ascéticon syriaque d'abba Isaïe I. Les témoins et leurs parallèles non-syriaques. Edition des logoi I–XIII. II. Edition des logoi XIV–XXVI.* Edited by R. Draguet. CSCO 289/Syr. 120 and 290/Syr. 121. Louvain, 1968.

———. *Les cinq recensions de l'Ascéticon syriaque d'abba Isaïe. I. Introduction au problem isaïen. Version des logoi I–XIII avec des parallèles grecs et latins. II. Version des logoi XIV–XXVI avec des parallèles grecs.* Edited by R. Draguet. CSCO 293/Syr. 122 and 294/Syr. 123. Louvain, 1968.

———. *L'Ascéticon Copte de 1'abbé Isaïe: fragments sahidiques*. Edited by A. Guillaumont. Bibliothèque d'Etudes coptes 5. Cairo, 1956.

———. *Paterica Armeniaca*. Edited by L. Leloir. CSCO/Subsidia 42–3, 47, 51. Louvain, 1974–76.

Athanasius. *Vita Antonii*. PG 26:838–976.

Barsanuphius and John. *Letters*. Translated by J. Chryssavgis and P. Penkett (forthcoming).

———. *Questions and Answers.* PO 31:3. Paris, 1966.

Basil. *The Ascetical Works*. Translated by W. K. L. Clarke. London, 1925.

Choricius of Gaza. *Opera*. Edited by R. Foerster and E. Richsteig. Stuggart, 1922, 1972r.

Commentaire du Livre d'abba Isaïe (fragments). CSCO 336/Syr. 150 and 337/Syr. 151. Louvain, 1973.

Dadišo Qatraya. *Commentaire du livre d'abba Isaïe (logoi I–XV)*. Edited by R. Draguet. CSCO 326/Syr. 144 and 327/Syr. 145. Louvain, 1972.

Enea of Gaza. *Epistole*. Edited by L. M. Positano. Naples, 1962.

Evagrius Ponticus. *The Praktikos and Chapters on Prayer.* Translated by J. E. Bamberger. Kalamazoo: Cistercian Publications, 1978.

Isaac of Nineveh. *Homily* 7. Edited A. J. Wensick. Wiesbaden, 1969.

Jerome. *Life of Hilarion*. PL 23:29–64.

Johannes von Gaza und Paulus Silentarius-Kunst-beschreibungen Justinianischer Zeit. Edited by P. Friedlander. Leipzig and Berlin, 1912.

John Cassian. *Conferences.* Translated by C. Luibheid. New York, 1985.

John of Gaza. *Anacreontica—Anecdota Graeca*. Edited by P. Matranga. Rome, 1850; Hildesheim, 1971r.

John Rufus (of Maïouma). *Plérophoriae*. PO 8/1. Paris, 1912.

Lives of the Desert Fathers. Edited by N. Russell and B. Ward. Oxford and Kalamazoo, 1981.

Mark the Deacon. *The Life of Porphyry, Bishop of Gaza*. Translated by G. F. Hill. Oxford, 1913.

Outtier, B. 'Un Patéricon arménien (*Vitae Patrum*, II, 505–635)', in *Le Muséon* 84 (1971) 299–351.

Pachomian Koinonia. Translated by A. Vielleux. 3 vols. Kalamazoo: Cistercian Publications, 1980–81.

Palladius. *Lausiac History*. Translated by R. T. Meyer. London and Maryland, 1965.

Paphnutius. *Histories of the Monks of Upper Egypt and The Life of Onnophrius*. Translated by T. Vivian. Kalamazoo: Cistercian Publications, 1993.

Paul Evergetinos. *Synagogē: A Collection of the inspired sayings of the godly and holy fathers gathered together from the entirety of divinely inspired literature*. 4 vols. Athens, 1986.

Petrus der Iberer. Edited by R. Raabe. Leipzig, 1895. See also, *Lives and Legends of the Georgian Saints*. London, 1956.

Philokalia. Edited by Nikodemus the Hagiorite and Makarios of Corinth. Translated by G. Palmer, P. Sherrard, and K. Ware. London, 1979 f.

Procopius of Gaza. *Epistolae et Declamationes*. Edited by A. Garzya and R. - J. Loenertz. Rome, 1963.

Sayings of the Desert Fathers: The Alphabetical Collection. Translated by B. Ward. Kalamazoo: Cistercian Publications, 1983r.

Timothy of Gaza. *On Animals*. Translated by F. Bodenheimer and A. Rabinowitz. Jersusalem, 1948.

Vies et Pratiques des saints Pères. 4 vols. Venice, 1855.

Vitae virorum apud Monophysitas celeberrimorum. Edited by E. W. Brooks. CSCO/Syr 25. Paris, 1907.

Wisdom of the Desert Fathers: Systematic Sayings from the Anonymous Series of the Apophthegmata Patrum. Translated by B. Ward. Oxford, 1986r.

World of the Desert Fathers: Stories and sayings from the Anonymous Series of the Apophthegmata Patrum. Translated by C. Stewart. Oxford, 1986.

Zacchariah of Mitylene. *The Chronicle*. Translated by E. W. Brooks. London, 1899.

Zacchariah Rhetor. *Historia Ecclesiastica.* Edited by E. W. Brooks. CSCO 83 and 84 (transl. in 87 and 88). Paris, 1919–1921.

Zacchariah the Scholar. *Historia Ecclesiastica.* Edited by E. W. Brooks. CSCO 55:6. Paris, 1919.

———. *Vitae Isaiae.* Edited by E. W. Brooks. CSCO 7 and 8. Paris, 1907.

———. *Vita Severi.* PO 2:1. Paris, 1907.

SECONDARY SOURCES

A: ON ABBA ISAIAH AND THE *DISCOURSES*

Astruc, C. 'Un recueil de textes ascétiques: le Parisinus Graecus 915', *RAM* 42 (1966) 181–191.

Aubert, R. 'Isaié de Scété', in *Dictionnaire d'Histoire et de Géographie Ecclésiastique*, fasc. 150 (1912-) cols. 120–24.

Bacht, H. 'Isaias der Jüngere', in *Lexikon für Theologie und Kirche.* Vol. 5 (1962) col. 782.

Bardenhewer, O. *Geschichte der altkirchlichen literatur.* n.p., 1913–32.

Bauer, W. *Die Severus—Vita des Zacharias Rhetor*, in *Aufsatze und kleine Schriften.* Tubingen, 1967.

Baumstark, A. *Geschichte der Syrischen Literatur mit Ausschluss der christlich-palastinischen Texte.* Bonn, 1922.

Binns, J. *Ascetics and Ambassadors of Christ: The Monasteries of Palestine (314–631).* Oxford, 1994.

Boumis, P. 'Isaias', in 'Ησαίας, in Θρησκευτικὴ καί 'Ηθικὴ 'Εγκυκλοπαιδεία. Vol. 6 (1965) col. 78.

Bouyer, L. *A History of Christian Spirituality, vol. 1: The Spirituality of the New Testament and the Fathers.* London and New York, 1982.

Brock, S. 'The Syriac Tradition', in *The Study of Spirituality.* Edited by C. Jones, G. Wainwright, and E. Yarnold. London, 1992r: 199–215.

Burton-Christie, D. *The Word in the Desert: scripture and the quest for holiness in early Christian monasticism*. New York and Oxford, 1993.

Chabot, M. *Pierre l'Ibérian évêque monophysite de Mayouma à la fin du V siècle*. Paris, 1895.

Chadwick, H. 'Eucharist and Christology in the Nestorian Controversy', *JTS* N.S. 2/2 (1951) 145–164.

Chitty, D. J. 'Abba Isaiah', *JTS* N. S. 22/1 (1971) 47–72.

———. 'The Books of The Old Men', *Eastern Churches Review* 6 (1974) 15–21.

———. *The Desert a City: An Introduction to the Study of Egyptian and Palestinian Monasticism under the Christian Empire*. London and Oxford, 1977r.

Chryssavgis, J. 'Abba Isaiah of Scetis and the Practice of Holiness', in N. Panou (ed.), *Orthodoxia and Economia: Festschrift for His All Holiness Ecumenical Patriarch Bartholomew* (Athens, 2000) 79–93. In Greek and English.

———. 'Aspects of Spiritual Direction in Abba Isaiah of Scetis', in *Studia Patristica* 35 (Louvain, 2001) 30–40.

———. 'Isaiah of Scetis and John Wesley', in *Wesleyan Theological Journal* 35, 2 (2000) 91–113. Also appeared in S. T. Kimbrough (Jr.), Orthodox and Wesleyan Spirutuality (New York, 2002) 75–94.

Couilleau, G. 'Entre Scété et Gaza, un monachisme en devenir: l'Abbé Isaïe', Appendix to the third edition of the French translation of Abba Isaiah, *Recueil ascétique* (1985) 337–367 (see Primary Sources).

———. 'Marc le Diacre', in *Dictionnaire de Spiritualité* 10 (1977) cols. 265–67.

D. I. D. (initials of reviewer of), 'Τοῦ ὁσίου πατρὸς ἡμῶν ἀββᾶ Ἠσαίου Λόγοι κθ', *Irénikon* 36 (1963) 142–143.

Devos, P. 'Quand Pierre 1'Ibère vint-il à Jérusalem?', *AB* 86 (1968) 337–50.

Draguet, R. 'A la source de deux *Apophtegmes* grecs, PG 65 Jean Colobos 24 and 32', *Byzantion* 32 (1962) 53–61.

———. 'Les Apophtegmes des moines d'Égypte: Problèmes littéraires', *Bulletin de la classe des lettres de 1'Académie de Belgique* 47 (1961) 134–149.

———. 'Notre édition des recensions syriaque de 1'[Ascéticon] d' Abba Isaïe', *Revue d' Histoire Ecclésiastique* 63/3–4 (1968) 843–857.

———. 'Parallèles macariens syriaques des logoi I et III de 1'Ascéticon isaïen syriaque', *Le Muséon* 83 (1970) 483–496.

———. 'Une lettre de Sérapion de Thumis aux disciples d'Antoine (AD 356)', *Le Muséon* 64 (1951) 1–25.

———. 'Une section isaïenne' d'apophtegmes dans le Karakallou 251', *Byzantion* 35 (1965) 44–61.

Elm, S. *Virgins of God: The Making of Asceticism in Late Antiquity*. Oxford, 1994.

Frend, W. H. C. *The Rise of the Monophysite Movement*. Cambridge, 1972.

Geerard, M. 'Isaias Gazaeus (Scetensis?)', in *Clavis Patrum Graecorum*. Turnhout, 1974-: 5555–5556.

Gould, G. *The Desert Fathers on Monastic Community*. Oxford, 1993.

Graf, G. *Geschichte der christlichen arabischen Literatur*. Studi e Testi 118. Vatican City, 1944.

Graffin, F. 'Un inédit de 1'abbé Isaïe sur les étapes de la vie monastique', *Orientalia Christiana Periodica* 29 (1963) 449–454.

Gribomont, J. 'Egyptian Spirituality' in *Christian Spirituality, vol. 1: Origins to the Twelfth Century*. Edited by B. McGinn, J. Meyendorff and J. Leclercq. New York, 1985: 89–112.

———. 'Isaiah of Scete (and Gaza)' in *Encyclopedia of the Early Church* (1992) 147.

Grillmeier, A. and H. Bacht, 'Das konzil von Chalkedon', in *Geschichte und gegenwart*. Wurzburg, 1951. Vol. 2, 273–74.

Guillaumont, A. 'Dadišo Qatraya' in *Dictionnaire de Spiritualité* 3/1 (1933-) 2–3.

———. 'La recension copte de 1''Ascéticon' de 1'abbé Isaïe' in *Coptic Studies in honor of Walter Ewing Crum*. Boston, 49–60.

———. 'Une notice syriaque inédite sur la vie de 1'abbé Isaïe', *AB* 67 (1949) 350–360.

Guy, J. -C. 'Le centre monastique de Scété dans la litterature du Ve siècle', *Orientalia Christiana Periodica* 30 (1964) 129–47.

———. *Recherches sur la tradition grecque des 'Apophthegmata Patrum'*. Subsidia Hagiographica 36. Brussels, 1962.

Hardy, Jr., E. R. 'A fragment of the works of the abbot Isaias', *Annuaire de l'Institut de philologie et d'histoire orientales et sklaves de l'Université Libre de Bruxelles* 7 (1944) 127–40.

Hausherr, I. 'L'imitation de Jésus-Christ dans la spiritualité byzantine', *Orientalia Christiana Analecta* 183 (1969) 217–245.

———. 'Le Météríkon de 1'abbé Isaïe', *Orientalia Christiana Analecta* 183 (1969) 105–120.

———. 'Le Pseudo-Denys est-il Pierre 1'Ibérien?', *Orientalia Christiana Analecta* 183 (1969) 247–260.

———. *Spiritual Direction in the Early Christian East.* Kalamazoo: Cistercian Publications, 1990.

———. *The Name of Jesus*. Kalamazoo: Cistercian Publications, 1978.

Honigmann, E. *Pierre l'Ibérian et les écrits du Pseudo-Denys l'Aréopagite*. Brussels, 1952.

Keller, H. 'L'abbé Isaïe-le-Jeune', *Irénikon* 16 (1939) 113–126.

Kirchmeyer, J. 'A propos d'un texte du pseudo-Athanase', *RAM* 40 (1964) 311–13.

Krüger, G. 'Wer War Pseudo-Dionysios?', *Byzantinische Zeitschrift* 8 (1899) 302–305.

Kugener, M. 'Observations sur la Vie de 1'ascète Isaïe et sur les Vies de Pierre l'Ibérien et de Théodore d'Antinoé par Zacharie le Scolastique', *Byzantinische Zeitschrift* 9 (1900) 464–70.

Lefort, L. -Th. 'Fragments coptes', *Le Muséon* 58 (1945) 97–120.

Lang, D. M. 'Peter the Iberian and his biographers', *Journal of Ecclesiastical History* 2 (1951) 158–68.

Mercati, S. 'Sur papiro greco dell'Archivio di Stato di Firenze', *Aegyptus* 32 (1952) 464–473.

Nau, F. 'Les récits inédits du moine Anastase', *Revue de l'Orient Chrétien* 22 (1920–21).

Neyt, F. 'Citations [isaïennes] chez Barsanuphe et Jean de Gaza', *Le Muséon* 84 (1971) 65–92.

———. *Les lettres a Dorothée dans la correspondance de Barsanuphe et de Jean de Gaza*, (Thesis) Louvain, 1969.

Penkett, P. and J. Chryssavgis. *In the Footsteps of the Lord: The Teaching of Abba Isaiah of Scetis.* Oxford, 2001.

Penkett, R. 'Towards a Theology of Tears: Penthos in the Writings of Abba Isaiah', *Fairacres Chronicle*, 30:2 (1997) 8–14.

Perrone, L. *La Chiesa di Palestina e le Controversie Cristologiche: dal concilio di Efeso (431) al secondo concilio di Constantinopoli (553)*, Testi e ricerche di Scienze religiose 18. Brescia, 1980.

Petit, L. 'Isaie' in *Dictionnaire de Théologie Catholique*, vol. 8 (1924) cols. 78–81.

Regnault, L. 'Isaïe de Scété ou de Gaza' in *Dictionnaire de Spiritualité* 7/2 (1971) cols 2083–2095.

———. 'Isaïe de Scété ou de Gaza?', *RAM* 46 (1970) 33–44.

———. *La Vie Quotidienne des Pères du Désert en Égypte au IVe Siècle.* Paris, 1990.

———. *Les Pères du désert à travers leurs apophtegmes*. n.p., 1987.

Sauget, J. -M. 'Les fragments de 1'Ascéticon de 1'abbé Isaïe du Vatican arabe 71', *Oriens Christianus* 48 (1964) 235–259.

———. 'La double recession arabe des Préceptes aux novices de l'abbé Isaïe de Scété' in *Melanges E. Tisserant* 3 (1964) 299–336.

———. 'Un fragment ascétique d'abba Isaïe en traduction arabe sous le nom d'abba Moïse', *Proche Orient Chrétien* 27 (1977) 43–70.

———. 'Un nouveau témoin de collection d'*Apophthegmatum Patrum*: Le *Paterikon* du Sinai arabe 547', *Le Muséon* 86 (1973) 14–16.

Scher, A. 'Notice sur la vie et les oeuvres de Dadišo Qatraya', *Journal asiatique*, 10/7 (1906) 103–18

Schwartz, E. *Johannes Rufus, ein monophysitischer Schriftsteller*. Heidelberg, 1912.

Spidlik, T. *The Spirituality of the Christian East*. Kalamazoo: Cistercian Publications, 1979.

Vailhé, S. 'Un mystique monophysite: le moine Isaïe', *Echos d'Orient* 9 (1906) 81–91.

Villecourt, L. 'Note sur une Lettre de l'abbé Isaïe à l'abbé Pierre', *Revue de l'Orient Chrétien* 22 (1920–21) 54–56.

Viller, M. and K. Rahner. *Aszese und Mystik in der Vaterzeit*. Freiburg, 1939.

White, H. G. Evelyn. *The Monasteries of the Wadi 'N Natrun*. New York, 1932.

Young, F. *From Nicaea to Chalcedon: A Guide to the Literature and its Background*. London, 1983.

B: GENERAL: Select

Abel, F. -M. *Géographie de la Palestine*. 2 vols. Paris, 1933 and 1938.

———. *Histoire de la Palestine*. 2 vols. Paris, 1952.

Avi-Yonah, M. 'Une école de mosaique à Gaza au sixième siècle' in *Art of Ancient Palestine*. Jerusalem, 1981.

Barasch, M. *The David Mosaic of Gaza*. (Typescript) Tel Aviv University Library.

Cohen, R. 'New light on the Petra-Gaza Road', *Biblical Archeologist* 45 (1982) 240–47.

Downey, G. *Gaza in the Early Sixth Century*. Oklahoma, 1963.

Glucker, C. A. M. *The City of Gaza in the Roman and Byzantine Periods,* BAR International Series 325. Oxford, 1987.

Hardy, E. R. *Christian Egypt*. Oxford, 1962.

Hunt, E. D. *Holy Land Pilgrimage in the Later Roman Empire AD 312–460*. Oxford, 1984.

Kasher, A. 'Gaza during the Greco-Roman Era', in *The Jerusalem Cathedra*. Edited by L. Levine. Jerusalem, 1982.

Mayerson, P. 'The desert of southern Palestine according to Byzantine Sources', *Proceedings of the American Philosophical Society* 107 (1963) 160–72.

———. 'The wine and vineyards of Gaza in the Byzantine period', *Bulletin of the American Schools of Oriental Research* 257 (1985) 75–80.

Meyer, M. *History of the City of Gaza*. New York, 1907.

Ovadiah, A. *Corpus of the Byzantine Churches in the Holy Land*. Theophaneia 22. Bonn, 1970.

———. 'Les mosaistes de Gaza dans 1'antiquité chrétienne', *Revue Biblique* 82 (1975) 552–57.

Rappaport, U. 'Gaza and Ascalon in the Persian and Hellenistic periods in relation to their coins', *Israel Exploration Journal* 20 (1970) 75–80.

Vööbus, A. *History of Asceticism in the Syrian Orient*. 2 vols. CSCO 184 and 197. Louvain, 1958 and 1960.

Wacht, M. *Aeneas von Gaza als Apologet: seine Kosmologie im Verhaltnis zum Platonismus*. Bonn, 1969.

Patristics Index

Scripture Index

Old Testament

Index of Names

Subject Index

C

D

E

I

J

K

T

V

W

CISTERCIAN TEXTS

Bernard of Clairvaux

- Apologia to Abbot William
- Five Books on Consideration: Advice to a Pope
- Homilies in Praise of the Blessed Virgin Mary
- In Praise of the New Knighthood
- Letters of Bernard of Clairvaux / by B.S. James
- Life and Death of Saint Malachy the Irishman
- Love without Measure: Extracts from the Writings of St Bernard / by Paul Dimier
- On Grace and Free Choice
- On Loving God / Analysis by Emero Stiegman
- Parables and Sentences
- Sermons for the Summer Season
- Sermons on Conversion
- Sermons on the Song of Songs I–IV
- The Steps of Humility and Pride

William of Saint Thierry

- The Enigma of Faith
- Exposition on the Epistle to the Romans
- Exposition on the Song of Songs
- The Golden Epistle
- The Mirror of Faith
- The Nature and Dignity of Love
- On Contemplating God: Prayer & Meditations

Aelred of Rievaulx

- Dialogue on the Soul
- Liturgical Sermons, I
- The Mirror of Charity
- Spiritual Friendship
- Treatises I: On Jesus at the Age of Twelve, Rule for a Recluse, The Pastoral Prayer
- Walter Daniel: The Life of Aelred of Rievaulx

Gertrud the Great of Helfta

- Spiritual Exercises
- The Herald of God's Loving-Kindness (Books 1, 2)
- The Herald of God's Loving-Kindness (Book 3)

John of Ford

- Sermons on the Final Verses of the Songs of Songs I–VII

Gilbert of Hoyland

- Sermons on the Songs of Songs I–III
- Treatises, Sermons and Epistles

Other Early Cistercian Writers

- Adam of Perseigne, Letters of
- Alan of Lille: The Art of Preaching
- Amadeus of Lausanne: Homilies in Praise of Blessed Mary
- Baldwin of Ford: The Commendation of Faith
- Baldwin of Ford: Spiritual Tractates I–II
- Geoffrey of Auxerre: On the Apocalypse
- Guerric of Igny: Liturgical Sermons Vol. I & 2
- Helinand of Froidmont: Verses on Death
- Idung of Prüfening: Cistercians and Cluniacs: The Case for Cîteaux
- In the School of Love. An Anthology of Early Cistercian Texts
- Isaac of Stella: Sermons on the Christian Year, I–[II]
- The Life of Beatrice of Nazareth
- Serlo of Wilton & Serlo of Savigny: Seven Unpublished Works
- Stephen of Lexington: Letters from Ireland
- Stephen of Sawley: Treatises
- Three Treatises on Man: A Cistercian Anthropology

MONASTIC TEXTS

Eastern Monastic Tradition

- Abba Isaiah of Scete: Ascetic Discourses
- Besa: The Life of Shenoute
- Cyril of Scythopolis: Lives of the Monks of Palestine
- Dorotheos of Gaza: Discourses and Sayings
- Evagrius Ponticus: Praktikos and Chapters on Prayer
- Handmaids of the Lord: Lives of Holy Women in Late Antiquity & the Early Middle Ages
- Harlots of the Desert
- John Moschos: The Spiritual Meadow
- Lives of the Desert Fathers
- Lives of Simeon Stylites
- Manjava Skete
- Mena of Nikiou: Isaac of Alexandra & St Macrobius
- The Monastic Rule of Iosif Volotsky (Revised Edition)
- Pachomian Koinonia I–III
- Paphnutius: Histories/Monks of Upper Egypt
- The Sayings of the Desert Fathers
- The Spiritually Beneficial Tales of Paul, Bishop of Monembasia
- Symeon the New Theologian: The Theological and Practical Treatises & The Three Theological Discourses
- Theodoret of Cyrrhus: A History of the

Monks of Syria
- The Syriac Fathers on Prayer and the Spiritual Life

Western Monastic Tradition

- Achard of Saint Victor: Works
- Anselm of Canterbury: Letters I–III / by Walter Fröhlich
- Bede: Commentary…Acts of the Apostles
- Bede: Commentary…Seven Catholic Epistles
- Bede: Homilies on the Gospels I–II
- Bede: Excerpts from the Works of Saint Augustine on the Letters of the Blessed Apostle Paul
- The Celtic Monk
- Gregory the Great: Forty Gospel Homilies
- Life of the Jura Fathers
- The Maxims of Stephen of Muret
- Peter of Celle: Selected Works
- The Letters of Armand Jean-deRancé I–II
- Rule of the Master
- Rule of Saint Augustine

CHRISTIAN SPIRITUALITY

- A Cloud of Witnesses...The Development of Christian Doctrine / by David N. Bell
- The Call of Wild Geese / by Matthew Kelty
- The Cistercian Way / by André Louf
- The Contemplative Path
- Drinking From the Hidden Fountain / by Thomas Spidlík
- Entirely for God / by Elizabeth Isichei
- Eros and Allegory: Medieval Exegesis of the Song of Songs / by Denys Turner
- Fathers Talking / by Aelred Squire
- Friendship and Community / by Brian McGuire
- Grace Can do Moore: Spiritual Accompaniment / by André Louf
- High King of Heaven / by Benedicta Word
- How Far to Follow / by B. Olivera
- The Hermitage Within / by a Monk
- Life of St Mary Magdalene and of Her Sister St Martha / by David Mycoff
- The Luminous Eye / by Sebastian Brock
- Many Mansions / by David N. Bell
- Mercy in Weakness / by André Louf
- The Name of Jesus / by Irénée Hausherr
- No Moment Too Small / by Norvene Vest
- Penthos: The Doctrine of Compunction in the Christian East / by Irénée Hausherr
- Praying the Word / by Enzo Bianchi
- Praying with Benedict / by Korneel Vermeiren
- Russian Mystics / by Sergius Bolshakoff
- Sermons in a Monastery / by Matthew Kelty
- Silent Herald of Unity: The Life of Maria Gabrielle Sagheddu / by Martha Driscoll
- Spiritual Direction in the Early Christian East / by Irénée Hausherr
- The Spirituality of the Christian East / by Thomas Spidlík
- The Spirituality of the Medieval West / by André Vauchez
- The Spiritual World of Isaac the Syrian / by Hilarion Alfeyev
- Tuning In To Grace / by André Louf

MONASTIC STUDIES

- Community and Abbot in the Rule of St Benedict I–II / by Adalbert de Vogüé
- The Hermit Monks of Grandmont / by Carole A. Hutchison
- In the Unity of the Holy Spirit / by Sighard Kleiner
- A Life Pleasing to God: Saint Basil's Monastic Rules / By Augustine Holmes
- Memoirs [of Jean Leclercq]: From Grace to Grace
- Monastic Practices / by Charles Cummings
- The Occupation of Celtic Sites in Ireland / by Geraldine Carville
- Reading St Benedict / by Adalbert de Vogüé
- Rule of St Benedict: A Doctrinal and Spiritual Commentary / by Adalbert de Vogüé
- The Venerable Bede / by Benedicta Ward
- Western Monasticism / by Peter King
- What Nuns Read / by David N. Bell

CISTERCIAN STUDIES

- Aelred of Rievaulx: A Study / by Aelred Squire
- Athirst for God: Spiritual Desire in Bernard of Clairvaux's Sermons on the Song of Songs / by Michael Casey
- Beatrice of Nazareth in Her Context / by Roger De Ganck
- Bernard of Clairvaux: Man, Monk, Mystic / by Michael Casey [tapes and readings]
- Catalogue of Manuscripts in the Obrecht Collection of the Institute of Cistercian Studies / by Anna Kirkwood
- Christ the Way: The Christology of Guerric of Igny / by John Morson
- The Cistercians in Denmark / by Brian McGuire
- The Cistercians in Scandinavia / by James France
- A Difficult Saint / by Brian McGuire
- The Finances of the Cistercian Order in the Fourteenth Century / by Peter King

- Fountains Abbey and Its Benefactors / by Joan Wardrop
- A Gathering of Friends: Learning & Spirituality in John of Ford / by Costello and Holdsworth
- The Golden Chain...Isaac of Stella / byBernard Mc Ginn
- Image and Likeness: Augustinian Spirituality of William of St Thierry / by David Bell
- Index of Authors & Works in Cistercian Libraries in Great Britain I / by David Bell
- Index of Cistercian Authors and Works in Medieval Library Catalogues in Great Britian / by David Bell
- The Mystical Theology of St Bernard / by Étienne Gilson
- The New Monastery: Texts & Studies on the Earliest Cistercians
- Monastic Odyssey / by Marie Kervingant
- Nicolas Cotheret's Annals of Cîteaux / by Louis J. Lekai
- Pater Bernhardus: Martin Luther and Bernard of Clairvaux / by Franz Posset
- Pathway of Peace / by Charles Dumont
- Rancé and the Trappist Legacy / by A. J. Krailsheimer
- A Second Look at Saint Bernard / by Jean Leclercq
- The Spiritual Teachings of St Bernard of Clairvaux / by John R. Sommerfeldt
- Studies in Medieval Cistercian History
- Three Founders of Cîteaux / by Jean-Baptiste Van Damme
- Towards Unification with God (Beatrice of Nazareth in Her Context, 2)
- William, Abbot of St Thierry
- Women and St Bernard of Clairvaux / by Jean Leclercq

MEDIEVAL RELIGIOUS WOMEN

A Sub-series edited by
Lillian Thomas Shank and John A. Nichols

- Distant Echoes
- Hidden Springs: Cistercian Monastic Women (2 volumes)
- Peace Weavers

CARTHUSIAN TRADITION

- The Call of Silent Love / by A Carthusian
- The Freedom of Obedience / by A Carthusian
- From Advent to Pentecost / by A Carthusian
- Guigo II: The Ladder of Monks & Twelve Meditations / by E. Colledge & J. Walsh
- Halfway to Heaven / by R.B. Lockhart
- Interior Prayer / by A Carthusian
- Meditations of Guigo I / by A. Gordon Mursall
- The Prayer of Love and Silence / by A Carthusian
- Poor, Therefore Rich / by A Carthusian
- They Speak by Silences / by A Carthusian
- The Way of Silent Love (A Carthusian Miscellany)
- Where Silence is Praise / by A Carthusian
- The Wound of Love (A Carthusian Miscellany)

CISTERCIAN ART, ARCHITECTURE & MUSIC

- Cistercian Abbeys of Britain
- Cistercian Europe / by Terryl N. Kinder
- Cistercians in Medieval Art / by James France
- Studies in Medieval Art and Architecture / edited by Meredith Parsons Lillich (Volumes II–V are now available)
- Stones Laid Before the Lord / by Anselme Dimier
- Treasures Old and New: Nine Centuries of Cistercian Music (compact disc and cassette)

THOMAS MERTON

- The Climate of Monastic Prayer / by T. Merton
- Legacy of Thomas Merton / by P. Hart
- Message of Thomas Merton / by P. Hart
- Monastic Journey of Thomas Merton / by Patrick Hart
- Thomas Merton/Monk / by P. Hart
- Thomas Merton on St Bernard
- Toward an Integrated Humanity / edited by M. Basil Pennington

CISTERCIAN LITURGICAL DOCUMENTS SERIES

- Cistercian Liturgical Documents Series / edited by Chrysogonus Waddell, ocso
- Hymn Collection from the…Paraclete
- The Paraclete Statutes:: Institutiones nostrae
- Molesme Summer-Season Breviary (4 vol.)
- Old French Ordinary & Breviary of the Abbey of the Paraclete (2 volumes)
- Twelfth-century Cistercian Hymnal (2 vol.)
- The Twelfth-century Cistercian Psalter
- Two Early Cistercian Libelli Missarum

FESTSCHRIFTS

- Bernardus Magister...Nonacentenary of the Birth of St Bernard
- The Joy of Learning & the Love of God: Essays in Honor of Jean Leclercq
- Praise no Less Than Charity in honor of C. Waddell
- Studiosorum Speculumin honor of Louis J. Lekai
- Truth As Gift... in honor of J. Sommerfeldt

BUSINESS INFORMATION

Editorial Offices & Customer Service

- Cistercian Publications
  WMU Station, 1903 West Michigan Avenue
  Kalamazoo, Michigan 49008-5415 USA

  Telephone 616 387 8920
  Fax 616 387 8390
  e-mail cistpub@wmich.edu

Please Note: As of 13 July 2002 the 616 area code becomes 269

Canada

- Novalis
  49 Front Street East, Second Floor
  Toronto, Ontario M5E 1B3 CANADA

  Telephone 1 800 204 4140
  Fax 416 363 9409

U.K.

- Cistercian Publications UK
  Mount Saint Bernard Abbey
  Coalville, Leicestershire LE67 5UL UK
- UK Customer Service & Book Orders
  Cistercian Publications
  97 Loughborough Road
  Thringstone, Coalville
  Leicestershire LE67 8LQ UK

  Telephone 01530 45 27 24
  Fax 01530 45 02 10
  e-mail MsbcistP@aol.com

Website

- www.spencerabbey.org/cistpub

Trade Accounts & Credit Applications

- Cistercian Publications / Accounting
  6219 West Kistler Road
  Ludington, Michigan 49431 USA

  Fax 231 843 8919

Cistercian Publications is a non-profit corporation. Its publishing program is restricted to monastic texts in translation and books on the monastic tradition.

A complete catalogue of texts in translation and studies on early, medieval, and modern monasticism is available, free of charge, from any of the addresses above.